PRACTICAL PROJECT
RISK MANAGEMENT

The ATOM Methodology

PRACTICAL PROJECT
RISK MANAGEMENT

The **ATOM Methodology**

David Hillson

Peter Simon

8230 Leesburg Pike, Suite 800
Vienna, Virginia 22182
Phone: 703.790.9595
Fax: 703.790.1371
www.managementconcepts.com

Printed in the United States of America
10 9 8 7 6 5 4 3 2 1

Library of Congress Cataloging-in-Publication Data

Hillson, David, 1955-
    Practical project risk management : the ATOM methodology / David Hillson and
Peter Simon.
        p. cm.
    Enhanced subtitle: Active Threat and Opportunity Management (ATOM)
    Includes bibliographical references and index.
    ISBN 978-1-56726-202-5
    1. Risk management--Methodology. 2. Project management. I. Simon, Peter, 1956-
II. Title. III. Title: Active Threat and Opportunity Management (ATOM).
HD61.H477 2007
658.15'5--dc22
                                                                                2007008623

ABOUT THE AUTHORS

Dr. David Hillson, PMP, FRSA, FAPM, FIRM, FCMI, is an international risk management consultant and Director of Risk Doctor & Partners (www.risk-doctor.com). He is a popular conference speaker and award-winning author on risk. David is recognized internationally as a leading thinker and practitioner in the risk field, and has made several innovative contributions to improving risk management. He is well-known for promoting the inclusion of proactive opportunity management within the risk process, and has developed a practical application of emotional literacy to risk psychology.

David is an active member of the Project Management Institute (PMI®) and was a founder member of its Risk Management Specific Interest Group. He received the PMI® Distinguished Contribution Award for his work in developing risk management over many years. He is a Fellow of the UK Association for Project Management (APM) and past chairman of its Risk Management Specific Interest Group. David is also a Fellow of the UK Institute of Risk Management (IRM), a Fellow of the Royal Society for the Encouragement of Arts, Manufactures and Commerce (RSA), and a Fellow of the Chartered Management Institute.

David can be contacted at david@risk-doctor.com.

Peter Simon, BSc, PMP, FAPM, has 30 years of experience as a project management consultant and practitioner across all industries and business sectors.

In his early career he worked for a variety of organizations across the oil and gas, utilities, and transportation sectors as a project management and project services practitioner and was responsible for all aspects of project planning and control and risk management for projects based in Europe, the United States, and the Middle East.

In his later career he has achieved significant success in building the project management consultancy and training arms of the PMProfessional group of companies, in addition to many years as a successful freelance project management consultant and a period as European Technical Director for ESI International. Peter is now Managing Partner of Lucidus Consulting Limited (www.lucidusconsulting.com).

Peter was Chairman of the UK Association for Project Management's (APM) Risk Management Specific Interest Group for four years and was Project Manager and Managing Editor of the APM PRAM Guide published in October 1997. He is a Fellow of APM, a member of the Project Management Institute (PMI®), and a Visiting Fellow of Cranfield University School of Management.

In addition to this book, Peter is coauthor of *Starting Out in Project Management,* a study guide for APM qualifications.

Peter can be contacted at peter@lucidusconsulting.com.

TABLE OF CONTENTS

TABLE OF CONTENTS

TABLE OF CONTENTS

TABLE OF CONTENTS

LIST OF FIGURES

LIST OF FIGURES

LIST OF FIGURES

LIST OF FIGURES

FOREWORD

....

It must be remembered that there is nothing more difficult to plan, more doubtful of success nor more dangerous to manage than the creation of a new system. For the initiator has the enmity of all who profit by the preservation of the old institution and merely lukewarm defenders in those who would gain by the new one.—Nicolo Machiavelli, 1532

Seneca (5 BC–65 AD) wrote that "The greatest loss of time is delay and expectation, which depend upon the future. We let go the present, which we have in our power, and look forward to that which depends upon chance, and so relinquish a certainty for an uncertainty." His insight could represent the start of risk management, or at least the beginnings of a debate which rages on today.

Simply put, risk management is the art/science of attempting to understand and manage that which hasn't happened yet. The philosophy of risk was put forth a thousand years ago and the principles, tenets, and maxims of risk management haven't changed much in the last one hundred years. So what is left for people to debate?

At present, the debate centers around two major issues. First is the issue of risk versus uncertainty. In his seminal work, *Risk, Uncertainty, and Profit* (1921), economist Frank Knight established the important distinction between risk and uncertainty:

> Uncertainty must be taken in a sense radically distinct from the familiar notion of Risk, from which it has never been properly separated. ... The essential fact is that "risk" means in some cases a quantity susceptible of measurement, while at other times it is something distinctly not of this character; and there are far-reaching and crucial differences in the bearings of the phenomena depending on which of the two is really present and operating. ... It will appear that a measurable uncertainty, or "risk" proper, as we shall use the term, is so far different from an unmeasurable one that it is not in effect an uncertainty at all. We ... accordingly restrict the term "uncertainty" to cases of the non-quantitative type.

Knight distinguished between risk and uncertainty, a distinction that explains why risk management has developed into its own discipline in modern times. However, the debate continues about how far we should be trying to manage uncertainty, or whether we must restrict our efforts to managing risk.

The second issue exciting debate today is the question of "positive" risk, commonly called opportunity. In the past, project risks have traditionally been seen as uncertainties that would have a negative impact to project objectives. However, current thinking expands the concept of risk to include "upside" risk, or opportunity. This book is an ambitious attempt to address the current paradigm shift in the field of project risk management, clarifying the difference between general uncertainty and risk, and showing how to tackle both threats and opportunities together.

Tools, techniques, powerful computers, and software have made many seemingly impossible tasks easy to do but, until now, there has always been one thing missing from the risk toolkit. Many textbooks exist, espousing particulars view or styles of risk management. As necessary as these books are, there has been an unfulfilled need for a "How to …" risk management manual. We have been waiting for "A Practitioner's Guide" to risk management … *Practical Project Risk Management: The ATOM Methodology,* by David Hillson and Peter Simon, is that book. This book is a simple, concise guide for practitioners of project risk management, at any level.

The Active Threat and Opportunity Management (ATOM) risk process addresses projects of any size, in any industry. ATOM offers a unique process that can be used to address both threats and opportunities. It minimizes the learning process and maximizes the return on investment for companies and organizations striving to improve their risk management process.

The major concepts in the ATOM approach are simple and repeatable on all projects. This book provides "commonsense" risk management in clear, concise writing that everyone can grasp, understand, and implement. It is a consistent process that can be applied across multiple project and industry standards. Using the same process for threat and opportunity management offers economies of scale and shortens the learning curve for practitioners.

This practitioners' guide follows the familiar structure of both the *PMBOK® Guide* and *PRAM Guide* by describing inputs and outputs at each phase of the process. ATOM is specifically designed for the "medium-sized project" but can be used to advantage on any size project. Tailoring the ATOM process is necessary depending upon your specific needs. Templates for small, medium, and large projects are included. ATOM also contains practical examples and solutions to common situations. This practitioners' guide optimizes the chance for project success, because it is practical … logical … useable!

David Hillson and Peter Simon have been working hard for many years to advance the state of the art and practice of project risk management. This book captures their insights, allowing practitioners of risk management to be better prepared and well-armed to get the job done. David and Peter have provided the risk community with a unique, thoughtful approach to risk management.

The debate surrounding risk management will doubtless go on, and some people may take issue with some or all of what is offered in this insightful new approach. But at least we now have a clear, concise, and complete "How to" practitioner's guide to project risk management.

Charles W. Bosler Jr., CPCM, 2007 Chairman, PMI Risk Management SIG
May 2007

PREFACE

Everyone agrees that managing risk is a core part of project management, because all projects are risky. Risk management focuses on addressing proactively the implications of uncertainty on the achievement of project objectives. Despite this shared view, for many project managers and their teams, as well as for risk practitioners, the problem comes when they try to make risk management work in practice. The training course has been attended, the theory is well understood, and the tools and techniques all make sense. There is no problem with "what, why, when, where, and who." But somehow it all seems different when it comes to your project. If only someone could show you how.

Through this book, we hope to make our expertise available to hard-pressed project management professionals, with practical advice on how to manage risk properly, efficiently, and effectively. This is not a book of academic theory or generic principles, although it is firmly based on current international best practices and reflects leading-edge thinking and developments. This book is about actually doing it, so that businesses and their projects can manage risk effectively, minimizing threats and maximizing opportunities in order to optimize achievement of objectives. This book will be helpful to someone with no prior knowledge of risk management who needs to implement a proven approach, as well as to someone who has some limited experience but needs guidance on how to apply risk management successfully. Risk management can really work in practice—this book shows how.

We have taken best practice guidelines and standards and translated them into a comprehensive, proven, practical methodology for managing project risk, presented as a simple stepwise process leaving no ambiguity about what should be done next. We call this methodology Active Threat and Opportunity Management (ATOM), reflecting our belief that risk management is about taking action and that risk management must be targeted equally at both downside risk (threats) and upside risk (opportunities). For each process step, practical advice, hints, and tips are offered on how to get the most out of the risk management process.

With our combined experience of over 40 years of managing risk on projects, we know that risk management works. It frustrates us to hear people saying that it's too hard, or not worth the effort, or just a waste of time. ATOM is our answer—a simple, scaleable risk process that applies to projects in all industries and business sectors. We hope that you will not just read this book, but that you'll put what you read into practice, since this is the only way of gaining the promised benefits. None of us has time to waste on processes and activities that don't work. Risk management does work, if it is done properly. But please don't take our word for it; try it for yourself and find out.

David Hillson and Peter Simon

ACKNOWLEDGMENTS

"There are risks and costs to a program of action. But they are far less than the long-range risks and costs of comfortable inaction." —John F. Kennedy (1917–1963)

We first met in 1985 at a conference for users of risk software, and since then risk management has formed an important part of our professional relationship. So it seemed obvious for us to write a book together, outlining our shared insights and approach to risk management on projects. As practitioners, it was natural for us to concentrate on practical guidelines outlining how to do it, especially since there are so few other books offering practical guidelines.

The risk process described in this book draws on our many years of experience and is honed through both failure and success. Along the way, we have learned much from each other, as well as from colleagues, competitors, and clients, that has shaped the way we now think and act. Some of these people have shown the way through their good practice, while others have shown us what not to do. To each we are grateful, though they are too many to mention individually.

Some do deserve special mention. Particular individuals in the risk specific interest groups (SIGs) of both the U.K. Association for Project Management (APM) and the Project Management Institute (PMI) have helped us to develop our understanding and practice, notably Philip Rawlings, Steve Grey, John Perry, David Vose, David Hulett, and Kik Piney. Among key clients, Roy Millard, Renata Crome, Andy Sallis, and Frank Millar provided early opportunities to implement and prove our approach. Our mutual friend and colleague Ruth Murray-Webster has provided consistent encouragement and support, without which we might never have finished the book. We would also like to thank the team at Management Concepts for their patience and encouragement during the writing process.

The approach to project risk management described here is our own, and we know it works. We remain responsible for any flaws or shortcomings, and welcome feedback from readers at contact@ATOM-risk.com.

David Hillson and Peter Simon

PART I

The Problem

....

CHAPTER 1

The Challenge
of Managing Risk

F ew would disagree that life is risky. Indeed, for many people it is precisely the element of risk that makes life interesting. However, unmanaged risk is dangerous because it can lead to unforeseen outcomes. This fact has led to the recognition that risk management is essential, whether in business, projects, or everyday life. But somehow risks just keep happening. Risk management apparently does not work, at least not in the way it should. This book addresses this problem by providing a simple method for effective risk management. The target is management of risks on projects, although many of the techniques outlined here are equally applicable to managing other forms of risk, including business risk, strategic risk, and even personal risk.

The book is divided into three parts, starting with defining the problem in an effort to understand the underlying reasons for the apparent failure of project risk management to deliver the promised or expected benefits. The main body of the book describes a generic risk management process applicable to most projects, focusing on simple guidelines to make risk management work in practice. Finally, the book considers implementation issues, applying the risk management process to different types of projects, and addressing the steps necessary to use risk management effectively.

But before considering the details of the risk management process, there are some essential ideas that must be understood and clarified. For example, what exactly is meant by the word *risk?*

Risk—The Definition Debate

Some may be surprised that there is any question to be answered here. After all, the word *risk* can be found in any English dictionary, and surely everyone knows what it means. But in recent years risk practitioners and professionals have been engaged in an active and controversial debate about the precise scope of the word.

Everyone agrees that risk arises from uncertainty, and that risk is about the impact that uncertain events or circumstances could have on the achievement of goals. This agreement has led to definitions combining two elements of uncertainty and objectives, such as, "A risk is any uncertainty that, if it occurs, would have an effect on achievement of one or more objectives." Traditionally risk has been perceived as bad; the emphasis has been on the potential effects of risk as harmful, adverse, negative, and unwelcome. In fact, the word *risk* has been considered synonymous with *threat.* But this is not the only perspective.

Obviously some uncertainties could be helpful if they occurred. These uncertainties have the same characteristics as threat risks (i.e., they arise from the effect of uncertainty on achievement of objectives), but the potential effects, if they were to occur, would be beneficial, positive, and welcome. When used in this way, *risk* becomes synonymous with *opportunity.*

Risk practitioners are divided into three camps around this debate, as illustrated by Figure 1-1.

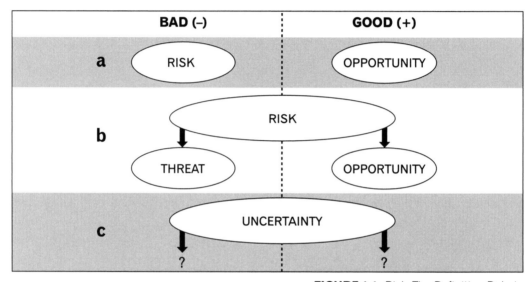

FIGURE 1-1: Risk–The Definition Debate

One group insists that the traditional approach must be upheld, reserving the word *risk* for bad things that might happen. This group recognizes that opportunities also exist, but sees them as separate from risks, to be treated differently using a distinct process (row a).

A second group believes that there are benefits from treating threats and opportunities together, broadening the definition of risk and the scope of the risk management process to handle both (row b).

A third group seems unconcerned about definitions, words, and jargon, preferring to focus on "doing the job." This group emphasizes the need to deal with all types of uncertainty without worrying about which labels to use (row c).

While this debate remains unresolved, clear trends are emerging. The majority of official risk management standards and guidelines use a broadened definition of risk, including both upside opportunities and downside threats. Some leading procedural standards, such as *A Guide to the Project Management Body of Knowledge (PMBOK® Guide)* from the Project Management Institute, and the Association for Project Management's *Project Risk Analysis and Management (PRAM) Guide,* also reflect this wider definition in their risk management processes, with tools and techniques to identify, assess, and manage both opportunities and threats. Following this trend, increasing numbers of organizations are widening the scope of their risk management approach to address uncertainties with positive upside impacts as well as those with negative downside effects.

Given the increasing popularity of the wider application of risk management to both threats and opportunities, as well as the attraction of using a single process to deal with two related concerns, this book adopts the inclusive position. Using a common process to manage both threats and opportunities has many benefits, including:

- *Maximum efficiency,* with no need to develop, introduce, and maintain a separate opportunity management process

- *Cost-effectiveness* (double "bangs per buck") from using a single process to achieve proactive management of both threats and opportunities, resulting in avoidance or minimization of problems, *and* exploitation and maximization of benefits

- *Familiar techniques,* requiring only minor changes to current techniques for managing threats so organizations can deal with opportunities

- *Minimal additional training,* because the common process uses familiar processes, tools, and techniques

- *Proactive opportunity management,* so that opportunities that might have been missed can be addressed

- *More realistic contingency management,* by including potential upside impacts as well as the downside, taking account of both "overs and unders"

- *Increased team motivation,* by encouraging people to think creatively about ways to work better, simpler, faster, more effectively, etc.

- *Improved chances of project success,* because opportunities are identified and captured, producing benefits for the project that might otherwise have been overlooked

Having discussed what a risk is ("any uncertainty that, if it occurs, would have a positive or negative effect on achievement of one or more objectives"), it is also important to clarify what risk is not. Effective risk management must focus on risks and not be distracted by other related issues. A number of other elements are often confused with risks but must be treated separately, such as:

- *Issues.* This term can be used in several different ways. Sometimes it refers to matters of concern that are insufficiently defined or characterized to be treated as risks. In this case an issue is more vague than a risk, and may describe an area (such as requirement volatility, or resource availability, or weather conditions) from which specific risks might arise. The term *issue* is also used (particularly in the U.K.) as something that has occurred but cannot be addressed by the project manager without escalation. In this sense an issue may be the result of a risk that has happened, and is usually negative.

- *Problems.* A problem is also a risk whose time has come. Unlike a risk that is a potential future event, there is no uncertainty about a problem—it exists now and must be addressed immediately. Problems can be distinguished from issues because issues require escalation, whereas problems can be addressed by the project manager within the project.

- *Causes.* Many people confuse causes of risk with risks themselves. The cause, however, describes existing conditions that might give rise to risks. For example, there is no uncertainty about the statement, "We have never done a project like this before," so it cannot be a risk. But this statement could result in a number of risks that must be identified and managed.

- *Effects.* Similar confusion exists about effects, which in fact only occur as the result of risks that have happened. To say, "The project might be late," does not describe a risk, but what would happen if one or more risks occurred. The effect might arise in the future (i.e., it is not a current problem), but its existence depends on whether the related risk occurs.

Using Risk Management on Projects

The widespread occurrence of risk in life, business, and projects has encouraged proactive attempts to manage risk and its effects. History as far back as Noah's Ark, the pyramids of Egypt, and the Herodian Temple shows evidence of planning techniques that include contingency for unforeseen events. Modern concepts of probability arose in the 17th century from pioneering work by Pascal and his contemporaries, leading to an improved understanding of the nature of risk and a more structured approach to its management.

Without covering the historical application of risk management in detail here, clearly those responsible for major projects have always recognized the potentially disruptive influence of uncertainty, and they have sought to minimize its effect on achievement of project objectives. Recently, risk management has become an accepted part of project management, included as one of the key knowledge areas in the various bodies of project management knowledge and as one of the expected competencies of project management practitioners.

Unfortunately, embedding risk management within project management leads some to consider it as "just another project management technique," with the implication that its use is optional, and appropriate only for large, complex, or innovative projects. Others view risk management as the latest transient management fad. These attitudes often result in risk management being applied without full commitment or attention, and are at least partly responsible for the failure of risk management to deliver the promised benefits.

To be fully effective, risk management must be closely integrated into the overall project management process. It must not be seen as optional, or applied sporadically only on particular projects. Risk management must be *built in not bolted on* if it is to assist organizations in achieving their objectives.

Built-in risk management has two key characteristics:

- First, project management decisions are made with an understanding of the risks involved. This understanding includes the full range of project management activities, such as scope definition, pricing/budgeting, value management, scheduling, resourcing, cost estimating, quality management, change control, post-project review, etc. These must take full account of the risks affecting the project, giving the project a risk-based plan with the best likelihood of being met.

• Secondly, the risk management process must be integrated with other project management processes. Not only must these processes use risk data, but there should also be a seamless interface across process boundaries. This has implications for the project toolset and infrastructure, as well as for project procedures.

Benefits of Effective Risk Management

Risk management implemented holistically, as a fully integral part of the project management process, should deliver benefits. Empirical research by Terry Cooke-Davies, gathering project performance data from benchmarking networks of major organizations across a variety of industries, shows that risk management is the single most influential factor in project success. Where risk management is well implemented, more projects meet their objectives (using a composite performance measure for schedule and cost, projects in organizations reporting "fully adequate" risk management completed on average at 95 percent of plan). Where risk management is poor, projects fail more often (projects where risk management was rated "not at all adequate" averaged 170 percent of plan). These conclusions are based on detailed examination of characteristics describing risk management approach and deployment. Figure 1-2 presents typical data (in this case, for assignment of risk owners to agreed actions).

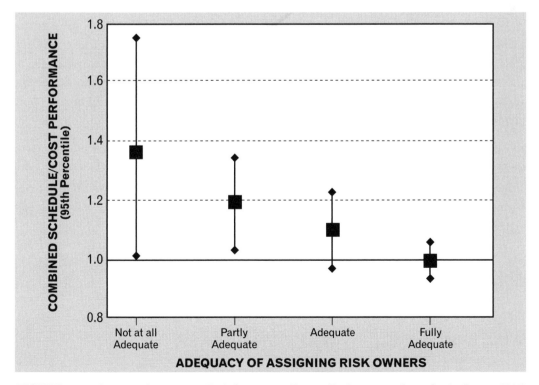

FIGURE 1-2: Influence of Assigning Risk Owners on Project Performance (from Cooke-Davies 2005)

Unfortunately, despite indications that risk management is very influential in project success, the same research found that risk management is the lowest scoring of all project management techniques in terms of effective deployment and use, suggesting that although many organizations recognize that risk management matters, they are not implementing it effectively. As a result, projects still fail, businesses still struggle, too many foreseeable downside threat-risks turn into real issues or problems, and too many achievable upside opportunity-risks are missed.

There is clearly nothing wrong with risk management in principle. The concepts are clear, the process is well defined, proven techniques exist, tools are widely available to support the process, and there are many training courses to develop risk management knowledge and skills. So where is the problem? If it is not in the theory of risk management, it must be in the practice. Despite the huge promise held out by risk management to increase the likelihood of project and business success by allowing uncertainty and its effects to be managed proactively, the reality is different.

The problem is not a lack of understanding the "why, what, who, or when" of risk management. Lack of effectiveness comes most often from not knowing "how to." Project managers and their teams face a bewildering array of risk management standards, procedures, techniques, tools, books, training courses—all claiming to make risk management work—which raises the questions: How to do it? Which method to follow? Which techniques to use? Which supporting tools?

The main aim of this book is to offer clear guidance on "how to" do risk management in practice. The next chapter discusses common barriers to risk management effectiveness and introduces a number of Critical Success Factors to overcome these barriers. This leads into Chapter 3, which outlines Active Threat and Opportunity Management (ATOM)—a generic risk management methodology, applicable to any type of project of any size in any industry. Implementation of ATOM for the typical project is described in Part II, where each step in the risk process is presented with sufficient detail to make implementation as easy as possible without oversimplifying. Techniques are explained step by step, with underlying theory where appropriate and relevant, and useful templates are contained in two appendices.

Of course not all projects are typical, so ATOM is scalable to fit both the simple and the more complex project. Part III of this book explains how to tailor the generic risk process to both small and large projects to ensure that the process meets the specific risk challenge.

Undoubtedly risk management has much to offer to both businesses and projects. People following the approach in this book will discover how to capture those promises for themselves, their projects, and their business.

CHAPTER 2

Making It Work

Risk management is too important to be left to chance. For risk management to work it must be applied consistently, and this is best achieved using a structured or formal approach that requires a number of components to be in place, including:

- A supportive organization

- Competent people

- Appropriate supporting infrastructure

- A simple to use, scalable, and documented process

These factors, which are discussed later in this chapter, are often referred to as Critical Success Factors (CSFs), for two reasons:

1. Their absence leads to a failure of risk management to deliver the full benefit to the organization.

2. Their presence increases the chances of risk management being effective and successful.

Putting Critical Success Factors in place may sound simple to achieve, but in practice making risk management work is a real challenge. This chapter explores some of the main reasons for this—not to be negative but to provide possible ways to counteract the most common reasons. Forewarned is forearmed.

A research project by Risk Doctor & Partners in collaboration with KLCI investigated how organizations perceive the value of risk management. The survey addressed several different aspects, but two questions were particularly interesting. The first question asked, "How *important* is risk management to project success," with possible answers including extremely important, very important, important, somewhat important, and not important. The second question asked, "How *effective* is risk management on your projects," with answers ranging from extremely effective to very effective, effective, somewhat effective, or ineffective.

With 561 responses, the raw data is interesting in itself, but the correlation between answers to these two questions is fascinating. Simplifying the answers to each question into two options (positive or negative) gives four possible combinations, presented below along with the percentage of respondents who fell into each category (Figure 2-1):

1   Risk management is *important* and *effective.*
2   Risk management is *important* but *not effective.*
3   Risk management is *not important* and *not effective.*
4   Risk management is *not important* but it is (somehow) *effective.*

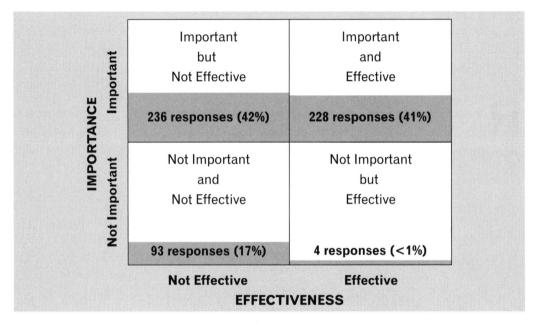

FIGURE 2-1: Importance and Effectiveness of Risk Management

Perhaps the fourth combination is not really feasible because it would be unusual for risk management to be effective if the organization does not consider it to be important; indeed, less than 1 percent of people responding to the research questionnaire believed themselves to be in this situation. Indeed, if risk management is viewed as unimportant it might not be done at all. But the other three combinations represent different levels of risk management maturity, and organizations in each of these three groups might be expected to act in very different ways.

Organizations that consider risk management to be important and effective in delivering the promised benefits (combination 1) could become champions for risk management, demonstrating how it can work and persuading others to follow their lead. These risk-mature organizations might be prepared to supply case studies and descriptions of best practice, allowing others to learn from their good experience. Encouragingly, more than 40 percent of respondents in the research project reported being in this position.

An organization that believes risk management is important but not effective in practice (combination 2), which is the position reported by about 41 percent of respondents (about the same as for combination 1), should consider launching an improvement initiative to benchmark and develop its risk management capability. Tackling the CSFs for effective risk management leads to enhanced capability and maturity, allowing the organization to reap the expected benefits.

Not surprisingly, risk management is ineffective in organizations that believe it is unimportant (combination 3), because it is not possible to manage risk effectively without some degree of commitment and buy-in. Only 17 percent of respondents admitted to this, perhaps recognizing that it is not a particularly good place to be. These risk-immature organizations should be persuaded and educated about the benefits of risk management to the business—a task best performed by convinced insiders who can show how to apply proactive management of risk to meet the organization's specific challenges.

It is a good idea for every organization to review its position on risk management against the two dimensions of importance and effectiveness, and to take appropriate action to move up the scale of risk management maturity. Risk management offers genuine and significant benefits to organizations, their projects, and their stakeholders, but these benefits will never be achieved without recognition of the *importance* of managing risk at all levels in the business, matched with operational *effectiveness* in executing risk management in practice.

Why Don't We Do It?

Most people would agree that risk management should be useful. If this is true, why is it not more widely used? Some of the more frequently cited reasons or excuses are listed in Figure 2-2 and described in the following paragraphs.

COMMON EXCUSES	PROPOSED SOLUTIONS
Process takes time and costs money.	Proper application saves time and money. Use the same argument as for quality management.
Responses cost money.	Explain that responses are an investment in the future—spending to save or spending to gain.
Risk management doesn't work.	Do it properly and demonstrate its effectiveness through example or pilot projects.
Risk management is just scaremongering.	Find the real risks (uncertainties that matter) and always include the positives—opportunities.
Managing issues is more fun.	Develop KPIs that measure the effectiveness of risk management and reward those who do it properly.
It's too late.	Remind everyone that it is never too late; failing to identify risks doesn't make them go away.
Too busy dealing with issues.	Risk management will prevent issues so starting the process will make for a better future.
It's just common sense.	Unfortunately it isn't to all. The framework of risk management will help those with less common sense.
Can't prove it works.	Demonstrate the benefits perhaps by emphasizing the management of opportunities. Seek evidence from outside.

FIGURE 2-2: Excuses and Solutions

The risk process takes time and money

Risk management is not a passive activity, and there is a cost associated with executing the upfront risk process—the cost of *assessing risk*. Risk management requires involvement of the project sponsor, project manager, members of the project team, and other stakeholders over and above what some would consider their normal level of commitment to the project. This causes a double problem: finding time for the risk process in an already overloaded working environment is difficult; and even when time is found, the risk process costs money as effort is spent in risk workshops and review meetings.

Risk responses cost money

A central purpose of the risk process is to identify risks and determine appropriate responses, which inevitably results in the need to do new and unplanned things. This introduces a second type of cost to the risk process: the cost of *addressing risk*. Risk responses are in reality new project activities that were not originally considered necessary. Because risk responses were not included in the original project scope, they add to the resource requirement and budget. As a result, risk management adds to the project workload while at the same time increasing the required budget.

Risk management doesn't work for us

Although risk management is not difficult, many people have unfortunately experienced it being applied ineffectively, leading them to believe that risk management doesn't work. This situation often arises when risk management is performed without proper commitment, perhaps by organizations merely complying with a regulatory, contractual or procedural requirement.

Risk management is just scaremongering

Until recently, risk management was commonly concerned only with threats. As a result the risk process focused only on the bad things that might occur, examining every possible cause of failure, and listing every potential problem. This can demotivate and create a sense of doom for the project team, which believes that the project cannot succeed given the number of identified negative risks. This can also affect senior management, project sponsors, and customers, who might believe that the project team is merely scaremongering, raising potential problems that might never happen, possibly trying to engender sympathy, or maybe even paving the way for project failure.

Managing issues is more fun and rewarding

Some believe that dealing with issues, problems, or even crises is more interesting and rewarding. Individuals might gain considerable satisfaction from solving a problem, especially if it's a big one, even if it could have been prevented by proactive risk management. In addition, many organizations reward those macho project managers who successfully resolve a major crisis and then deliver their project in line with its objectives. By contrast, the project manager who has avoided all problems by effectively applying risk management is often ignored, with the implication that "it must have been an easy project because nothing went wrong."

It's too late to carry out risk management

Some projects simply involve implementing predefined solutions in which all key objectives (time, cost, and quality) are pre-agreed and unchangeable. Where this is true, the project manager might see little point in taking time to identify risks that require additional work and more money to manage, when neither more resources nor more budget will be made available because the objectives are fixed and agreed upon in advance. The risk process might even reveal that achieving the agreed project objectives is impossible—an "unacceptable" conclusion. Although many would say that part of the purpose of risk management is to expose unachievable objectives, in reality this could put the project manager in a difficult position and could result in statements like, "Don't give me problems, just give me solutions," or, "Stop complaining, just do it."

I'm too busy dealing with issues

When projects are badly planned in the first place, issues and problems will quickly arise that can dominate the project's day-to-day management. In these situations project managers easily become consumed with the "now" problems and find it difficult, if not impossible, to worry about potential future events, even though identifying and proactively managing them would clearly be beneficial to the project. Frequently the result is that risk management never even gets started.

It's just common sense

Everyone looks both ways when they cross the road, don't they? Nobody would ever consider climbing a mountain without ropes, would they? The majority of people should surely carry out risk management on a day-to-day basis; it's just common sense. If this is true then we should expect that risk management will be applied intuitively to all projects, and that project managers will always do it without needing a formal or structured risk process.

We can't prove that risk management works

Some risks that are identified never materialize, and as a result some people think that considering things that might not happen is just a waste of time. In addition, it is difficult to prove that risk management is working on a project because there is never an identical project that can be run without risk management as a control. And where the risk process only addresses threats, successful risk management means nothing happens! Since it is impossible to prove a negative, the absence of unusual problems cannot be firmly linked with the use of risk management—the project might just have been lucky that no problems occurred.

Turning Negatives into Positives

Each of the excuses described above represents a potential barrier to implementing effective risk management. Where project stakeholders hold these views, it is important to address their concerns, correct their misperceptions, and allay their fears so that they can engage with the risk process and make it work. The following paragraphs outline possible approaches to deal with each point (summarized in Figure 2-2).

The risk process takes time and money

Implementing risk management does take time and does cost money. However, when applied properly, risk management actually saves time, saves money, and produces outputs of the required quality. The argument is similar to that supporting the use of quality procedures in project management, where proactive attention to potential problems ensures the best possible results by reducing wasted effort and materials caused by rework or solving problems.

Risk responses cost money

The cost of implementing new activities in order to manage risks is a fundamental part of applying the risk process. Failing to respond to risks through planned response activities means that risks will go unmanaged, the risk exposure will not change, and the risk management process will not be effective. The cost of risk responses should be seen as an investment in the project's success—"spending to save." A similar argument exists for the cost of quality, where rework or fixing noncompliances is recognized as being more expensive than doing the job right the first time. Equally for risk management, addressing a threat proactively usually costs less than it does to resolve a problem when it happens. And addressing an opportunity is clearly more cost-effective than missing a potential benefit.

Risk management doesn't work for us

Ineffective or badly applied risk management can cause more problems than it solves. Where this is the case, measures must be put in place to make the risk management process more effective, perhaps by training project team members or improving risk processes. Once these changes have been made then the organization must ensure proper application of the changed ways of working. If the excuse that "risk management doesn't work" is based on poor practice, the answer is to do it properly and it will work. Sometimes the belief that risk management is not applicable or helpful arises from a view that "our projects are different," a feeling that risk management might work for others but "it doesn't work for us." Here, a pilot project can be particularly useful in demonstrating the benefits of doing it properly on a real project.

Risk management is just scaremongering

Overemphasis on identifying every potential threat to the project can be overcome in two ways. The best solution is to ensure that the risk process also proactively identifies and addresses upside risks (opportunities) that counteract the threats. This also helps the project stakeholders realize that the project is not all "doom and gloom," and that things might get better as well as worse. The second part of the answer is to ensure that identified threats really do matter. Often many so-called threats may have little or no impact on the project, or might not even be risks at all. And of course where threats are identified that really could affect the project adversely, effective responses must be developed to reduce the risk exposure. The answer to the charge that risk management is merely scaremongering is to ensure that the risk assessment is realistic and presents genuine threats and opportunities together with appropriate responses.

Managing issues is more fun and rewarding

It is undoubtedly stimulating to tackle problems and crises, and it is right for organizations to reward the staff who have the skills to rescue troubled projects. However, the reward scheme should not incentivize macho behavior at the expense of prudent risk management. Organizations should also find ways to reward project managers who successfully manage the risks on their project. This may be through the creation of key performance indicators (KPIs) that measure the effectiveness of the risk process, linked to a risk-based bonus. One KPI related to effective risk management might be the number of issues that arise during the project: the greater the number of issues, the less effectively the risk management process has been applied.

It's too late to carry out risk management

The reality is it's never too late, because failing to identify risks doesn't make them go away; a risk identified is a risk that can be managed. Failing to identify and manage risks means that projects are taking risks blindfolded, leading to a higher number of problems and issues, and more missed opportunities. Even where project objectives are presented as "fixed," this does not guarantee that they are achievable, and the aim of the risk process is to maximize the chances of achieving objectives.

I'm too busy dealing with issues

This excuse can become a self-fulfilling prophecy. If risk management never starts, then more issues will arise that require immediate attention, reinforcing the problem. This downward spiral must be nipped in the bud. Making risk management mandatory might solve the problem, though there is a danger that imposing a risk process will result in project teams only paying lip service to it. A better strategy is to make a convincing argument that risk management is actually good for the project, and that carrying it out will prevent further issues and make life easier.

It's just common sense

The problem with common sense is that it's not very common. Risk management cannot be left to intuition because the stakes are too high. Of course, some people are very good at managing risk intuitively, and these individuals might be able to trust their common sense instead of following a structured approach to risk management. However, most people require some assistance in taking the necessary steps to identify and manage risk effectively. For the majority, having a framework within which to conduct the risk process is both helpful and necessary. A structured approach to risk management helps everyone do what the best practitioners do intuitively.

We can't prove that risk management works

This excuse might exist where the risk process is focused entirely on threats, since it is difficult to prove unambiguously that an absence of problems resulted from successful risk management. However, when the risk process also addresses upside risks (opportunities), a successful risk process results in measurable additional benefits, including saved time, reduced cost, reduced rework, etc. We recommend a broad approach to risk management covering both threats and opportunities; where this is implemented, evidence that risk management works can be gathered. It should also be recognized that risk management delivers a range of "soft" benefits in addition to those that are directly measurable, as reflected in Figure 2-3, which

"HARD" BENEFITS	"SOFT" BENEFITS
Generic Benefits of Risk Management	
Enables better informed and more believable plans, schedules, and budgets.	Improves corporate experience and general communication.
Increases the likelihood of a project adhering to its schedules and budgets.	Leads to a common understanding and improved team spirit.
Leads to the use of the most suitable type of contract.	Helps distinguish between good luck/good management and bad luck/bad management.
Allows a more meaningful assessment of contingencies.	Helps develop the ability of staff to assess risks.
Discourages the acceptance of financially unsound projects.	Focuses project management attention on the real and most important issues.
Contributes to the buildup of statistical information to assist in better management of future projects.	Facilitates greater risk-taking, thus increasing the benefits allowed.
Enables a more objective comparison of alternatives.	Demonstrates a responsible approach to customers.
Identifies and allocates responsibility to the best risk owner.	Provides a fresh view of the personnel issues in a project.
Organizational Benefits of Risk Management	
Compliance with corporate governance requirements.	Better reputation as a result of fewer headline project failures.
A greater potential for future business with existing customers.	Better customer relations due to improved performance on current projects.
Reduced cost base.	A less stressful working environment.

Source: *Project Risk Analysis and Management Guide.* 2nd Edition, APM Risk SIG.
© APM Publishing Limited 2004. Reproduced with permission.

FIGURE 2-3: Benefits of Risk Management

presents "hard" and "soft" benefits of risk management as listed in the *APM PRAM Guide*. Many of these benefits offer demonstrable proof of risk management's value to an organization and its projects. Finally, evidence can be sought from either within the organization or other similar organizations by reviewing case studies of successful projects where the results are attributed to effective risk management.

The Critical Success Factors for Risk Management

All of the common reasons/excuses for not applying risk management can be overcome by focusing on CSFs. It is possible to generate a long list of CSFs (for example, Figure 2-4); these have been grouped into four main categories for discussion in the following paragraphs.

Supportive organization

A supportive organization behaves in such a way that it is seen to be fully behind risk man-

SUPPORTIVE ORGANIZATION	COMPETENT PEOPLE
• Clear objectives for risk management • Availability of adequate resources • Buy-in from all stakeholders • A culture that recognizes that uncertainty is inevitable • Accept the need to change in response to risk management • Suitable contractual framework to support the risk process	• Shared understanding of the key concepts and principles of risk management • A common language and agreement of key risk management terms • Recognize the need for continuous training of staff • Skilled and competent staff • Combination of theoretical knowledge, effective behaviors, and appropriate attitudes
APPROPRIATE METHODS TOOLS, AND TECHNIQUES	**SIMPLE, SCALABLE PROCESS**
• Required level of infrastructure and software tools to support appropriate level of implementation • Training in the selected methods, tools, and techniques • Integrated toolkit, both internally coherent and interfacing with project management and business tools	• Recognize that "one size fits all" is the wrong approach • Efficient procedural framework • A documented process • Clear instruction on "what to do"

FIGURE 2-4: Critical Success Factors for Effective Risk Management

agement and all it entails. The organization "walks the talk." It ensures that there are clear objectives for risk management and that these objectives are bought into by all stakeholders, who also contribute inputs and commit to using the outputs of the process. The organization allows time in the schedule for risk management and it ensures that risk management occurs as early as possible in the project life cycle. The organization also provides the necessary resources and funding to carry it out. Supportive organizations recognize that the extra work identified to manage risks is fundamental to ensuring project success and needs to be adequately resourced. These organizations also accept the need to change in response to risk, and, where appropriate, provide a suitable contractual framework to facilitate the process.

In the same way that individuals have an attitude to risk that affects their participation in the risk process, organizations also have a "risk culture" that reflects their preferred approach to dealing with uncertainty. There is a range of organizational risk cultures, as illustrated in Figure 2-5. Organizations with a negative attitude to risk might be labeled as "risk-averse"; those with no strong response could be called "risk-tolerant;" "risk-seeking" organizations have a positive attitude toward risk. A fourth type of organizational risk culture is "risk-neutral," displaying a short-term risk aversion combined with a longer-term willingness to seek risk. These cultures have a significant influence on the risk management process. For example, extreme risk aversion can sometimes develop into hostility: "We don't have risk in our projects; we're professionals/engineers/scientists…." Denial results in important risks being ignored, and decisions being made without cognizance of the associated risks. At the other end of the scale, the risk-seeking organization might adopt a "gung ho" attitude to risk, which will likely lead to disaster if the amount of risk exposure taken on exceeds the organization's ability to manage it.

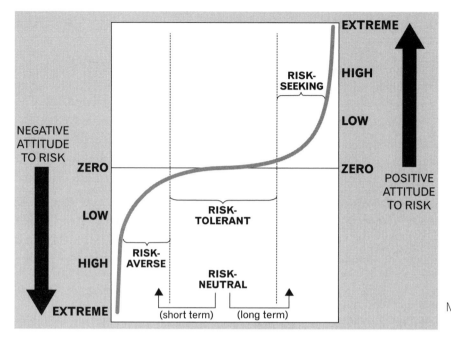

FIGURE 2-5: Range of Organizational Risk Cultures (Based on Hillson and Murray-Webster 2007)

The preferred risk attitude for an organization is neither risk-averse nor risk-seeking; rather, it is "risk-mature". This attitude produces a supportive culture in the organization, which recognizes and accepts that uncertainty is inevitable, and welcomes it as an opportunity to reap the rewards associated with effective risk management. These organizations set project budgets and schedules with the knowledge that uncertain events can influence project progress and outcomes, but also with a commitment to provide the necessary resources and support to manage these events proactively. Project managers and their teams are rewarded for managing risks appropriately, with the recognition that some unwelcome risks occur in even the best-managed project.

Culture is the total of the shared beliefs, values, and knowledge of a group of people with a common purpose. Culture therefore has both an individual and a corporate component. For risk management to be effective, the culture must be supportive, meaning that individuals' risk attitudes must be understood and managed, and the organization's overall approach must value risk management and commit to making it work.

Competent people

For many people, risk management seems to be neither common sense nor intuitive. Project sponsors, project managers, team members, and stakeholders must be trained in applying the process and/or participating in it. Training also needs to be at the right level and depth to suit the role involved. Effective training creates a shared understanding of the key concepts and principles of risk management. It enables the establishment of a common language and agreement on key risk management terms. Properly delivered training also helps to convince participants of the benefits of the process.

Training should not be viewed as a one-off event carried out when formal risk management is first introduced. It must be a continual process, bringing new members of the organization up to speed as soon as is practical. The end benefit of effective training is skilled and competent staff who contribute effectively to the risk process.

Attention should also be paid to ongoing competence development, with on-the-job training, job rotation, mentoring, coaching, etc., in addition to focused formal training courses. The aim is to develop practical skills as well as theoretical knowledge, encouraging effective behaviors and appropriate attitudes.

Appropriate methods, tools, and techniques

Different organizations may implement risk management in varying levels of detail, depending on the type of risk challenge they face. The decision about implementation level may also be driven by organizational risk appetite—the overall willingness or hunger to expose the organization to risk—and by the availability of funds, resources, and expertise to invest in risk management. The objective is for each organization to determine a level of risk management implementation that is appropriate and affordable. Having chosen this level, the organization then needs to provide the necessary infrastructure to support it.

Having selected the level of implementation, providing the required level of infrastructure to support the risk process is then possible. This might include choosing techniques, buying or developing software tools, allocating resources, providing training in both knowledge and skills, developing procedures that integrate with other business and project processes, producing templates for various elements of the risk process, and considering the need for support from external specialists. The required level for each of these factors will be different depending on the chosen implementation level.

Failure to provide an appropriate level of infrastructure can cripple risk management in an organization. Too little support makes efficient implementation of the risk process difficult, while too much infrastructure and process can be overly bureaucratic and fail to add value, in fact reducing the overall benefit. Getting the support infrastructure right is therefore a Critical Success Factor for effective risk management, because it enables the chosen level of risk process to deliver the expected benefits to the organization and its projects.

A simple, scalable process

Risk management is not "one size fits all." While all projects are risky, and risk management is an essential feature of effective project management, there are different ways of putting risk management into practice. At the simplest level is an informal risk process in which all the phases are undertaken, but with a very light touch. In this informal setting, the risk process might be implemented as a set of simple questions. For example:

- What are we trying to achieve?

- What could hinder or help us?

- Which of these are most important?

- What shall we do about it?

If these questions are followed by action and repeated regularly, the full risk process will have been followed, though without use of formal tools and techniques.

At the other extreme is a fully detailed risk process that uses a range of tools and techniques to support the various phases. For example, using this in-depth approach, stakeholder workshops might be used for the definition phase, followed by multiple risk identification techniques involving a full range of project stakeholders. Risk assessment would be both qualitative (with a Risk Register and various structural analyses) and quantitative (using Monte Carlo simulation, decision trees, or other statistical methods). Detailed response planning at both strategic and tactical levels might include calculation of risk-effectiveness, as well as consideration of secondary risks arising from response implementation.

Both of these approaches represent extremes, and the typical organization will wish to implement a level of risk management somewhere in between these two. These approaches do, however, illustrate how it is possible to retain a common risk methodology while selecting very different levels of implementation. Each organization wanting to adopt risk management consistently must first decide what level of implementation is appropriate.

A simple to use, scalable, and documented process ensures that each project does not have to work out the best way to apply risk management in its situation. An efficient procedural framework that supports the process and outlines "what to do" ensures support from the organization, and makes the most of the investment in training, tools, and techniques.

Conclusion

This chapter presented some of the common difficulties expressed by people who feel that risk management belongs in the "too difficult" category. It also offered counterarguments to each objection, suggesting that attention to CSFs can make the difference between wasting time on an ineffectual process and implementing risk management that works. If any of these supporting elements (see Figure 2-6) are weak or missing then the implementation of risk management becomes unstable and may even fall over.

Out of the four groups of CSFs discussed, the one that seems easiest to address is the last—implementation of a simple scalable process. This CSF allows project teams to apply risk management theory to their particular risk challenge. It also deals most directly with the main difficulty expressed by so many: "How exactly do we do risk management?" The rest of this book presents a detailed answer to this question, describing a simple scalable risk process that can be applied on any project in any industry. The next chapter introduces this process, known as Active Threat and Opportunity Management (ATOM), and Part II of the book describes the ATOM process in detail.

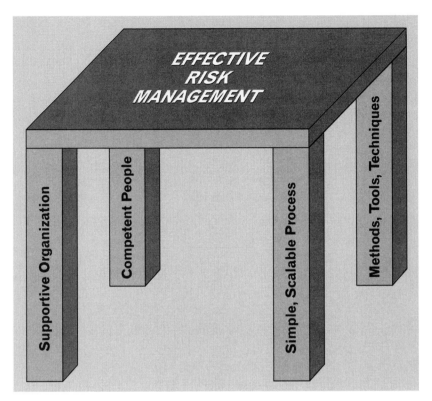

FIGURE 2-6:
Critical Success
Factors to Support
Effective Risk
Management

··

CHAPTER 3

Active Threat and Opportunity Management—The ATOM Risk Process

The benefits of formal risk management are undeniable and clear for all those who care to see. Even though this fact is recognized by many organizations, the reality is that risk management is rarely implemented effectively, often despite well-defined processes, the existence of proven tools and techniques, and many training opportunities for those who need it. If this is the case, then where is the problem? It appears that ineffectiveness stems largely from project managers and their teams not knowing how to actually do risk management. Clear, practical "how to" guidance is obviously needed; this also meets one of the four Critical Success Factors (CSFs) for risk management outlined in the previous chapter: a simple to use, scalable, and documented process that removes many of the barriers to the use of risk management for projects, and provides invaluable help to those who believe it to be important but are struggling to make it effective.

First we must determine what such a simple, scalable process should cover. A number of important steps must be included:

- If risk is defined as "any uncertainty that, if it occurs, would have a positive or negative effect on achievement of one or more objectives," then clearly the first step in a risk management process is to ensure that the objectives at risk are well defined and understood. These objectives might have been clarified outside the risk process (for example, in a project charter, business case, or statement of work), but risk management cannot begin without them, so if there is no clear list of project objectives, the risk process must produce one.

- After defining objectives, determining the uncertainties that might affect them is possible. As discussed in Chapter 1, potentially harmful uncertainties (threats) must be identified, as must those that might assist the project in achieving its objectives (opportunities).

- Of course, not all of the uncertainties identified in this way are equally important, so the risk process must include a step for filtering, sorting, and prioritizing risks to find the worst threats and the best opportunities. Examining groups of risks to determine whether there are any significant patterns or concentrations of risk is also useful. It might also be good to determine the overall effect of all identified risks on the final project outcome.

• Once risks have been identified and prioritized, the risk challenge faced by the project will be clear and the risk process can move from analysis to action. At this point attention turns to deciding how to respond appropriately to individual threats and opportunities, as well as considering how to tackle overall project risk. A range of options exists, from radical action such as canceling the project to doing nothing. Between these extremes lies a wide variety of action types: attempting to influence the risk, reducing threats, embracing opportunities, etc.

• The important step of planning responses is not enough to actually change risk exposure, of course; it must be followed by action, otherwise nothing changes. Planned responses must be implemented in order to change the risk exposure of the project, and the results of these responses must be monitored to ensure that they are having the desired effect.

• These steps in a risk process might be undertaken by just a few members of the project team, but the results are important for everyone, so it is essential to communicate what has been decided. Key stakeholders should be kept informed of identified risks and their importance, as well as what responses have been implemented and the current risk exposure of the project.

• Clearly the risk challenge faced by every project is dynamic and changing. As a result, the risk process must continually revisit the assessment of risk to ensure that appropriate action is being taken throughout the project.

• A fully effective risk process does not end at this point, because the learning organization wants to take advantage of the experience of running this project to benefit future projects. The normal Post-Project Review step must, of course, include risk-related elements so that future threats are minimized and opportunities captured in the most efficient and effective manner.

Introducing ATOM

The logical story outlined above is not rocket science, but it does offer a simple, structured way to deal with the uncertainties that might affect achievement of project objectives. Any project risk management process should follow these eight steps:

1. Define objectives

2. Identify relevant uncertainties

3. Prioritize uncertainties for further attention

4. Develop appropriate responses

5. Report results to key stakeholders

6. Implement agreed actions

7. Monitor changes to keep up to date

8. Learn lessons for the future

Active Threat and Opportunity Management (ATOM) is designed to meet the need for a simple scalable risk management process and to be applicable to all projects. It also embodies the steps described above in a generic risk management process that can be applied to all projects in any industry or business sector, whatever their size or complexity. ATOM brings together recognized best practices and tried-and-tested methods, tools, and techniques, combining them into an easy-to-use yet structured method for managing project risk.

The ATOM process is composed of the following eight steps:

1. Initiation

2. Identification

3. Assessment

4. Response Planning

5. Reporting

6. Implementation

7. Review

8. Post-Project Review

The Assessment step might also include quantitative risk analysis to determine the effect of risks on overall project outcome, though this is not always required (as discussed below). Figure 3-1 shows how these steps fit together into a cohesive process, which is described in detail for a typical project later in this chapter.

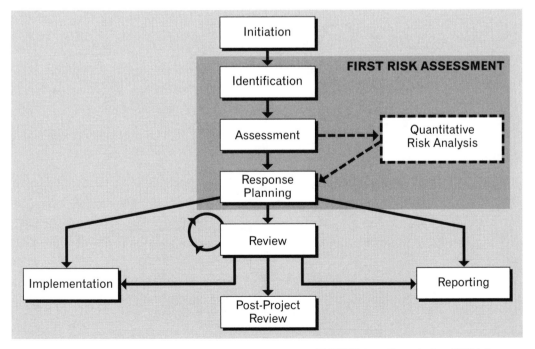

FIGURE 3-1: Steps in the ATOM Process

Of course risk does not appear just at the beginning of a project and then go away, so a risk management process cannot be performed just once. The ATOM approach recognizes the undeniable need to carry out risk management throughout the project life cycle, from concept to completion, or from the business justification to handover, as shown in Figure 3-2. Risk management is all too often seen as something done at the beginning of the project and then cast aside as other "proper project management processes" take over. This is clearly wrong. ATOM demands that, following an initial risk assessment, a series of reviews are undertaken through the life cycle of the project to keep the process alive. It is also important to recognize that part of any project's value is the organizational learning it offers to the business, which is why ATOM places emphasis on lessons learned as an essential part of project management. The ATOM risk management process also includes a final step to capture risk-related lessons at the end of a project, concluding with a formal Post-Project Review.

Figure 3-2 shows how the ATOM risk process might be conducted through the various phases of the project life cycle. For a typical project ATOM starts before the project is sanctioned or approved, by undertaking the Initiation step leading to a Risk Management Plan, followed by a First Risk Assessment to determine the risks associated with implementing the project. After the project sanction or approval, ATOM continues with a series of reviews throughout the project life cycle. The project life cycle is different for a contracting organization, which bids for work and only conducts the project if it wins it. For some contractors, ATOM starts when they win the work, which is when they undertake the Initiation and First Risk Assessment steps. For other contractors, ATOM starts during the bid process and is an integral part of putting the bid together. It is likely that a contractor that carries out Initiation and First Risk Assessment as part of the bid process will repeat the process if the bid is successful.

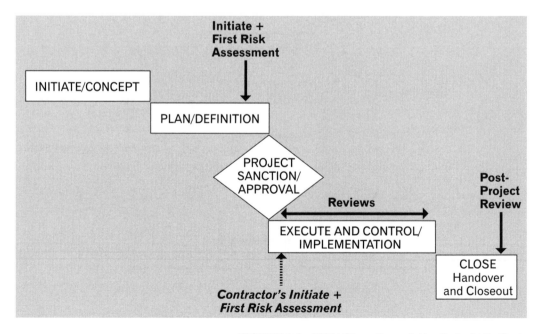

FIGURE 3-2: ATOM Steps through the Project Life Cycle

Project Sizing

No two projects are the same. Projects vary vastly in size and complexity. Some projects are started and finished in a few weeks, while others take a decade or more to complete. Some projects have budgets of a few thousand dollars (or even no budget at all), while others cost billions. Some projects are relatively routine, using tried and tested strategies, while others are totally innovative and groundbreaking.

In response to this wide variety of projects, ATOM offers a fully scalable risk management process that recognizes that simple or low-risk projects may need just a simple risk process, while complex or high-risk projects require more rigor and discipline. ATOM provides scalability in three ways: through the number and type of reviews required during the project life cycle, through the optional use of quantitative risk analysis techniques, and through the range of tools and techniques used during each of the ATOM steps.

- *Reviews.* Sometimes simply revisiting the risk process to determine changes to existing risks and whether any new risks have arisen is sufficient. At other times a full repeat of the entire risk process might be appropriate. ATOM uses two types of reviews to meet these needs: a Major Review and a Minor Review. These can be used in various combinations depending on the size of the project.

- *Quantitative risk analysis.* ATOM suggests reserving use of quantitative analysis for projects that are large or high-risk, where the investment in such techniques can be justified.

- *Tools and techniques:* Many techniques exist for the identification and assessment of risks. An appropriate set of techniques should be selected to meet the risk challenge of a particular project.

Figure 3-3 presents the full scalable ATOM risk process, indicating where reviews and quantitative risk analysis (QRA) might occur. Broken lines in Figure 3-3 indicate the optional nature of QRA.

With a scalable process, a method of deciding what level of process is appropriate for any particular project is clearly important. "Project size" is a multidimensional concept, with many factors to be considered. It is also a continuous variable, rather than one with a small number of discrete values. However, it is useful to have a simple tool that uses various criteria to characterize a given project, perhaps dividing projects into three groups that we can call "small, medium, or large." This tool has several uses, not just relating to risk management, because many project management processes can also be scalable depending on the size of the project.

One key question is how many criteria should be used in such a sizing tool. If too few criteria are used then it is difficult to distinguish between projects of different sizes. On the other hand, too many criteria can become overly complex and can lead to insufficient discrimination due to the averaging effect. Experience suggests that ten to 12 criteria is about right, giving a good compromise between detail and usability. Each organization should define those criteria that best describe the relative size and importance of a project within the business. One organization's "small" will be another organization's "large."

Even where sizing criteria are well defined, an organization may wish to allow shortcuts to

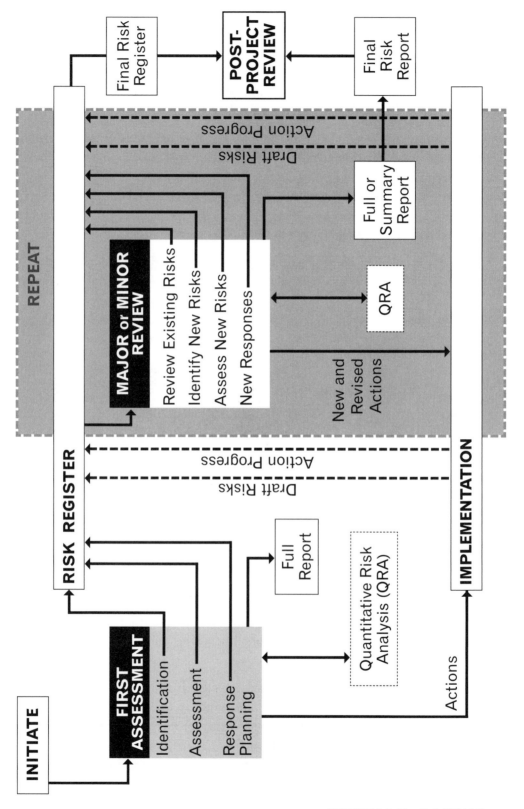

FIGURE 3-3: The Full ATOM Process

describe circumstances in which project size can be determined without use of the project sizing tool. For example, projects of very low value or very short duration might always be deemed small, while business-critical projects might always be large.

Figure 3-4 presents a sample project sizing tool to illustrate the approach that an organization might adopt in order to size a project. This example uses a Likert scale to translate qualitative descriptions of the sizing criteria into quantitative values that can be combined into a sizing score. Thresholds are then set to define small, medium, and large. Any given project can then be scored against the criteria in order to determine its size.

The example in Figure 3-4 is specific to a particular business, but can be tailored by another organization to include those criteria that reflect the types of projects it undertakes, because the general principles should apply.

This project sizing tool divides projects into three categories (small, medium, and large), to indicate the appropriate level of risk management process. Two shortcuts are used: Projects with value less than $50K are automatically defined as small, and projects valued at more than $5M are defined as large. Projects valued between $50K and $5M are assessed against the ten criteria below. For each criterion the closest description is selected, and the corresponding criterion score is recorded at the right of the row (one of 2, 4, 8, or 16). Criterion scores are totaled to give an overall project score, indicating project size as follows:

≥75	*Large project*	An extended ATOM risk management process is required.
35–74	*Medium project*	A standard ATOM risk management process is required.
<35	*Small project*	A reduced ATOM risk management process is required.

CRITERION	CRITERION VALUE= 2	CRITERION VALUE= 4	CRITERION VALUE= 8	CRITERION VALUE= 16	CRITERION SCORE
Strategic importance	Minor contribution to business objectives	Significant contribution to business objectives	Major contribution to business objectives	Critical to business success	
Commercial/ contractual complexity	No unusual commercial arrangements or conditions	Minor deviation from existing commercial practices	Novel commercial practices, new to at least one party	Groundbreaking commercial practices	
External constraints and dependencies	None	Some external influence on elements of the project	Key project objectives depend on external factors	Overall project success depends on external factors	
Requirement stability	Clear, fully defined, agreed objectives	Some requirement uncertainty, minor changes during project	Key project objectives depend on external factors	Requirements not finalized and subject to negotiation	
Technical complexity	Routine repeat business, no new technology	Enhancement of existing product/ service	Novel product/ project with some innovation	Groundbreaking project with high innovation	
Market sector regulatory characteristics	No regulatory requirements	Standard regulatory framework	Challenging regulatory requirements	Highly regulated or novel sector	
Project value	Small project value (<$250K)	Significant project value ($250K–$1M)	Major project value ($1M–$3M)	Large project value (>$3M)	
Project duration	Duration <3 months	Duration 3–12 months	Duration 1–3 years	Duration >3 years	
Project resources	Small in-house project team	Medium in-house project team	Large project team including external contractors	International project team or joint venture	
Post-project liabilities	None	Acceptable exposure	Significant exposure	Punitive exposure	
				OVERALL PROJECT SCORE	

FIGURE 3-4: Example Project Sizing Tool

Of course, there are exceptions to every rule, and it is important not to be process-driven when making important decisions on projects. There will always be projects that score as medium or small using a project sizing tool, but that are so strategically important or commercially sensitive that it would be foolhardy not to treat them as large. Such decisions to contradict the output of the project sizing tool should only be made by the project sponsor in consultation with the project manager.

Most project-based organizations have a portfolio of projects of various sizes, including small, medium, and large ones, all of which require active management of risk, though at different levels. A reduced level of risk management attention is appropriate for small projects because they matter less to the business and the potential for variation is usually small. By contrast, large projects require a higher level of risk management attention because any variation is likely to be significant.

The typical ATOM process is designed for medium-size projects, though it is scalable for small and large ones. Taking the basic ATOM process as shown in Figure 3-3, the main differences for the three project sizes are as follows:

- Small projects require a reduced ATOM risk management process that is integrated into the normal day-to-day management of the project without using dedicated risk meetings.

- Medium projects require the application of the standard ATOM risk process with risk-specific activities in addition to the normal project process. These are led by a risk champion who oversees use of specific risk meetings, including workshops, interviews, and ongoing reviews.

- Large projects require an extended ATOM process, which includes quantitative risk analysis and a more rigorous review cycle in addition to the elements applied for medium projects.

It is important for the depth of the risk process to match the risk challenge of the project. For example, applying a reduced risk process to a medium or large project is likely to result in the failure to properly resource the process and ineffective management of risk.

The ATOM process for a medium-size project is described in detail in Part II (Chapters 4 through 12) and is summarized below. Recommended variations in using ATOM for small and large projects are covered in Chapters 13 and 14, respectively.

ATOM for the Typical Project

The ATOM process for a typical medium-size project requires a structured approach, as follows.

Like most other risk management processes, ATOM starts with an Initiation step. This step, described in Chapter 4, considers project stakeholders and their relationship to the project. A fundamental part of the Initiation step is confirmation of the project objectives to ensure that they are clearly understood and documented, and as a result the uncertainties that matter can be determined and subsequently prioritized. The size of the project, and therefore the degree to which ATOM should be applied, is also confirmed. Initiation culminates with the preparation of a Risk Management Plan.

This is followed by three sequential steps that make up the First Risk Assessment, namely Identification, Assessment, and Response Planning. A formal two-day risk workshop is used to identify project risks (see Chapter 5) as well as to assess their probability and impacts against predefined scales as set out in the Risk Management Plan (see Chapter 6). The aim of the Identification step is to identify and properly describe relevant uncertainties, including both positive opportunities and negative threats that could affect project objectives. Assessment provides the means to determine which uncertainties matter most to the project, by considering the probability of the risk occurring and its potential impact on the defined project objectives. During Identification and Assessment, all identified risks and their assessment data are recorded in a newly created project Risk Register. Following the risk workshop, Response Planning takes place via a series of interviews with identified risk owners, during which responses are identified with their associated actions (see Chapter 7). The appropriateness of the response is paramount to this step to ensure that responses are not only physically effective but also timely and cost-effective.

Once the First Risk Assessment step is complete, the next two steps in the ATOM process take place in parallel. A risk report documenting the results from the First Risk Assessment is prepared and disseminated to those who need to receive it; this Reporting step is described in Chapter 8. Reporting is one of the ways in which the dynamic nature of risk is communicated, because reports highlight significant changes to project risk exposure.

At the same time as the Reporting step, the ongoing step of Implementation of responses via their associated actions also starts (see Chapter 9). Implementation of responses continues throughout the project, only concluding when the project ends. Without effective implementation, the risk exposure of the project remains unchanged.

Fundamental to keeping the process alive throughout the project life cycle is the use of formal risk reviews. At predetermined points in the life cycle, as set out in the Risk Management Plan, a Major Review (see Chapter 10) takes place that includes the same elements as the First Risk Assessment but on a reduced scale. All key stakeholders attend a risk workshop to review existing risks, and identify and assess new risks, resulting in an update to the Risk Register. Risk responses and their associated actions are identified by interviewing risk owners as soon as possible after the risk workshop. Agreed responses and actions are recorded in the Risk Register. New and revised actions are implemented through the ongoing Implementation step. A full report is produced at the end of the Major Review.

At regular points in the project, usually in line with the normal project reporting cycle, risk management is formally revisited as part of a Minor Review (see Chapter 11). A Minor Review may take place as part of a normal project review or as a separate meeting. During a Minor Review all high-priority risks are reviewed, new risks are identified and assessed, and responses are planned; the Risk Register is then updated. As for the Major Review, new and revised actions are implemented through the ongoing Implementation step. A summary report is produced at the end of each Minor Review.

The ATOM process concludes either at the formal Post-Project Review meeting or at a separate meeting, during which a "risk lessons learned" report is produced and the final Risk Register agreed. Chapter 12 describes this conclusion to the ATOM process.

The ATOM process for the typical medium-size project is purely qualitative, with no use of statistical processes to predict the overall effect of risk on project outcome. Quantitative risk analysis techniques are an important part of project risk management, but ATOM suggests that they should only be mandatory for large projects. This does not, however, mean that quantitative risk analysis cannot be used effectively on medium or even small projects, but this analysis should be at the discretion of the project manager and considered during the ATOM Initiation step. Quantitative risk analysis is valuable because it models the effect of identified risks on the project schedule and budget, calculating the range of possible completion dates (and interim milestones) and final project cost. It is also possible to predict ranges of outcomes for other project criteria, such as Net Present Value (NPV) and Internal Rate of Return (IRR). This information can be beneficial when determining the correct strategy for the project and for understanding the effects of managing individual risks. Chapter 15 describes how to apply quantitative risk analysis to projects.

Comparison to Existing Standards

A number of standards documents in the project risk management area offer different approaches to the subject. The most popular of these include:

- *Guide to the Project Management Body of Knowledge* (PMBOK®), from the Project Management Institute (PMI®), particularly Chapter 11, "Project Risk Management"

- *Project Risk Analysis and Management (PRAM) Guide,* from the Association for Project Management (APM)

- *Management of Risk* (M_o_R), from the U.K. Office of Government Commerce (OGC)

- AS/NZS 4360:2004 *Risk Management*

- IRM/ALARM/AIRMIC *Risk Management Standard*

- *Risk Analysis and Management for Projects (RAMP),* from the U.K. Institution of Civil Engineers, Faculty of Actuaries and Institute of Actuaries

- BS IEC 62198:2001 *Project risk management. Application guidelines*

- BS6079-3:2000 *Project management—Part 3: Guide to the risk management of business related project risk*

Although several different standards cover the topic, there is good agreement among their content, with the main differences being terminology. Those familiar with these standards should have no problem understanding or applying the ATOM process, since ATOM is fully consistent with them all. The key differences between ATOM and the standards are summarized in Figure 3-5, which compares their use of terminology, the different constituent stages of each process (mapped to ATOM steps labeled A through H), and the unique aspects of each approach.

The fact that ATOM is consistent with the main project risk management standards raises the question of why it should be used instead of what already exists. The main difference is that ATOM is not a standard. Rather, it is a practical methodology describing how to do risk management for a real project, rather than a theoretical framework or set of principles. ATOM is

	DEFINITION OF RISK	RISK MANAGEMENT PROCESS	UNIQUE ASPECTS AND EMPHASIS
ATOM	Any uncertainty that, if it occurred, would have a positive or negative effect on achievement of one or more objectives	A Initiation B Identification C1 Assessment C2 (Quantitative risk analysis) D Response planning E Reporting F Implementation G Review H Post-project review	• Totally scalable • Can be used on all projects • Practical "how to" methodology
Guide to the Project Management Body of Knowledge (PMBOK®), Third edition (2004)	An uncertain event or condition that, if it occurred, would have a positive or negative effect on a project's objectives	A Risk management planning B Risk identification C1 Qualitative risk analysis C2 Quantitative risk analysis D Risk response planning E/G Risk monitoring and control	• Strong process orientation (inputs/tools and techniques/outputs) • Addresses opportunities as well as threats
Project Risk Analysis and Management (PRAM) Guide, Second edition (2004)	**Risk event:** An uncertain event or set of circumstances that, should it or they occur, would have an effect on the achievement of one or more of the project's objectives **Project risk:** The exposure of stakeholders to the consequences of variations in outcome	A Initiate B Identify C Assess D Plan responses E Implement responses ? Manage process	• Includes chapters on benefits of managing risks (2), establishing a risk management organization (5), behavioral aspects (6), and implementation/ application issues (7) • Addresses threats and opportunities • Defines risk at two levels: risk event and project risk
Management of Risk—Guidance for Practitioners (M_o_R) (2007)	An uncertain event or set of events that, should it occur, will have an effect on the achievement of objectives. A risk is measured by a combination of the probability of a perceived threat or opportunity occurring and the magnitude of its impact on objectives	A Identify - context B Identify – identify the risks C1 Assess - estimate C2 Assess - evaluate D Plan F Implement ? Embed and review ? Communicate	• Entire chapters on management of risk principles and embedding and reviewing management of risk. • Applicable to strategic, program, project, and operational risk • Part of a larger suite of methods including Managing Successful Programmes and PRINCE2
AS/NZS 4360: 2004 Risk Management (2004)	The chance of something happening that will have an impact on objectives	A Establish context B Identify risks C Analyse risks C Evaluate risks D Treat risks G Monitor and review E Communicate and consult	• Applicable to business and projects • Entire chapter (2) devoted to embedding risk management in the organization • Lists communication and consultation as a main element of the process

FIGURE 3-5: Comparison of Different Standards

	DEFINITION OF RISK	RISK MANAGEMENT PROCESS	UNIQUE ASPECTS AND EMPHASIS
IRM/ALARM/ AIRMIC Risk Management Standard (2002)	The combination of the probability of an event and its consequences	A The organization's strategic objectives B Risk identification B Risk description C Risk estimation C Risk evaluation E Risk reporting D Risk treatment G Monitoring and review	• Applicable to business and projects • Link to organization strategic management • Chapter 9 devoted to roles of various functions in the organization
Risk Analysis and Management for Projects (RAMP), Second edition (2005)	A threat (or opportunity) that could affect adversely (or favorably) achievement of the objectives of an investment	A Process launch B Plan and initiate risk review B Identify risks C Evaluate risks D Devise measures for responding to risks D Assess residual risks and decide whether to continue D Plan responses to residual risks E Communicate risk response strategy and response plan F Implement strategy and plans G Control risks H Process closedown	• Considers opportunities as well as threats • Focus is on whole life assets, with emphasis on capital projects
BS IEC 62198: 2001 Project risk management. Application guidelines (2002)	Combination of the probability of an event occurring and its consequences on project objectives	A Establishing the context B Risk identifications C Risk assessment D Risk treatment F/G Risk review and monitoring H Post-project	• Originated as part of dependability standard • Focus on projects with technological content
BS6079-3:2000 Project management— Part 3: Guide to the risk management of business related project risk (2000)	Uncertainty inherent in plans and the possibility of something happening (i.e., a contingency) that can affect the possibility of achieving business or project goals	A Context B Risk identification C Risk analysis C Risk evaluation D Risk treatment E/F/G Communicate/monitor and review/update plans	• Focus on link to business objectives and strategy • Roles of perception and stakeholder analysis

FIGURE 3-5: Comparison of Different Standards (*continued*)

intended to make project risk management accessible to all and easy to use, with enough detail to support practical implementation on any project in any organization or industry type.

Conclusion

One of the main Critical Success Factors for effective risk management is a simple scalable process. ATOM offers such a process, and following it allows any organization to identify and manage risks to its projects in a way that is appropriate and affordable. Using ATOM provides assurance that the main risks will be exposed, thereby minimizing threats, maximizing opportunities, and optimizing the chance of achieving project objectives.

PART II

Applying **ATOM** to a Typical Project

....

CHAPTER 4

Start at the Beginning
(Initiation)

Everyone recognizes that risks must be *managed,* and that managing risks requires development and implementation of appropriate *responses.* Determining the appropriate type of response is not possible without first *assessing and/or analyzing* the characteristics and significance of a risk—of course this assumes that risks have actually been *identified.* This logical chain of reasoning forms the basis for the core steps in the ATOM risk management process (see Figure 3-1), namely Identification, Assessment, Response Planning, Reporting, Review, and Implementation.

It seems obvious that the first task in a risk management process is to identify the risks, and until recently the first step in most risk management processes was Identification. However, Chapter 1 points out that risk can only be defined in relation to objectives, which means that one cannot identify any risks until objectives are defined and agreed. In reality, in many cases project objectives are either not clear, not agreed, or not documented. Projects are still launched prematurely, with the intention to "tidy up loose ends later." This lack of definition makes it impossible to identify risks properly, leading to confusion and conflict, disagreement and disillusionment, and ultimately ineffective risk management. This shortfall must be rectified before the risk process can start. It is also necessary to decide which objectives are to be included within the scope of the risk process, because the boundary can be drawn in various places. For example, a project might decide to perform only a technical risk assessment, or to focus instead on schedule risk exposure, budget uncertainties, or organizational reputation.

Something else is required before risk identification can commence. Simply defining the project objectives and then getting on with the risk management process is not enough. Organizations and projects must recognize that there cannot be a "one size fits all" approach to risk management. While ATOM offers a standardized risk management process, the depth at which it is implemented can vary. It is possible to do risk management very simply, perhaps only involving the project manager stepping through the process informally and quickly, using the minimum of tools and techniques. On the other hand, the risk management process can be performed in some detail, involving all project stakeholders, using a variety of approaches and tools, including sophisticated analysis and simulation. Significant amounts of time, effort, and money can be spent on understanding, assessing, and managing the risks. In fact, there is a spectrum of possible implementation levels at which risk management can be undertaken, and one must decide the appropriate level for a particular project. In ATOM this is determined by using a project sizing tool.

It is important to involve key stakeholders in decisions about scope and objectives, and the appropriate process level. However, it is not always clear who these stakeholders are, or who can make such decisions on behalf of the project. Stakeholder analysis answers these questions, and often forms part of the pre-project definition and planning phase—but not always. If key stakeholders have not already been identified it is important to undertake a stakeholder analysis to determine who should be involved in setting the parameters of the risk process.

To address these potential problems, most current risk management processes include a step prior to risk identification; in ATOM this is called Initiation. The purpose of this step is to:

- Clarify which stakeholders should set the parameters of the risk process

- Decide on the appropriate level of risk process for this project

- Define the scope and objectives of the risk process

The Initiation step requires the following inputs:

- List of key stakeholders, if available

- Defined project objectives, usually documented in the business case, project charter and scope statement, or bid documentation

- Project sizing tool (if project sizing has not already been done)

In ATOM, Initiation requires the following activities:

- Stakeholder analysis (if it has not already been done for this project)

- Project sizing, to confirm the appropriate level of risk process

- Facilitated Initiation meeting to decide the parameters of the risk process

The Initiation step produces the following outputs:

- List of key stakeholders and their relationship to the project (unless this was previously available)

- Agreed level of risk process appropriate to the project size

- Risk Management Plan, which records decisions on the scope, objectives, and parameters of the risk process

These inputs, activities, and outputs are illustrated in Figure 4-1, and described in detail in the following sections.

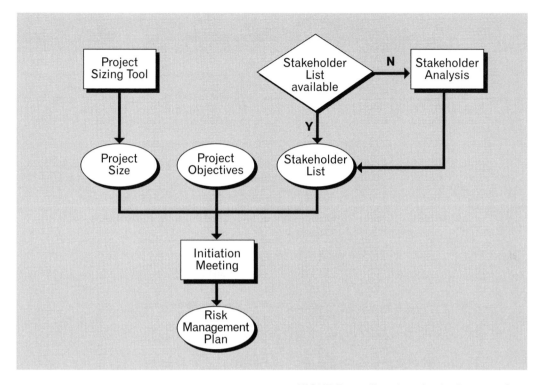

FIGURE 4-1: Flowchart for the Initiation Step

Inputs

Key stakeholders are responsible for making important decisions about how the project should be managed, including the risk process. It is therefore essential to identify these people and understand their relationship to the project. Stakeholder analysis is commonly performed before the project is formally sanctioned, and documented in the business case or project charter. When this analysis is completed prior to the Initiation step, information on key stakeholders can be used directly to determine their input to the risk process. Otherwise a stakeholder analysis must be undertaken during Initiation.

Similarly, project objectives should be clearly recorded in the business case or project charter; for external projects they may form part of the bid documentation, such as an invitation to tender (ITT) or request for proposal (RFP). If project objectives are already unambiguously defined, they can form an input to Initiation, otherwise they must be clarified as part of this step.

Activities

Stakeholder analysis

The first activity of the ATOM Initiation step is determining the key stakeholders, because these people will provide essential input on future decisions. If a prior stakeholder analysis is available, the results should be used directly, otherwise such an analysis must be undertaken here. A recommended method for stakeholder analysis is based on assessing three dimensions for each stakeholder (as illustrated in Figures 4-2 and 4-3):

Stakeholder	Area of Interest	Attitude (+/–)	Power (+/–)	Interest (+/–)	Stakeholder Type

Instructions:
- List all key stakeholders and their interest (or stake) in the project in the first two columns.
- For each stakeholder, identify whether their attitude toward the project is supportive or resistant (+ or –), whether their power to influence the project is high or low (+ or –), and whether their level of interest in the project is high or low (+ or –).

FIGURE 4-2: Stakeholder Analysis Template

- Their *attitude* toward the project, either supportive or resistant

- Their *power* to influence the project for better or worse

- Their level of *interest* in the project and its success or failure

Assessment of these three dimensions can be recorded using a stakeholder analysis template similar to that shown in Figure 4-2. Figure 4-3 shows how this assessment maps stakeholders in one of eight positions: Savior, Friend, Sleeping Giant, Acquaintance, Saboteur, Irritant, Time Bomb, or Tripwire. These positions are described in detail in Figure 4-4.

Having completed a stakeholder analysis, the project sponsor and project manager identify the key stakeholders and therefore who should contribute to decisions about the risk process. All Saviors are definitely invited to attend the Initiation meeting, and it is worth inviting Sleeping Giants in order to engage their interest. The project sponsor and project manager might seek the views of Saboteurs and Time Bombs (outside the meeting) if they feel able to contain any possible negative input and convert these stakeholders into supporters. Although Friends and Acquaintances support the project, their contribution is limited by their low power or low interest levels, so they need not be included. Irritants and Tripwires are also excluded.

The project manager decides how the role of risk champion will be fulfilled for the project. The risk champion is responsible for facilitating the risk process (see Figure 4-7).

Project sizing

The assumption is that the organization has prepared a project sizing tool for use in all projects, as discussed in Chapter 3 (see Figure 3-4). This tool lists criteria that determine the importance of the project to the organization and that give an indication of the level of risk. Projects can then be scored on a consistent basis, and ranked relative to one another. Projects that are strategically important or particularly risky require a more robust risk process than smaller projects, where a simpler process can be employed.

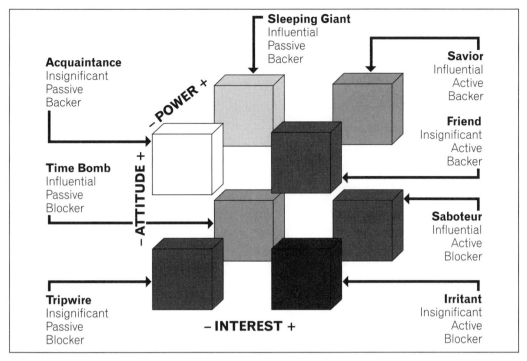

FIGURE 4-3: Stakeholder Mapping Cube (from Murray-Webster and Simon 2006)

When a project sizing tool exists, the project sponsor and project manager together complete it for the project to determine whether the project rates as small, medium, or large. This information is used during the Initiation meeting to inform decisions about how detailed the risk process should be.

If the organization does not have a project sizing tool, the project may wish to develop one that can be used more widely within the business. Alternatively, key stakeholders' views can be sought to determine whether this project should be treated as small, medium, or large. Whichever method is used, project sizing should be done prior to the Initiation meeting and then confirmed as part of the meeting. The rest of this chapter assumes that the project is medium-size.

Initiation meeting

Key decisions about the risk process for a particular project are made at the Initiation meeting, which is attended by key stakeholders and facilitated by the risk champion. For a medium-size project, this meeting might be expected to last a day. Before the meeting, the risk champion briefs the attendees on its content and format as well as their expected contribution. A typical agenda for the Initiation meeting is given in Figure 4-5.

The Initiation meeting is required only for medium and large projects; small projects are handled differently (see Chapter 13). The project size of either medium or large should have been determined prior to the meeting. Assuming this has been done, the Initiation meeting starts with a brief discussion among key stakeholders, facilitated by the risk champion, to confirm the project size. If size has not been predetermined, a discussion is held to determine the project size using the project sizing tool.

TYPE	ATTITUDE	POWER	INTEREST	DESCRIPTION
Savior	+	+	+	Powerful, with a high interest level and a positive attitude toward the project. It is important to pay attention to these stakeholders; harness their support and do whatever is necessary to keep it.
Friend	+	−	+	Low power, but high interest and positive attitude, these stakeholders can be used as confidants or sounding boards. Maintain their support in case they gain additional power within the organization.
Sleeping Giant	+	+	−	Powerful stakeholders who support the project but displaying low levels of interest; they need to be awakened to raise their commitment to the project and maximize their positive input.
Acquaintance	+	−	−	Low-power, low-interest backers who should be kept informed, but need not be a top priority unless their levels of power or interest increase.
Saboteur	−	+	+	Powerful, with a high interest level in the project, but display a negative attitude; they must be actively engaged to prevent them causing significant disruption to the project. The aim is to make their attitude toward the project more supportive and to use their influence to benefit the project.
Irritant	−	−	+	Very interested in the project but do not support it, though they have little power to influence things. Their negative attitude must be contained and countered where possible.
Time Bomb	−	+	−	Powerful but with low interest levels and a negative attitude toward the project; these stakeholders must be understood so they can be "defused before the bomb goes off." Efforts should be made to improve their attitude and engage active input.
Tripwire	−	−	−	Low-power, low-interest, negative-attitude stakeholders who are likely to hinder the project; their interaction with the project should be minimized as much as possible.

FIGURE 4-4: Descriptions of Different Stakeholders

Having sized the project, it is then possible to define the appropriate level of risk management process to be used. This definition should address the following process characteristics:

- Scope and objectives of the risk management process

- The degree to which ATOM should be applied

- Schedule of planned ATOM activities

- Tools and techniques to be used

TIME ALLOWANCE (hours)	CONTENT
½	1. Introductions
¼	2. Background to the project
½–1	3. Clarification of project objectives: scope, time, cost, quality, other objectives
¼	4. Scope and objectives of the risk management process
¼	5. Application of the ATOM risk management process
¼	6. Tools and techniques to be used
½	7. Roles and responsibilities for risk management
¼	8. Reporting and review requirements
¼	9. Definitions of scales for probability and impacts (P-I scales)
¼	10. Risk thresholds
¼	11. Potential sources of risk to this project
¼	12. Next steps

FIGURE 4-5: Typical Agenda for an Initiation Meeting

- Roles and responsibilities for risk management

- Reporting and review requirements

- Definitions of probability and impact scales for qualitative assessment

Everyone involved with the project must be clear about each of these aspects before they try to manage risk on the project. Therefore, decisions about each item must be documented and made available to all project stakeholders. This is done in a process description document called the Risk Management Plan, which details how risk management will be performed on a particular project. (Some organizations may use other names for this document, such as the Risk Strategy Statement or Risk Policy Document.) The content of a typical Risk Management Plan for a medium-size project is described in the following section of this chapter, with a template in Appendix A-1.

The previous elements are considered by key stakeholders in the Initiation meeting, which is facilitated by the risk champion.

CLARIFICATION OF PROJECT OBJECTIVES

Of course, project objectives should be defined and documented before the project starts, and should be included in the business case or project charter, or in the ITT/RFP for external projects. These documents should record project objectives, link them to the business case and strategic goals of the organization, and prioritize them to indicate which takes precedence if trade-offs are required. If this prior definition of objectives has already been completed, the Risk Management Plan can simply refer to the document that contains the statement of objectives. If, however, the project does not already have clearly stated objectives, they must be defined at the start of the Initiation meeting because the risk process cannot continue without them.

Project objectives usually cover the scope, time, cost, and quality requirements of the project.

There is, however, a range of other possible objectives that might be set for a particular project. These objectives might include: technical performance, reputation, safety, regulatory compliance, maintainability, operability, reliability, etc.

To define, clarify, or confirm project objectives, the following questions are considered during the meeting:

- *Scope:* What is included and excluded in the project scope? What are the project deliverables?

- *Time:* Is there a date by which this project must be completed? Are there any intermediate milestones during the project? Are any interim deliverables required before project completion?

- *Cost:* What budget has been set for this project? How much contingency and/or management reserve is set aside? Are there targets for cash flow, margin, profitability, Return on Investment (ROI), etc.?

- *Quality:* Are there specific quality requirements for this project? What are the acceptance criteria?

- *Other objectives:* Are these clearly defined, agreed, and documented?

The answers to these questions are documented in the Risk Management Plan, which forms the output from this Initiation step.

SCOPE AND OBJECTIVES OF THE RISK MANAGEMENT PROCESS

Clearly defined project objectives, either from a preexisting document or following a definition exercise during the Initiation meeting, make it possible to consider the scope of the risk management process. The key stakeholders discuss and agree on which of the project objectives are to be included in the risk process, and they define the boundary of what is included and excluded. It is also important to consider risk process scope in organizational terms. For example, will the risk process address risks only within the main project, or will it also include supplier risks, subcontract risks, program risks, corporate risks, etc.?

Deciding which objectives are in scope is essential to risk identification, because risks are defined in terms of the objectives that would be affected should the risk occur. For example, it might be decided to undertake a purely technical risk assessment, identifying and managing only those uncertainties that could affect technical performance objectives. Or the risk process might be expected to include all project objectives, including scope, time, cost, quality, etc. Alternatively it might be decided to use the risk process to address risks to both this project and the program or portfolio to which it belongs.

Finally, in this part of the Initiation meeting, clear objectives are set for the risk process itself, against which the performance of the risk process can be measured.

APPLICATION OF THE ATOM RISK MANAGEMENT PROCESS

Like most risk methods, ATOM can be tailored to meet the specific requirements of a particular project, and such tailoring is discussed and agreed on by key stakeholders during the meeting; decisions are documented in the Risk Management Plan.

TOOLS AND TECHNIQUES TO BE USED

The organization might apply a standard set of risk tools and techniques during the risk process, and it might decide during the Initiation meeting simply to use the standard approach. Alternatively there may be a case for changing the tools and techniques, and this is discussed, agreed, and documented in the Risk Management Plan.

ROLES AND RESPONSIBILITIES FOR RISK MANAGEMENT

The contribution of the key participants in the risk process is defined and agreed during the meeting. This can be done simply by discussion, listing the various tasks and agreeing who will do what. A more structured analysis might be more useful; for example, using a responsibility assignment matrix (RAM) in the format of a RACI chart, which allocates one or more stakeholders to each of four responsibilities:

- Responsible for performing the activity

- Accountable for the task (and may also Approve the output)

- Consulted about the task (or Contributes to it)

- Informed about the task

An example RACI chart is given in Figure 4-6. The list of agreed roles and responsibilities is

	PROJECT SPONSOR	PROJECT MANAGER	RISK CHAMPION	RISK OWNER	ACTION OWNER	PROJECT TEAM MEMBERS	OTHER STAKEHOLDERS
Produce and maintain Risk Management Plan	C	A	R	I	I	I	I
Facilitate risk process (workshops, interviews, risk review meetings, etc.)		A	R				
Identify risks	R	R	A	I		R	R
Assess risks		R	A	I		R	R
Develop responses		A	C	R	C	C	I
Implement responses		I	I	A	R	C	I
Report progress on actions (individual risks)		I	A	R	R		
Produce and maintain Risk Register	I	A	R	C	I	I	I
Produce and maintain risk reports	I	A	R	C	I	I	I
Key:							
R= Responsible **A**= Accountable/Approve **C**= Consult/Contribute **I**= Inform							

FIGURE 4-6: Example RACI Chart

documented in the Risk Management Plan, together with the RACI chart if one is produced. Figure 4-7 lists the key roles associated with the ATOM process: project sponsor, project manager, risk champion, risk owner, action owner, project team members, and other stakeholders.

REPORTING AND REVIEW REQUIREMENTS

The information needs of key stakeholders are considered in order to define what outputs are required from the risk process. This information is captured in the Risk Management Plan, and also forms part of the project communication plan, if one exists. For a medium-size

---

Project sponsor
Has overall accountability for the project and for delivering the project's promised benefits, and as such is considered by many to be the ultimate risk taker and perhaps risk owner. The project sponsor ensures that resources and funds for risk management are provided to the project.
The role of the project sponsor, in relation to risk management, includes:
- Actively supporting and encouraging the implementation of a formal risk management process on the project
- Setting and monitoring risk thresholds and ensuring these are translated into acceptable levels of risk for the project
- Attending risk workshops, identifying risks and ownership of risks
- Reviewing risk outputs from the project with the project manager to ensure process consistency and effectiveness
- Reviewing risks escalated by the project manager that are outside the scope or control of the project or that require input or action from outside the project
- Making decisions on project strategy in light of current risk status in order to maintain acceptable risk exposure
- Ensuring that adequate resources are available to the project to respond appropriately to identified risks
- Releasing management reserve funds to the project where justified to deal with exceptional risks
- Regularly reporting risk status to senior management

Project manager
Has overall responsibility for delivering the project on time, within budget, and to the agreed level of quality such that the project's outputs will allow the promised benefits to be achieved. The project manager is accountable for the day-to-day management of the project, and, as part of this, makes sure that risk management takes place and that risks are identified and managed through effective risk management.
The role of the project manager includes:
- Determining the acceptable levels of risk for the project by consulting with the project sponsor
- Approving the Risk Management Plan prepared by the risk champion
- Promoting the risk management process for the project
- Participating in risk workshops and review meetings, and identifying and owning risks
- Approving risk response plans and their associated risk actions prior to implementation
- Applying project contingency funds to deal with identified risks that occur during the project
- Overseeing risk management by subcontractors and suppliers
- Regularly reporting risk status to the project sponsor and project board/steering committee, with recommendations for appropriate strategic decisions and actions to maintain acceptable risk exposure
- Highlighting to senior management any identified risks that are outside the scope or control of the project, or that require input or action from outside the project, or where release of management reserve funds might be appropriate
- Monitoring the efficiency and effectiveness of the process in conjunction with the risk champion
The project manager reports to the project sponsor.

Risk champion
(This role might be full-time or part-time.) Responsible for overseeing and managing the risk management process on a day-to-day basis.
The role of the risk champion includes:
- Preparing the Risk Management Plan
- Facilitating risk workshops and risk reviews, at which risks are identified and assessed
- Creating and maintaining the Risk Register
- Interviewing risk owners to determine risk responses
- Ensuring the quality of all risk data
- Analyzing data and producing risk reports
- Reviewing progress of risk responses and their associated actions with risk owners
- Advising the project manager on all matters relating to risk management
- Coaching and mentoring team members and other stakeholders on aspects of risk management
The risk champion reports to the project manager.

FIGURE 4-7: Roles and Responsibilities within ATOM

Risk owner
Appointed by the project manager in liaison with the risk champion as the best person to manage an identified risk. The risk owner's role is temporary, in that once a risk has been closed his role ceases. A risk owner can be a member of the project team, a stakeholder who is not part of the project team, or specialist from outside the project. The role of the risk owner includes:
- Developing responses to risks in the form of risk actions, which they then assign to action owners
- Monitoring the progress on their risk responses
- Reporting progress on responses to the risk champion via the Risk Register

Action owner
Appointed by risk owners to perform the actions that make up a response to a risk. Like the role of the risk owner, the role of the risk action owner is temporary, as once the action has been completed their role ceases. Several action owners may contribute to the response to one risk.
- Implementing agreed actions to support response strategies
- Reporting progress on actions to the risk owner and recommending other actions needed to manage the risk

Project team members
Report to the project manager, and ensure that they and others who report to them follow the Risk Management Plan and risk management process. They are inevitably stakeholders in the project and therefore participate in risk workshops and risk review meetings as required.
- Participating actively in the risk process, proactively identifying and managing risks in their areas of responsibility
- Providing inputs to the project manager for risk reports

Other stakeholders
Some of these people might be classified as key stakeholders. All stakeholders are important to the project and must be involved in risk management where appropriate. Stakeholders are often themselves both causes of risks and possible sources of responses to risks. Key stakeholders are required to participate in risk workshops throughout the project.

FIGURE 4-7: Roles and Responsibilities within ATOM (*continued*)

project, the First Risk Assessment concludes when the risk champion issues a full risk report, which is distributed to the project sponsor, project manager, and key project team members (including all risk owners). This report includes the current Risk Register as well as analysis of the current risk exposure of the project. The executive summary from this report can be extracted for other key stakeholders.

The review and update cycle is also agreed and documented, deciding how often the risk assessment for this project will be repeated. The use of Major and Minor Reviews is agreed, as discussed in Chapter 3, and decisions are made regarding when Major Reviews will be performed and how often Minor Reviews are required. For the typical medium-size project, a First Risk Assessment is performed prior to project start, if possible, otherwise immediately afterward. The Major Review is repeated at key points in the project; for example, on major changes to scope or requirements and at key phase changes or stage gates. Regular Minor Reviews are undertaken periodically between Major Reviews, timed to match the normal project reporting cycle—typically monthly.

DEFINITIONS OF SCALES FOR PROBABILITY AND IMPACTS (P-I SCALES)

The key stakeholders discuss and agree on the meanings of the labels used during the Assessment step when estimating the probability and impacts of an individual risk.

For a medium-size project, use of five-point scales is recommended for both probability and impact; i.e., very high (VHI), high (HI), medium (MED), low (LO), and very low (VLO). The use of five-point P-I scales should be confirmed, and may be simplified to four points or

SCALE	PROBABILITY	+/- IMPACT ON PROJECT OBJECTIVES		
		TIME	COST	QUALITY
VHI	71–99%	>20 days	>$200K	Very significant impact on overall functionality
HI	51–70%	11–20 days	$101K–$200K	Significant impact on overall functionality
MED	31–50%	4–10 days	$51K–$100K	Some impact in key functional areas
LO	11–30%	1–3 days	$10K–$50K	Minor impact on overall functionality
VLO	1–10%	<1 day	<$10K	Minor impact on secondary functions
NIL	<1%	No change	No change	No change in functionality

FIGURE 4-8: Example Probability-Impact Scales

A project for the release of a new product has a planned timeline of 10 months and a budget of $4M. Delivery more than two months late would miss the market window and if the costs were anticipated to grow above $5M it would be cancelled. The earliest feasible delivery date to meet market requirements would be four weeks ahead of schedule. Cost savings of more than $500K would double the expected margin. Variations in schedule or budget of up to +/– 15% are acceptable.

Impact scales for this project might be:

	THREAT IMPACTS					
	STEP 1: Define VHI		STEP 3: Define VLO		STEP 3: Set Intermediate Values	
	TIME	COST	TIME	COST	TIME	COST
VHI	>8 wks	>$1M				
HI					4-8 wks	$501K-$1M
MED					2-4 wks	$101K-$500K
LO					1-2 wks	$10K-$100K
VLO			<1 wk	<$10K		

	OPPORTUNITY IMPACTS					
	STEP 4: Define VHI		STEP 5: Define VLO		STEP 6: Set Intermediate Values	
	TIME	COST	TIME	COST	TIME	COST
VHI	>4 wks	>$500K				
HI					3-4 wks	$251K-$500K
MED					2-3 wks	$81K-$250K
LO					1-2 wks	$10K-$80K
VLO			<1 wk	<$10K		

FIGURE 4-9: Examples of How to Set Impact Scales

three points if a more simple risk process can be justified for this project. Figure 4-8 shows an example set of probability and impact scales.

After the number of scale points are determined, the meanings of each must be agreed. Probability terms are defined in terms of percentage ranges. Impact terms are defined against each of the project objectives that are in scope for the risk process, translating each term into ranges of effects on time, cost, quality, etc. Many organizations use a common scale for probability definitions across all projects, but impact scales must be project-specific. Figure 4-9 illustrates the process of determining project-specific impact scales. The highest level of impact on each scale (VHI) is defined as the level of impact that cannot be ignored; e.g., a showstopper or catastrophic impact for a threat, or a golden "must-have" opportunity. The lowest impact scale (VLO) is defined as a degree of impact that does not need active management and is considered acceptable for this project. Intermediate scale points are set between these two limits. The three points in between are established by selecting a nonlinear scaling, usually based on a doubling of value at each point.

The same set of P-I scales are often used for both threats and opportunities, treating impacts as negative for threats (delays, additional cost, performance shortfall, etc.) and as positive for opportunities (saving time or cost, enhancing performance, etc.). It may, however, be decided to use different P-I scales for threats and opportunities if the sensitivities of the project are significantly different for each type of risk; for example, a catastrophic delay might be three months, but a time saving of just one month might be regarded as exceptional.

During the Assessment step, the probability and impacts of each risk are evaluated using these scales, then risks are positioned on a Probability-Impact Matrix to determine their relative importance, as described in Chapter 6. ATOM uses a default double P-I Matrix with the thresholds shown in Figure 4-10.

RISK THRESHOLDS

It is important to confirm the risk thresholds to which the organization generally works, or those that are appropriate to this project. The default scheme used in ATOM has three zones: "red" top-priority risks require urgent attention; "amber" risks are medium priority and require active monitoring, and "green" risks are low-priority. The position of the boundaries between these three zones on the matrix is confirmed during the Initiation meeting. Most projects will use the default scheme; changes to that scheme should be justified, agreed, and documented.

POTENTIAL SOURCES OF RISK TO THIS PROJECT

The organization may have defined typical sources of risk on its projects, either as a list of risk categories or as a hierarchical risk breakdown structure (RBS). Where a generic category list or RBS exists, it should be reviewed during the Initiation meeting, and key stakeholders should confirm that it includes all possible sources of risk to the project, making modifications where necessary. A sample risk breakdown structure is shown in Figure 4-11.

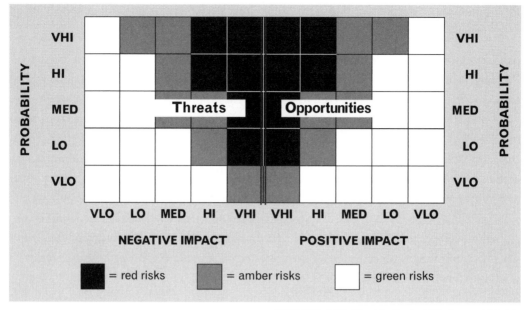

FIGURE 4-10: Double Probability-Impact Matrix

Outputs

If a stakeholder analysis is performed as part of the Initiation step, the results are captured in a report written by the project sponsor or project manager and distributed to key stakeholders, as appropriate.

The main output from the Initiation step is the Risk Management Plan, which documents the decisions reached during the Initiation meeting. The Risk Management Plan is drafted by the risk champion and approved by the project manager.

A sample contents list for a typical Risk Management Plan for a medium-size project is shown in Figure 4-12, and the contents and purpose of each paragraph is expanded below. (See also the template in Appendix A-1.)

- *Introduction.* Describe the purpose of the Risk Management Plan, with essential document reference information, including author, issue date, etc.

- *Project description and objectives.* Summarize the project, including its purpose, scope, objectives, and other relevant background information. Refer to existing project documentation wherever possible to avoid unnecessary duplication. Explicitly list all project objectives (scope, time, cost, quality, etc.) and comment on their relative priority in case of conflict.

- *Aims, scope, and objectives of risk process.* Describe the purpose of risk management for this project. Clearly state the scope of the risk process, defining what is in or out of scope. It may also be useful to include a glossary of risk terms or refer to a standard document.

- *Application of the ATOM risk management process.* Outline how ATOM will be used for this project, either summarizing each process step or by referring to a standard process description document. Any adjustments or tailoring of the ATOM process

RBS LEVEL 0	RBS LEVEL 1	RBS LEVEL 2
0. PROJECT RISK	1. TECHNICAL RISK	1.1 Scope definition 1.2 Requirements definition 1.3 Estimates, assumptions and constraints 1.4 Technical processes 1.5 Technology 1.6 Technical interfaces 1.7 Design 1.8 Performance 1.9 Reliability and maintainability 1.10 Safety 1.11 Security 1.12 Test and acceptance
	2. MANAGEMENT RISK	2.1 Project management 2.2 Program/portfolio management 2.3 Operations management 2.4 Organization 2.5 Resourcing 2.6 Communication 2.7 Information 2.8 HS&E 2.9 Quality 2.10 Reputation
	3. COMMERCIAL RISK	3.1 Contractual terms and conditions 3.2 Internal procurement 3.3 Suppliers and vendors 3.4 Subcontracts 3.5 Client/customer stability 3.6 Partnerships and joint ventures
	4. EXTERNAL RISK	4.1 Legislation 4.2 Exchange rates 4.3 Site/facilities 4.4 Environmental/weather 4.5 Competition 4.6 Regulatory 4.7 Political 4.8 Country 4.9 Social/demographic 4.10 Pressure groups 4.11 Force majeure

FIGURE 4-11: Sample Risk Breakdown Structure

should be noted. State the schedule for planned risk activities during the project.

• *Risk tools and techniques.* List the tools and techniques to be used for each step in the risk management process, either describing them briefly or referring to another process description document.

• *Organization, roles, and responsibilities.* State who is responsible for the various elements of the risk management process for this project and describe their contribution, possibly using a responsibility assignment matrix. Where possible use the names of individuals rather than job titles to encourage ownership.

INTRODUCTION

PROJECT DESCRIPTION AND OBJECTIVES

AIMS, SCOPE AND OBJECTIVES OF RISK PROCESS

APPLICATION OF THE ATOM PROCESS

RISK TOOLS AND TECHNIQUES

ORGANIZATION, ROLES, AND RESPONSIBILITIES
FOR RISK MANAGEMENT

RISK REVIEWS AND REPORTING

APPENDICES

A   PROJECT-SPECIFIC DEFINITIONS OF PROBABILITY
    AND IMPACTS

B   PROJECT-SPECIFIC SOURCES OF RISK
    (RISK BREAKDOWN STRUCTURE)

FIGURE 4-12: Sample
Contents List for a Risk
Management Plan

- *Risk reviews and reporting.* State how often risks will be reviewed on this project, and whether risk reviews will be undertaken as part of other project meetings or in a separate forum. Describe the deliverables from the risk management process, including types of report, their purpose, and distribution.

- *Project-specific definitions of probability and impacts.* Define the terms to be used for qualitative assessment of risks on this particular project. Confirm thresholds on the P-I Matrix to be used when prioritizing risks.

- *Project-specific sources of risk.* List the types of risk that the risk management process is expected to address for this project. This may be structured as a simple list of risk categories, or in a hierarchical RBS, either using a generic RBS or a project-specific version.

A Risk Management Plan template is presented in Appendix A-1, indicating typical content for a medium-size project. This template can be easily modified to apply to any particular project by replacing the text contained in <angle brackets>.

Once project objectives and process characteristics are defined in the Risk Management Plan, the project manager issues the plan to all key stakeholders so that everyone understands how risk management will be undertaken on their project. The Risk Management Plan becomes a formal configuration item, subject to configuration management. It is reviewed at key points during the project to determine whether the process is still appropriate and effective. It may be necessary to revise some of the decisions made at the start of the project, so that the risk management process remains capable of addressing the degree of emergent risk faced by the project. If the risk process is modified during the project, then the Risk Management Plan is revised and reissued.

Summary

The Initiation step, by defining the parameters and boundaries of how risk management will be undertaken for this particular project, provides all the necessary information for the next step in the risk process. Completing this step requires the following activities:

- Determine key stakeholders who will provide input to this step

- Size the project to determine the appropriate level of risk process

- Hold an Initiation meeting with key stakeholders in order to:

    - Confirm project size

    - Clarify project objectives

    - Set the scope and objectives for the risk process

    - Confirm the tools and techniques to be used

    - Allocate roles and responsibilities for risk management tasks

    - Agree on reporting and review requirements

    - Define scales for probability and impacts

    - Identify potential sources of risk to the project

- Document the decisions from the Initiation meeting in a Risk Management Plan, and distribute to key stakeholders

Completing the Initiation step makes it possible to move on to risk identification, as detailed in the next chapter.

CHAPTER 5

....

Exposing the Challenge (Identification)

Once the Initiation step is complete and the project's Risk Management Plan has been produced and distributed, the First Risk Assessment in the ATOM process can commence. This is the first opportunity for the project team to explore the risk exposure of the project in a structured manner, and therefore requires a high level of attention and effort. The First Risk Assessment has a number of subsidiary steps, including Identification, Assessment, and Response Planning. Identification is described in this chapter; the subsequent steps are described in Chapters 6 and 7.

The initial element of the First Risk Assessment is Identification; some think that this is the most important step in the process, because "a risk identified is a risk that can be managed," or, alternatively, "failing to identify a risk means taking it with your eyes closed." The need to carry out the preceding Initiation step formally and effectively cannot be overemphasized, because without clear project objectives and agreement of the scope for the risk management process, risk identification can find itself open-ended and without any clear purpose.

The aim of risk identification must be to identify all knowable risks; i.e., all risks that are practically and realistically identifiable. These are sometimes described as *known unknowns*, reflecting the unfortunate fact that there will always be unknowable or unidentifiable risks, or *unknown unknowns*—things that have never happened before and cannot be foreseen no matter which identification technique is used. This does not mean that project teams can rush through this step without applying the necessary amount of effort to do a good job, thinking that complete identification is not achievable. Certainly, over time, as participants in the process become more familiar with the tools and techniques, the identification of risks will get better. Perhaps initially only a portion of the knowable risks will be identified, but by employing the appropriate techniques and involving the right participants this situation will be improved significantly and quickly. However, a false sense of security must never be allowed, because it is impossible to identify all risks. There is always the potential for something else, an u*nknown unknown,* to arise that might either kill the project or make a fortune. Therefore, the same level of effort in risk identification must be applied to all projects.

Numerous tools and techniques can be used to identify risks. However, for a medium-size project ATOM recommends a facilitated workshop incorporating three standard techniques to identify risks:

- Structured brainstorming

- Analysis of assumptions and constraints

- Use of a standard risk checklist

ATOM also recommends continuing the same risk workshop after Identification and into the Assessment step of the First Risk Assessment, as described in Chapter 6.

The purpose of the Identification step is to:

- Identify and describe all knowable risks, including threats and opportunities

- Where possible and relevant, identify initial responses to identified risks

Doing this requires the following inputs:

- Risk Management Plan outlining project objectives and scope of the risk process

- Risk breakdown structure (RBS)

- Work breakdown structure (WBS)

- Project assumptions and constraints

- Standard risk checklist

- Risk tool (spreadsheet, database, or proprietary software)

In ATOM, Identification requires the following activities:

- Pre-workshop preparation, including agreeing on attendees, and preparing the workshop agenda and workshop prebrief

- The risk workshop itself, which includes:

  - Initial scene-setting: introductions, project background, objectives, explanation of the risk management process, etc.

  - Brainstorming, analyzing assumptions and constraints, and identifying all knowable risks through use of a checklist. Initial risk responses may also be identified.

  - Rationalizing risks to remove duplicates and nonrisks (i.e., risks that do not affect project objectives or that have been wrongly described).

  - Describing risks clearly and unambiguously.

  - Recording all identified risks.

The Identification step produces the following outputs:

- A consolidated agreed list of risks described using risk metalanguage
- A list of initial responses

These inputs, activities, and outputs are illustrated in Figure 5-1, and described in detail in the following sections.

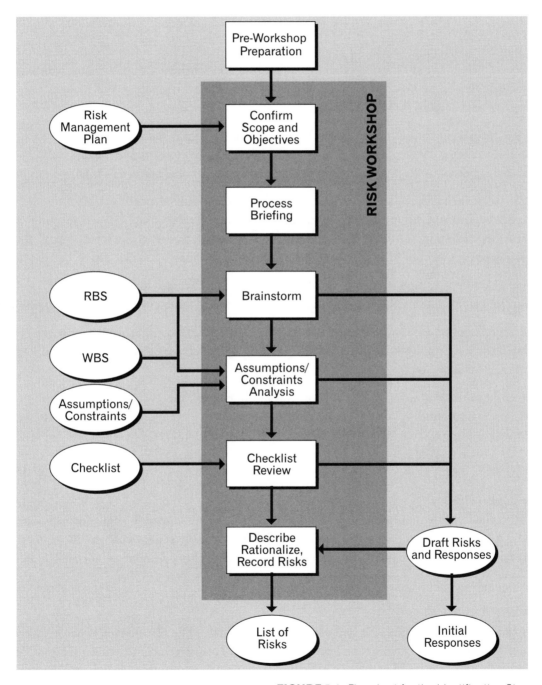

FIGURE 5-1: Flowchart for the Identification Step

Inputs

ATOM's term for the first risk pass through the risk process is the *First Risk Assessment* (as discussed in Chapter 3). It is recognized that further passes through the risk process will take place throughout the life cycle of the project, following the steps outlined in Chapter 3 and described in detail below.

The risk identification step at the beginning of the First Risk Assessment requires a number of inputs. The first is the Risk Management Plan for the project (see Chapter 4), listing the project objectives derived from the business case or project charter, or, for external projects, from the invitation to tender (ITT) or request for proposal (RFP). Project objectives must be known before any risks can be identified. The Risk Management Plan also states which of these objectives are in scope for the risk process, and defines the tools and techniques to be used as part of the ATOM process.

Also included in the Risk Management Plan is a list of key project stakeholders involved in the risk process. For the Identification step, these people are invited to participate in the risk workshop (see below), as their perspectives on the project enable identification of a wide range of risks.

The RBS, included as part of the Risk Management Plan, is another key input because it is used as a structure for the risk identification techniques. Similarly, the WBS for this project provides a structure for mapping the effects of risks, though this normally forms part of the Assessment element of the risk workshop (see Chapter 6).

Project assumptions and constraints should already have been included in the business case, project charter, or bid documentation. These can be analyzed during the risk workshop to identify risks.

The organization may have developed a standard risk checklist to capture organizational learning on generic risks that affected previous projects. This checklist can be used as a final step to ensure completion of coverage in risk identification.

Using a risk tool to support the risk process is recommended; this tool may be a spreadsheet, database, or proprietary software package that records all identified risks and initial responses, as well as outputs from the Assessment element of the workshop. Recording might be done during the risk workshop itself, or after the workshop is finished.

Activities

The primary activity in this step is the risk workshop, which is used for both Identification and Assessment. For the Identification step, activities can be divided into preworkshop preparations and the first part of the workshop itself, as detailed below. The remainder of the risk workshop is used for the Assessment step, as described in Chapter 6.

Pre-workshop preparation

The first task is to decide who should attend the workshop. The risk champion, in consultation with the project manager and project sponsor, should agree on the list of people to be invited, in addition to themselves. Other attendees should include key stakeholders (as previously identified during stakeholder analysis) and important members of the project team.

Although the ideal number for a workshop is ten to 16, too many people attending is better than too few. With a larger number, subgroups can be used at key points in the workshop to maximize participation and productivity. Whatever the number, a good facilitator will be able to make the session work.

An effective risk workshop can last from one to three days. An agenda is drawn up that covers the whole duration; see Figure 5-2 for a sample agenda for a two-day workshop. The agenda must be circulated sufficiently in advance of the workshop to ensure that all invited attendees are available and are aware of the workshop's purpose and timetable. Additionally, any workshop prebriefing information must be circulated, possibly including the workshop objectives and any preliminary reading, such as a summary of the project's business case or project charter. It is often helpful to ask attendees to consider in advance the biggest threats and opportunities in the project. As a result of these actions, attendees are more easily drawn into the Identification part of the workshop, which allows it to get off to a flying start.

The Risk Workshop

The importance of the risk workshop cannot be underestimated. It is often a costly and time-consuming exercise and therefore must be as effective as possible. To ensure that the workshop meets its objectives, it should be facilitated by the risk champion, although using another

---

DAY 1

Morning
1. Introductions
2. Confirm project objectives
3. Confirm scope of risk process for this workshop
4. Workshop ground rules
5. Risk management briefing (if required)
6. Expectations and results
7. Identify risks
   Brainstorm risks using the risk breakdown structure

Afternoon
   Analysis of assumptions and constraints to generate further risks
   A standard risk checklist to identify any further/final risks
8. Rationalize risks
9. Describe risks using risk metalanguage
10. Record identified risks (during workshop or after meeting)

DAY 2

Morning
11. Explanation of assessment scheme (recap)
12. Assessment of probability and impacts
13. Risk categorization

Afternoon
14. Nomination of risk owners
15. *If there is time, develop initial response to priority risks*
16. Close the workshop

FIGURE 5-2: Sample Agenda for a First Risk Assessment/Two-day Risk Workshop
(Including Identification and Assessment Steps)

specialist facilitator is possible. Effective facilitation is fundamental to the success of the workshop. The published agenda should be followed as closely as possible and all elements of the agenda addressed. The following sections describe the workshop elements relevant to the Identification step of the ATOM process.

INTRODUCTIONS

All attendees must be aware of each other's role in the project. The risk champion (or other facilitator) ensures that this does not absorb too much time in the workshop. This is often helped by asking participants to answer six specific questions:

- What is your name?

- What is your role on the project (as they understand it)?

- What previous experience do you have in the risk management process?

- What are your personal expectations for the both the project and the workshop?

- What is your biggest fear for the project?

- What do you believe could dramatically benefit the project?

CONFIRM PROJECT OBJECTIVES

Confirm the project's objectives as recorded in the Risk Management Plan. The importance of understanding the project's objectives is described in Chapter 4. Confirming project objectives as part of the workshop has two additional benefits:

- It removes any ambiguity or misunderstanding that participants might have about the specified objectives of the project.

- It allows identification of other, perhaps previously omitted, objectives that are considered important by the workshop participants.

CONFIRM SCOPE OF RISK PROCESS FOR THIS WORKSHOP

A risk workshop can focus on risks affecting all or a subset of the project's objectives; e.g., only those likely to impact schedule or quality objectives. The Risk Management Plan states which objectives are in scope, and the risk champion ensures that workshop participants understand the boundaries within which they are being asked to identify risks.

OUTLINE GROUND RULES

Workshop ground rules are outlined by the risk champion to ensure that all participants understand and accept them, so that the workshop is successful and effective. These rules include adhering to the agenda and timing, allowing all participants to speak, showing mutual respect and active listening, and deferring to the facilitator on process matters.

RISK MANAGEMENT BRIEFING

If this is the first workshop for a significant number of participants, it is probably worth having the risk champion present the main aspects of project risk management, including:

- Definitions of risk and risk management

- The ATOM risk management process: Initiation, Identification, Assessment, Response Planning, Reporting, Implementation, and Reviews (Major and Minor)

- Describing risks using the risk metalanguage

Because this workshop is also for assessing risks, this briefing must also cover:

- The use of probability and impacts to prioritize risks

- The role of the risk owner

EXPECTATIONS AND RESULTS

The risk champion clarifies workshop expectations both in terms of direct outputs as well as actions from individual participants. On completion of the risk workshop—i.e., after both Identification and Assessment steps—the main output is a list of prioritized, properly described risks that have each been assigned to appropriate risk owners. As a useful by-product, individual participants may gain a better understanding of the project and their role in it.

IDENTIFICATION OF RISKS

The Identification step of the First Risk Assessment uses three techniques: brainstorming, assumptions/constraints analysis, and a checklist. Each of the three main risk identification techniques is summarized below:

Brainstorm. A brainstorming session is facilitated by the risk champion, who ensures that all participants contribute, that the process is effective, and that all contributions are recorded. It is essential that the "golden rules" of brainstorming are followed:

- No criticism of ideas (there are no wrong answers)

- Go for large quantities of ideas (quantity not quality)

- Build on each other's ideas (hitchhike)

- Encourage wild and exaggerated ideas (if you think it, say it)

Risks identified during the brainstorm should be recorded immediately by the risk champion, usually using a flipchart. Data might be entered directly into the selected risk tool during the workshop in parallel with use of the flipchart, or data entry may be undertaken on completion of both the Identification and Assessment elements of the workshop.

To aid brainstorming, the ATOM process recommends using the RBS as a framework, both as a prompt to identification and as a means to ensure completeness. An example RBS is shown in Figure 4-11.

Analysis of assumptions and constraints. Assumptions are statements taken for granted as "facts" upon which the project was justified and is being planned. Constraints are things associated with the project that are considered "fixed," and either "must happen" or "must not happen." The project's business case, project charter, or bid documentation should identify all assumptions and constraints. Unfortunately this is not always the case, because many assumptions and constraints are not explicit and are held implicitly by project stakeholders. Implicit assumptions and constraints must be exposed as much as possible during the risk workshop. These can be identified in a short discussion structured around either the RBS or WBS, and facilitated by the risk champion, who encourages participants to challenge the accepted project boundaries. Figure 5-3 presents a template for recording identified assumptions and constraints.

Assumption or Constraint	Could this assumption/constraint prove false? (Y/N)	If false would it affect project? (Y/N)	Convert to a risk?
Instructions:			
List all project assumptions and constraints in the first column.			
Identify whether each might prove false (Y/N), and whether a false assumption/constraint might affect the project (Y/N).			
Where both answers are yes, mark the assumption/constraint as a risk.			

FIGURE 5-3: Assumptions and Constraints Analysis Template

Once assumptions and constraints are identified and listed, the validity of each is tested through a facilitated discussion during the workshop. Some assumptions can be considered safe and unlikely to prove false, based on previous experience. Some constraints will be fixed and unlikely to change during the project. Safe assumptions and fixed constraints are excluded as potential risks. The discussion may also expose some false assumptions or constraints, which need to be addressed outside the workshop by the project manager and project sponsor. However, there will be some assumptions that participants believe may prove to be false, and some constraints that could be relaxed or removed. Each of these is considered to determine the extent to which they might affect project objectives. Risks are then raised for false assumptions that might pose a threat to achievement of project objectives, and constraints that could be relaxed or removed and present an opportunity. Risks raised in this way will be considered in the Assessment part of the risk workshop.

A standard risk checklist. The identification element of the workshop concludes with use of a standard risk checklist, if one exists, in order to identify any additional risks not exposed by the other techniques. The checklist ensures consideration of risks that occurred on previous comparable projects in order to determine whether they might also pose a risk to this project. Workshop participants consider each item on the checklist, and answer the question, "Could this risk affect our project?" with either yes, no, don't know, or not applicable. Items with an answer of yes or don't know are recorded as risks. An example checklist is presented in Appendix A-2, based on an RBS

After using the structured risk identification techniques, workshop participants are invited to identify any additional risks not yet raised.

People in the risk workshop naturally want to develop solutions as soon as possible, and so it is expected that initial responses to identified risks will be suggested during the Identification step. These proposed responses should not be ignored, but should be recorded for use in the later Response Planning step of the First Risk Assessment (see Chapter 7).

RATIONALIZE RISKS

This stage of the workshop merges duplicate risks and removes items identified as not risks (for example, causes of risks, effects on objectives, issues, or problems). During Identification, risks inevitably will be identified that are similar to or the same as others, particularly when creative techniques such as brainstorming are used. It is far better to allow this to happen during the workshop than to try to eliminate them during the process, which would stifle the creative process and hinder effective risk identification. Likewise, nonrisk items are also recorded because they may prove useful later in the risk process. However, before proceeding to the Assessment step, duplicates and nonrisks are discarded in order to prevent unnecessary effort. In addition, some risks may have been identified which do not affect project objectives but which are relevant to another part of the organization or other projects. The project manager notes these risks and escalates them after the workshop to the person who should manage them. This is either the owner of the objective(s) that would be affected, or the person best able to manage the escalated risk, if known. These risks are then excluded from the project risk process.

Once all duplicates, nonrisks and escalated risks have been removed, each risk is given a unique risk identifier. This can be derived from its position in the RBS; for example, using the example RBS in Figure 4-11, the first reputation risk would be numbered 2.10.1.

DESCRIBE RISKS USING RISK METALANGUAGE

As a concluding element of the Identification part of the workshop, all identified risks are clearly and unambiguously described using risk metalanguage. Such descriptions create a shared understanding of the true nature of the risk, enabling it to be properly assessed and managed. This provides a three-part structured description of a risk that separates cause, risk, and effect, in the form:

> *"As a result of <definite cause>, <uncertain event> may occur, which would lead to <effect on objective(s)>."*

By requiring each element to be explicitly and precisely stated, confusion between the three is minimized, and the focus is placed on identifying the risk itself. In addition, understanding cause and effect allows the grouping of risks in the Assessment step, using the RBS as a cause framework and the WBS to map effects, as discussed in Chapter 6. Cause and effect information can also assist when planning responses, as described in Chapter 7. Examples of risk descriptions using metalanguage are shown in Figure 5-4.

The risk metalanguage provides a three-part structured description of a risk, which separates cause, risk, and effect, as follows:

"As a result of <cause>, <risk> may occur, which would lead to <effect on objective(s)>."

Example risk description linking these three elements using risk metalanguage might be:

CAUSE (a definite fact)	RISK (an uncertain event or set of circumstances)	EFFECT (a direct impact on a project objective)
As a result of using novel hardware…	…unexpected system integration errors may occur…	…which would lead to overspend on the project.
Because our organization has never done a project like this before…	…we might misunderstand the customer's requirement…	…which would mean that our solution would not meet the quality acceptance criteria.
We have to outsource production…	…[so] we may be able to learn new practices from our selected partner…	…which would lead to increased productivity and profitability.
Because we have no experience of using this technology…	…we might not have the necessary skilled staff to carry out the design work…	…which would lead to a delay in the project while we train our existing staff or recruit new skilled staff.
The project is planned to take place during the summer…	…[so] we may be able to recruit additional skilled student labor…	…which could save time on all activities that take place during that period.
Because there are three other projects taking place in the same timeframe…	…we may be able to utilize skilled staff as they become available from another project…	…which would allow us to deliver early to the customer.

FIGURE 5-4: Examples of Risk Metalanguage

RECORD IDENTIFIED RISKS

Following use of the risk identification techniques, rationalization to remove duplicates and nonrisks, and proper description of risks using risk metalanguage, a consolidated, agreed list of risks is produced. It may be possible to record this directly into the risk tool during the risk workshop, if suitable administrative support is available. If not, information from both the Identification and Assessment elements of the risk workshop is taken from the facilitator's notes and flip charts and recorded into the risk tool as soon as possible afterward, in order to generate the initial Risk Register.

Outputs

The main output from the Identification step is a consolidated, agreed list of properly described risks and, when possible, this is recorded in the risk tool during the risk workshop or in the facilitator's notes. In addition, if identified, a list of initial responses to identified risks is also recorded. These are used as an input during the Response Planning step.

As the first major part of the workshop, Identification delivers a better understanding of the project and its objectives, and sets the tempo for the rest of the workshop. It is therefore crucial that the risk champion or facilitator maintains enthusiasm, momentum, and commitment to the task, and of course keeps to the agenda's published timetable.

Summary

The Identification part of the First Risk Assessment ensures that all knowable risks, both threats and opportunities, are identified and recorded. In addition, properly describing the risks aids in the next step when assessing their importance and in the planning of suitable responses. Performing the Identification step requires the following activities:

- Agree on workshop attendees; prepare a workshop agenda and workshop prebrief

- Facilitate a risk workshop to identify all knowable risks, which are then properly described using the risk metalanguage

- Consolidate risks to remove duplicates and nonrisks

- Record all risks in a suitable risk tool

- Record any initial responses to identified risks

Having completed the Identification step, it is possible to move on to the Assessment part of the risk workshop, which is detailed in the next chapter.

···

CHAPTER 6

Understand the Exposure (Assessment)

The output from the Identification part of the First Risk Assessment is a list of properly described risks, which can be quite long, especially as an organization becomes good at risk identification. It is easy to identify 50 to 100 risks on a project, and perhaps considerably more on some "risky" projects. (Of course, it is also possible to identify too many risks—i.e., risks at too low a level or too detailed to be managed effectively—one project known to the authors had more than 4,000 identified risks!) Clearly an organization cannot actively respond to all identified risks at the same time or with the same level of attention. It may be pointless or even impossible to develop a response for some low-priority risks. To avoid developing unnecessary responses, all identified risks must be prioritized before responses are planned. Therefore, the next step in the First Risk Assessment is to understand the exposure of the project to uncertainty and determine priorities for identified risks. The ultimate aim of this Assessment step is to determine the most important (worst) threats and (best) opportunities in order to enable focused, active management.

Effective risk assessment must treat threats and opportunities with equal emphasis, determining their relative priority in a holistic, nonprejudiced manner. The two key factors for prioritizing risks are their probability of occurrence (sometimes referred to as *likelihood*) and their potential impact on objectives should they occur (also known as *consequence*). Each risk can have only one probability, but it might have multiple impacts because it could affect more than one project objective. This needs to be taken into account when assessing the relative priorities of risks.

Another key part of the Assessment step is understanding how identified risks are grouped together. Common causes can be exposed by mapping identified risks to a risk breakdown structure (RBS), and common effects are shown by mapping to the work breakdown structure (WBS).

ATOM recommends continuing the risk workshop used to identify risks (described in Chapter 5) into the Assessment step, because the people who have identified risks are usually well placed to assess them. Additionally, because getting people together for any workshop can be difficult, once all the appropriate participants are assembled in one place it would be fool-hardy to let them disappear.

The purpose of the Assessment step is to:

- Prioritize risks so that those requiring the most urgent attention are addressed first

- Identify low-priority risks that may not need to be addressed at all

- Assign appropriate risk owners to all risks

- Determine "hot spots" of risk exposure

Doing this requires the following inputs:

- Risk Management Plan, which includes the agreed project-specific probability and impact scales, as well as risk thresholds

- RBS, defining possible causes of risk

- WBS, summarizing the work to be done during the project

- Consolidated list of properly described risks from the Identification part of the workshop, preferably already recorded in the risk tool

- Risk tool (spreadsheet, database, or proprietary software)

ATOM requires the following activities in the Assessment step:

- Continuation of the risk workshop itself, including:

    - Explanation of the scoring scheme used to assess risks (if not done earlier in the workshop)

    - Assessment of the probability of occurrence and impact against defined objectives for each identified risk

    - Categorization of risks using the RBS and WBS

    - Nomination of risk owners

- After the workshop, the risk champion ensures that all data is recorded in the risk tool (if this was not done during the workshop), and then prepares standard assessment outputs

The Assessment step produces the following outputs:

- List of risks held in the risk tool, each with a proper risk description, agreed assessments of probability and impacts, and nominated risk owners. Outputs produced from the risk tool include:

    - Risk Register

    - Prioritized risk list

- List of top threats and opportunities

- RBS categorization

- WBS categorization

• Double Probability and Impact Matrix showing number of risks per cell—in some cases the risk tool may produce this automatically

These inputs, activities, and outputs are illustrated in Figure 6-1, and described in detail in the following sections.

Inputs

Because the Assessment step is the second part of the risk workshop, many inputs are carried over from the Identification step. These include the Risk Management Plan for the project (see Chapter 4), which not only lists the project objectives against which risks have been identified, but also sets out the agreed scales for probability and impacts to be used during the Assessment step. Examples of these are in Figure 6-2. In addition, the Risk Management Plan

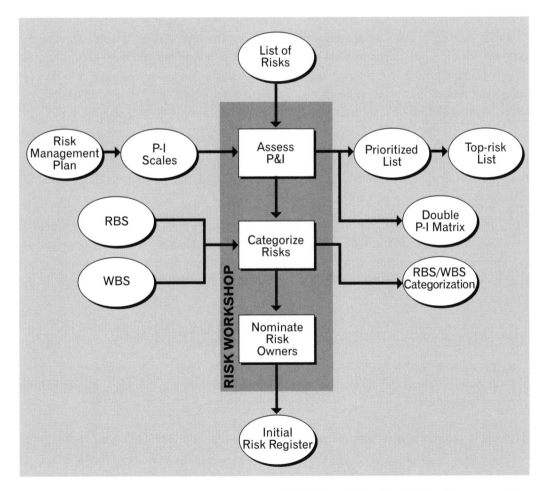

FIGURE 6-1: Flowchart for the Assessment Step

SCALE	PROBABILITY	+/– IMPACT ON PROJECT OBJECTIVES		
		TIME	COST	QUALITY
VHI	71–99%	>20 days	>$200K	Very significant impact on overall functionality
HI	51–70%	11–20 days	$101K–$200K	Significant impact on overall functionality
MED	31–50%	4–10 days	$51K–$100K	Some impact in key functional areas
LO	11–30%	1–3 days	$10K–$50K	Minor impact on overall functionality
VLO	1–10%	<1 day	<$10K	Minor impact on secondary functions
NIL	<1%	No change	No change	No change in functionality

FIGURE 6-2: Example of Project-specific Probability-impact Scales

defines the risk thresholds to be used in setting zones on the Probability-Impact Matrix.

The RBS defined in the Risk Management Plan might have been used as a structure for the risk identification part of the workshop. It can now also be used to categorize identified risks to determine whether there are any common causes. In the same way, the project WBS provides a framework for mapping the effects of risks to determine whether any parts of the project are particularly exposed to risk.

The consolidated list of identified risks produced during Identification is clearly the key input to this Assessment step. It is therefore of paramount importance that risks have been properly described using the risk metalanguage of cause, risk, and effect. Without proper descriptions, assessing risks with any confidence is not possible.

The same risk tool is usually used to support the whole risk process . If a risk tool was used to record identified risks and initial responses during the Identification part of the workshop, it can now be used to record assessments of probability and impact(s) for each risk, as well as the nominated risk owner and any modifications to risk descriptions that may arise during the Assessment step.

Activities

The prime activity is the continuation of the risk workshop used to identify risks—see Figure 5-2 for a sample agenda. Assessment step activities are divided into the risk workshop itself and post-workshop activities.

The risk workshop (continued)

An underlying assumption of the ATOM risk process is that the same risk workshop is used for both Identification and Assessment, with the same group of stakeholders and other team members present for both steps. It is important that effective facilitation continues into this part of the workshop, either by the risk champion or a specialist facilitator. The following sections describe the Assessment elements of the workshop.

EXPLANATION OF THE ASSESSMENT SCHEME

The concepts of probability and impact as the two dimensions of risk assessment should have been outlined previously, as part of the general introduction to the workshop (described in Chapter 5). However, the Assessment step will likely take place on the second day of the workshop; therefore, the facilitator quickly recaps those concepts. The probability and impact scales defined in the Risk Management Plan are displayed on a flip chart and the facilitator answers any questions about how to use them.

ASSESSMENT OF PROBABILITY AND IMPACTS

Ideally the assessment of probability and impact involves all workshop attendees in a single group. However, it may be beneficial to split the group into two, based on the following criteria:

- If the group is very large, perhaps in excess of 20, splitting it gives everyone the chance to participate equally and not be excluded by the more vocal members.

- If there are time pressures to complete the workshop, dividing the group significantly reduces the time required.

Should the decision be made to split the group, the facilitator ensures that each group contains approximately equal numbers and a balanced mix of members, considering field of expertise, relevant experience, seniority in the organization, etc. Because the facilitator cannot be with both subgroups simultaneously, each assigns a scribe to record the agreements. If they need assistance in overcoming a conflict in the group, the scribe requests it from the facilitator.

Once the group or subgroups are prepared, they then consider each risk in turn. At this point, the group members may realize that they lack a clear understanding of some of the risks that they are trying to assess, due to ambiguous or vague risk descriptions. Using risk metalanguage to describe risks during the risk identification step should prevent this problem, but if the group members are not clear about the nature of a particular risk, they may rephrase it before assessing it. They may request assistance from the facilitator if necessary.

Assessment is done in two steps and must ignore possible responses:

- The probability of occurrence is first estimated as one of the five points of very high, high, medium, low, or very low. Since the risk is an uncertain event or set of circumstances, it has just one probability, representing the level of uncertainty associated with the risk.

- Secondly, the participants imagine that the risk occurs, and determine its impacts against project objectives, again choosing one from the scale of very high, high, medium, low, or very low. Of course, a risk may have different levels of impact against different objectives; for example, a risk may have a medium probability of occurrence, and if it happened it might then have a low impact on project timescale, high impact on project budget, and no impact on quality.

The facilitator ensures that workshop participants refer constantly to the definitions of these scale points (as in Figure 6-2), and avoid unthinking or unjustifiable assessments. People commonly call out "high, high" or "low, low" without translating risks using the agreed definitions, and this must be avoided if assessments are to be realistic.

Clearly, different people will have different opinions about how to rate the probability and impacts of a particular risk. These differences can usually be resolved through discussion and exploration of underlying assumptions. However, if there is a large difference of opinion between workshop attendees, the facilitator clarifies the underlying reasons and seeks consensus. In addition, the facilitator identifies any subconscious bias during assessment that might arise from perceptual factors or heuristics. Heuristics are shortcuts or "rules of thumb" used to make decisions or judgments in cases of uncertainty. The three main heuristics that might operate in the Assessment step are:

- Availability (or "most recent is most memorable"). A person's belief that a risk has a high probability or high impact may stem from the risk having occurred recently in their experience.

- Representativeness (or "the same risk will always occur in similar circumstances"). Although this might be true, it might not take into account any local differences or change in circumstances.

- Anchoring and adjustment (or "the first answer is always nearly right"). This can make the group reluctant to disagree on or change the first value expressed by someone, even if they feel it is wrong.

Knowledge of heuristics allows the facilitator to identify when they are coming into play. When the facilitator believes that one or more heuristic is in evidence, he or she should challenge workshop attendees. This must be done sensitively, without personal criticism or offense; for example, using questions such as the following:

- Availability
  - When did that risk last occur? And previous to that?
  - Could it really happen again on this project?
- Representativeness
  - When was the last time you experienced this risk?
  - Could things have changed since then?
- Anchoring and adjustment
  - Are you sure? Why do you say that?
  - What do the rest of you think?

In the unlikely event that reaching agreement on assessments of probability and impact during the workshop proves impossible, then the highest estimates of both are recorded. This maximizes the level of attention given to these uncertain risks, rather than underplaying them. In these cases the nominated risk owner (see below) is tasked to clarify the risk and produce an agreed assessment as soon as possible after the workshop.

Once workshop attendees have agreed on the probability and impact(s) of each risk, the risks are plotted on the double Probability-Impact (P-I) Matrix to determine their priority. The matrix is drawn on a flip chart, and as each risk is assessed, its identifier number is entered into the appropriate matrix cell. The P-I Matrix is typically divided into three zones, using a traffic-light system: red, or high priority; amber, or medium priority; and green, or low priority. The thresholds for these zones are defined in the Risk Management Plan (see Chapter 4). The double P-I Matrix shows threats on the left side and opportunities on the right, with the worst threats and best opportunities appearing in the red zone at the center of the matrix. An example is shown in Figure 6-3.

It is also possible to refine the prioritization of risks beyond just three priority zones. A P-I scoring scheme can calculate a risk score for each risk, based on the assessed probability and impacts. Figure 6-4 shows the ATOM P-I scoring scheme; the resulting scores for the double P-I Matrix are shown in Figure 6-5. If a risk affects more than one objective, its risk score is set using the objective with the highest impact.

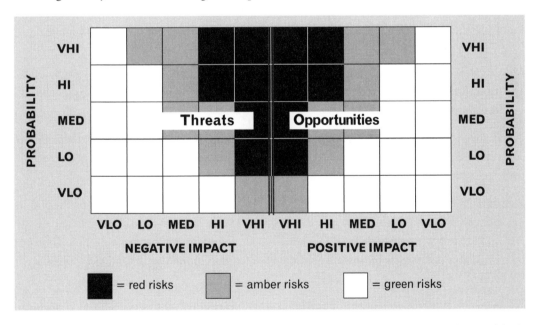

FIGURE 6-3: Double Probability-Impact Matrix

RANK	PROBABILITY	IMPACT
VHI	0.9	0.8
HI	0.7	0.4
MED	0.5	0.2
LO	0.3	0.1
VLO	0.1	0.05

FIGURE 6-4: Probability-Impact Scoring Scheme

VHI 0.90	0.045	0.09	0.18	0.36	0.72	0.72	0.36	0.18	0.09	0.045	**VHI** 0.90	
HI 0.70	0.035	0.07	0.14	0.28	0.56	0.56	0.28	0.14	0.07	0.035	**HI** 0.70	
MED 0.50	0.025	0.05	0.10	0.20	0.40	0.40	0.20	0.10	0.05	0.025	**MED** 0.50	
LO 0.30	0.015	0.03	0.06	0.12	0.24	0.24	0.12	0.06	0.03	0.015	**LO** 0.30	
VLO 0.10	0.005	0.01	0.02	0.04	0.08	0.08	0.04	0.02	0.01	0.005	**VLO** 0.10	
	0.05 **VLO**	0.10 **LO**	0.20 **MED**	0.40 **HI**	0.80 **VHI**	0.80 **VHI**	0.40 **HI**	0.20 **MED**	0.10 **LO**	0.05 **VLO**		

PROBABILITY (left and right)

NEGATIVE IMPACT   **POSITIVE IMPACT**

FIGURE 6-5: Probability-Impact Scoring Scheme on Double Probability-Impact Matrix

In the event of a tie between two or more risks, two basic rules should be followed in order to differentiate between them:

- In a tie between two risks where one risk impacts only one objective and the other impacts more than one objective, then the multiple-impact risk is the most important.

- If both risks impact more than one objective, then the impact on the second objective should be considered; the higher second-impact score determines the more important risk.

Proprietary risk tools commonly implement a P-I scoring scheme automatically to prioritize risks; however, if a bespoke spreadsheet or database risk tool is used, then the scoring scheme must be created in the tool.

Assessments of probability and impacts for each risk ideally are entered into the risk tool during the workshop, preferably by a scribe rather than the facilitator. This allows participants to see immediately the effects of their assessments and how each risk has been ranked alongside others. (If this is not possible, assessment data is recorded immediately after the workshop—see below.)

When two subgroups assess risks, it is important to consolidate the outputs of each group in such a way that both subgroups can see what has been done. The temptation to revisit each risk and the agreements made by the other group should be resisted as this will not only delay the workshop but also negate the reason for splitting the larger group in the first place. However, any obvious and clear-cut conflict should be dealt with immediately by the facilitator in order to avoid future repercussions and lingering disagreement.

RISK CATEGORIZATION

After the probability and impacts of all risks have been assessed, risks are categorized using the RBS and WBS. The prime purpose of doing this is to identify risk hot spots, common causes of risks (via the RBS), and common affected areas of the project (via the WBS). Identifying hot spots provides valuable information for developing effective risk responses, and may also influence the overall management of the project.

RBS categorization is simplified if the RBS was used to structure the risk identification step (as recommended in Chapter 5). In this case, workshop attendees simply confirm that allocation of the risk to an RBS element is correct. However, a risk might be better understood as a result of the Assessment step, or its description may have been changed, resulting in a need to reallocate it to a different RBS element. A risk may also have more than one cause and therefore could theoretically belong in several RBS elements, in which case workshop attendees choose the one RBS element that seems to be the primary cause. A single risk should not appear in more than one RBS element. Risks are commonly mapped into Level 2 of the RBS because lower levels of detail can create too many categories. Figure 6-6 shows an example categorization by RBS.

LEVEL 0	LEVEL 1	LEVEL 2	# RISKS
Project risk **68 risks**	1. Technical content **37 risks**	1.1 Scope definition	8
		1.2 Technical interfaces	4
		1.3 Test and acceptance	10
		1.4 Business processes	2
		1.5 Development life cycle	4
		1.6 Data migration	5
		1.7 Knowledge transfer	3
		1.8 Organizational change management	0
		1.9 Hardware acquisition	1
	2. Management **24 risks**	2.1 Supplier/customer relationship	3
		2.2 Resourcing	8
		2.3 Communication	2
		2.4 Program management organization	8
		2.5 Facilities and infrastructure	3
	3. Commercial **7 risks**	3.1 Contract management	5
		3.2 Subcontract issues	2

FIGURE 6-6: RBS Categorization

Mapping into the WBS is similar, with workshop attendees being asked to determine which work packages or activities would be affected if the risk were to occur (again, usually done at Level 2 of the WBS). However, the process differs from RBS categorization in that when a risk might affect several work packages, all affected work packages are recorded. As a result, it is not possible to roll the total number of risks from Level 2 work packages into the higher WBS elements. An example is shown in Figure 6-7.

The initial result of both RBS and WBS categorization is a total of the number of risks mapped into each RBS Level 2 element and into each WBS work package. However, this does not take account of the relative priority of risks, so proper determination of "hot spots" should be based on totals of P-I scores for mapped risks, rather than the simple number of risks. For example, RBS element 1.2 might have just one mapped risk, whereas RBS element 4.2 might have four risks—but if the one risk in RBS 1.2 is rated as high priority it might be more -

LEVEL 0	LEVEL 1	LEVEL 2	# RISKS
Project	1. Software	1.1 Requirements	18
		1.2 Programming	10
		1.3 User testing	6
		1.4 Training	7
		1.5 Warranty support	2
	2. Hardware and comms	2.1 Specifications	10
		2.2 Procurement	8
		2.3 Assembly	1
		2.4 Load testing	2
		2.5 User testing	4
		2.6 Warranty support	2
	3. Management and commercial	3.1 Project management	4
		3.2 Commercial management	3
		3.3 Communication	6

FIGURE 6-7: WBS Categorization (Level 2 Only)

important than four low-priority risks in RBS 4.2. An RBS categorization by P-I score is shown in Figure 6-8.

A final important part of risk categorization is separating threats and opportunities and producing different hot-spot analyses for each, rather than combining them into a single assessment.

Agreed categorizations for each risk ideally are entered into the risk tool during the workshop; if this is not possible, data is recorded immediately after the workshop (see below).

NOMINATION OF RISK OWNERS

The final element of the risk workshop is to nominate a risk owner for each risk. The target is to have an agreed risk owner for every risk by the end of the workshop. If time is limited, as a minimum, risk owners must be assigned to all high-priority risks (those that are in the red zone of the P-I Matrix) during the workshop.

A risk owner is the person within the project best placed to manage the risk. It is essential that this is a named individual, not a group of people or a functional department. The workshop participants agree on each nominated risk owner. Most potential risk owners are likely to be at the workshop. However, if this is not the case, the proposed risk owner is contacted by the risk champion as soon as possible after the workshop in order to gain his agreement.

It is important to avoid the natural tendency to nominate the person who identified the risk as the risk owner. Likewise, neither the project manager nor the risk champion should take ownership unless they are truly the person best placed to manage the risk.

The risk owner must have the appropriate level of authority to appoint action owners, who implement the necessary actions, as detailed in Chapter 7.

The names of agreed risk owners for each risk are entered into the risk tool during the workshop when possible; otherwise, this is recorded immediately after the workshop (see below).

LEVEL 0	LEVEL 1	LEVEL 2	
Project risk **4.28**	1. Technical content **2.55**	1.1 Scope definition	0.55
		1.2 Technical interfaces	0.48
		1.3 Test and acceptance	0.62
		1.4 Business processes	0.06
		1.5 Development life cycle	0.48
		1.6 Data migration	0.20
		1.7 Knowledge transfer	0.15
		1.8 Organizational change management	0.00
		1.9 Hardware acquisition	0.01
	2. Management **1.47**	2.1 Supplier/customer relationship	0.25
		2.2 Resourcing	0.41
		2.3 Communication	0.08
		2.4 Program management organization	0.46
		2.5 Facilities and infrastructure	0.27
	3. Commercial **0.26**	3.1 Contract management	0.20
		3.2 Subcontract issues	0.06

FIGURE 6-8: RBS Categorization by P-I Score

CLOSE THE WORKSHOP

In concluding the workshop, all participants are given the opportunity to give feedback on the workshop. Any unmet objectives or remaining concerns are aired and addressed. The risk champion closes the workshop by summarizing the outputs and next steps, and particularly ensuring that nominated risk owners are clear about their role in the Response Planning step (as described in Chapter 7).

The risk champion invites all attendees to raise any additional matters after the workshop, if necessary, which may mean that further risks are identified. It is essential that these new risks are brought into the overall ATOM process without delay. To ensure that this happens, the risk champion nominates a risk owner for each new risk, and the risk owner then confirms the risk description and assesses the risk for its probability and impact, passing information to the risk champion to be recorded in the risk tool.

Post-workshop

The activities following the workshop depend on what took place within it. If assessment information was not entered into the risk tool during the workshop, the risk champion ensures that all additional data is entered into the risk tool immediately afterward to enable preparation of the required outputs. This data includes the probability and impact(s) for each risk, risk categorizations by RBS and WBS, and the nominated risk owners. Any agreed modifications to the risk description are also recorded.

If any nominated risk owners did not attend the workshop, the risk champion obtains their agreement to take on the role, explaining what is expected of them and ensuring that they both understand and accept responsibility for the risks that have been allocated to them. In the unlikely event that a risk owner refuses the role, the risk champion, in liaison with the project manager, nominates an alternative.

Project Number:			Client:
Project Title:			Project Manager:
Risk Ref.	RBS Ref.	WBS Ref.	Risk Owner:
Risk Type: (T/O)	Risk Status: (Draft/Active/Closed/Deleted/Expired/Occurred)		
Risk Title:			
Risk Description:			

Cause of Risk	Effect on Objectives		
	Objective	Impact Rating Nil/VLO/LO/MED/HI/VHI	Impact Description
	Time		
	Cost		
	Quality		
Probability Rating Nil/VLO/LO/MED/ HI/VHI	Other		
Date Risk Raised:	Date Risk Closed/Deleted/Expired/Occurred:		

Risk Response—Preferred Strategy:			
Action(s) to Implement Strategy	Action Owner	Action by Date	Status
Comment/Status:			

Copyright 2004. From Effective Opportunity Management for Projects by David Hillson. Reproduced by permission of Taylor & Francis, a division of Informa plc.

FIGURE 6-9: Sample Risk Register Format

Outputs

The outputs from the Assessment step are provided by the risk tool. If the risk tool is unable to provide the necessary outputs, the risk champion produces them using any appropriate methods. The main outputs are listed below.

INITIAL RISK REGISTER

The initial Risk Register lists all currently known information about every identified risk; see Figure 6-9 for an example Risk Register format. At this point the Risk Register will contain

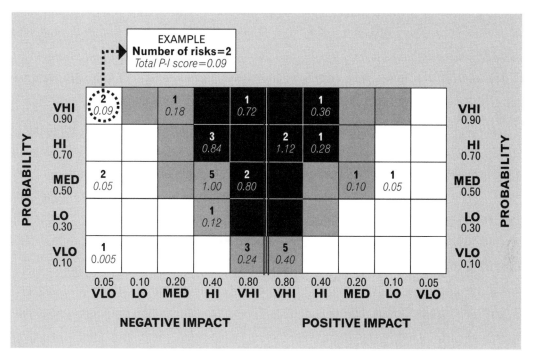

FIGURE 6-10: Double Probability-Impact Matrix Showing Risk Density

only risk descriptions, cause and effect information, assessments of probability and impacts, allocation to RBS and WBS elements, and nominated risk owners. It may also contain initial risk responses developed during the risk identification part of the risk workshop.

PRIORITIZED RISK LIST

The prioritized risk list includes all risks—both threats and opportunities—in their order of importance, as derived by their combined probability and impact scores. For clarity and emphasis it is helpful to divide the list into three sections using the agreed risk thresholds: red/high, amber/medium, and green/low. This allows the red/high priority risks to be addressed first.

LIST OF TOP THREATS AND TOP OPPORTUNITIES

These are taken from the risk list and can be used as both an immediate and future reporting tool. The term "top ten" is often used loosely to describe these lists, but this raises the danger of ignoring an important eleventh risk. A better solution is to focus on all red/high-priority risks, rather than artificially choosing a fixed number such as ten.

ANALYSIS OF CAUSES VIA THE RBS

A simple table is produced that lists the Level 2 elements of the RBS and the number of risks associated with each element, as well as the total P-I score.

ANALYSIS OF EFFECTS VIA THE WBS

Like the RBS, a simple table is produced to show each Level 2 or 3 element of the WBS (the level depends on how the WBS is constructed) and the risks associated with it.

DOUBLE P-I MATRIX

A double P-I Matrix shows the number of risks in each cell and/or total P-I score; see Figure 6-10. This matrix clearly illustrates the risk exposure of the project by showing the distribution of risks across the P-I Matrix. A high density of risks in the red zone clearly indicates a risky or highly uncertain project. However, this initial post-assessment version of the P-I Matrix shows the risk distribution only prior to response planning. A useful comparison can be made if the same output is produced taking into account planned responses (see Chapter 7).

Summary

The Assessment step prioritizes the identified risks such that the important or high-priority ones can be addressed first, and ensures that appropriate risk owners are nominated. Both actions are fundamental inputs to Response Planning. Carrying out the Assessment step requires the following activities:

- Assess probability for each risk based on a five-point scale

- Assess impact(s) for each risk based on a five-point scale

- Combine probability and impact to provide an overall probability-impact score, which will be used to determine priority

- Categorize risks using the RBS (causes) and WBS (effects) to determine "hot spots"

- Nominate risk owners, who will later develop appropriate risk responses and appoint action owners

- Record all additional risk data in the risk tool

- Prepare a set of outputs that will inform the continued risk management process as well as the overall project management process

Once the Assessment step of the First Risk Assessment is complete, it is possible to move onto the preparation of responses, as described in the next chapter.

....

CHAPTER 7

Options and Actions
(Response Planning)

The steps in the First Risk Assessment of the ATOM risk process described so far (Identification and Assessment) can be viewed as analysis, scoping the extent of the risk challenge for the project, seeking to understand the risks to which the project is exposed. However, simply understanding and describing the risks does not change them. It is vital that the risk process moves on to action, actually dealing with the risks in order to change the project's risk exposure. This is the purpose of the last element of the First Risk Assessment, which in ATOM is called Response Planning.

In many ways Response Planning is the most important step of the risk process, because effective risk responses result in minimized threats and maximized opportunities, optimizing the project's chances of achieving its objectives. Conversely, poor response planning can worsen the position, by not only failing to address identified risks but also introducing new risks as a result of ineffective actions. This step is where key decisions are made on how to manage risks, using risk information to modify project strategy where necessary, and positioning the project to gain the benefits offered by the risk process.

The key word in Response Planning is *appropriateness*. Recognizing that risks include both threats and opportunities, the aim of the project team is to make the negative risk exposure from threats as small as possible while increasing the positive risk exposure from opportunities. The appropriate response to each type of risk is clearly different. For some threats it might be appropriate to panic, or even cancel the project. It could be right to embrace some opportunities and actively seek the additional benefits they offer. For other risks the appropriate response may be to do nothing and wait to see what happens. Obviously the project should not panic over risks where the appropriate thing is to do nothing, or do nothing when a risk should be actively embraced. Choosing the appropriate response is an important decision requiring careful judgment, and is best done by people with the necessary level of experience and expertise.

As a result, it is vital that sufficient attention and effort is applied to Response Planning. Time and effort invested at this step in the process pays dividends in process effectiveness, whereas shortcuts have negative repercussions.

The purpose of the Response Planning step in ATOM is to:

- Consider all identified risks and select an appropriate response strategy for each

- Develop specific actions that put into practice each response strategy, with enough definition to allow effective implementation

- Ensure that each action is assigned to an action owner

In order to do this, the following inputs are required:

- Risk Management Plan, defining risk tools and techniques for this project

- Initial Risk Register, containing information on identified risks from the risk workshop, including the following:

  - Prioritized list of risks, each with a proper risk description and agreed assessments of probability and impacts

  - Nominated risk owner for each risk

  - Initial responses proposed during the Identification step

- Information on available generic response strategies

In ATOM, Response Planning requires the following activities:

- Response strategy selection

- Action development

- Assessment of post-response risk exposure

- Consideration of secondary risks

The Response Planning step produces the following outputs:

- Appropriate response strategy and agreed actions for each risk

- Nominated action owners for each agreed action

- Updated Risk Register containing response information for all identified risks

- Updated assessment results reflecting the post-response situation

- Updates to the project plan (both schedule and budget) to include agreed risk actions

These inputs, activities, and outputs are illustrated in Figure 7-1, and described in detail in the following sections.

Inputs

Like other steps in the risk process, the Risk Management Plan defines the detail for the risk process as it is to be applied for this project. Where necessary, the risk champion refers to the Risk Management Plan to clarify the requirements for this step.

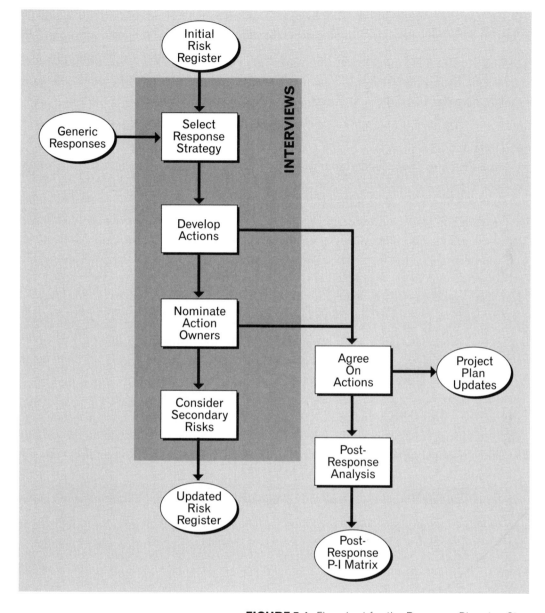

FIGURE 7-1: Flowchart for the Response Planning Step

The Assessment step allows identified risks to be prioritized, using the Probability-Impact (P-I) Matrix, into at least three groups (red or high priority, amber or medium priority, green or low priority), and possibly with more detailed prioritization using a P-I scoring scheme, as discussed in Chapter 6. Assessment also allocates to each identified risk a single risk owner, who is responsible for determining how the risk will be managed. This information is held in the Risk Register, which forms the main input to the Response Planning step. It is, however, recommended that the risk champion prepare subsets of the Risk Register, listing risks by risk owner, so that each owner can receive a list of their risks prior to the risk interview.

For some risks, initial responses may have been identified during the Identification step, and these will also have been recorded in the Risk Register. These responses are presented to risk owners for validation during this Response Planning step to confirm that they are appropriate and acceptable.

The final Response Planning input is information on what response strategies are available to risk owners. This information might exist within the organization as part of a knowledge base, or might be prepared by the risk champion as a prebrief for risk owners.

Activities

Response Planning can be undertaken as part of the risk workshop if there is sufficient time available. However, workshop time is frequently limited and may run out before responses can be considered for any or all identified risks. When time is available for Response Planning during the workshop, risks are considered in priority order, dealing first with the worst threats and best opportunities. Following the risk workshop, the risk champion holds a series of interviews with risk owners to deal with those risks not covered during the workshop. This section describes risk interviews, assuming that the risk workshop time is fully taken up by the Identification and Assessment steps, and that all response planning will take place this way.

Activities relating to risk interviews can be divided into three groups: preparation, interviewing, and post-interview tasks. These are described in the following paragraphs.

Preparing for risk interviews

The risk champion schedules interviews with all risk owners immediately after the risk workshop, with the goal of completing all interviews within one week. Each interview should be scheduled for two hours, though the full time may not be required, depending on the number and difficulty of risks to be addressed in each interview. When scheduling interviews with risk

---

GENERIC RESPONSES TO THREATS

Avoid: A response to a threat that eliminates either its probability or impact on the project. This can often be achieved by changing the project management plan for the project or by addressing the cause of the risk.
Transfer: A response to a threat that transfers the risk to a third party who is better able to manage it. The act of transfer does not itself change the risk, but the new owner should be able to take action to avoid or reduce it.
Reduce: A response to a threat that reduces its probability and/or impact on the project, aiming to reduce the risk to an acceptable level. This may be achieved by addressing key risk drivers.

GENERIC RESPONSES TO OPPORTUNITIES

Exploit: A response to an opportunity that ensures that the opportunity is taken by guaranteeing that it will definitely occur.
Share: A response to an opportunity that shares the risk with a third party better able to manage it, either by exploiting or enhancing the opportunity.
Enhance: A response to an opportunity that increases its probability and/or impact on the project.

GENERIC RESPONSE TO THREATS AND OPPORTUNITIES

Accept: A response where either no proactive action is taken (perhaps because it is not worth doing anything or it is not possible to) or where responses are designed that are contingent upon a change in circumstances. Alternatively, a contingency reserve (time, money, and resources) can be established to deal with the risk should it occur.

FIGURE 7-2: Generic Response Strategies

owners, the risk champion sends an extract from the Risk Register containing the risks assigned to them, listed in priority order, as well as practical arrangements for the interview, including time, venue, agenda, etc. For risk owners new to the process it might also be useful to send a reminder of the generic response strategies available. An example is given in Figure 7-2.

Prior to the risk interview, each risk owner prepares by considering their risks and possible options for responses and actions. This maximizes productivity during the interview.

Conducting risk interviews

At the start of each interview, the risk champion confirms the interview's purpose and agenda, and emphasizes its confidential nature. For each risk, the risk owner in discussion with the risk champion will:

- Select an appropriate response strategy

- Identify possible actions to implement that strategy

- Assign action owners to each action

- Assess post-response probability and impacts

- Identify any secondary risks

The role of the risk champion is to prompt and encourage the risk owner, facilitate the interview to maintain momentum and ensure good time-keeping, answer questions relating to the risk process or risk management theory and practice, and suggest possible response strategies and actions based on his own experience. However, it is the risk owner's responsibility to decide which response strategy and actions are appropriate for the risks that they own.

Each risk allocated to the risk owner is considered in turn, working through them in priority order as follows:

1. Red/high-priority opportunities

2. Red/high-priority threats

3. Amber/medium-priority opportunities

4. Amber/medium-priority threats

5. Green/low-priority opportunities

6. Green/low-priority threats

Considering opportunities before threats is recommended because people are less familiar with including opportunity in the risk process.

When addressing high-priority risks, often the proposed response strategies also addresses some of the medium- or low-priority risks. The risk champion must bear in mind this potential risk management efficiency when carrying out further interviews and developing responses to less important risks.

Initial responses to particular risks proposed during the Identification step are considered first. The risk owner decides whether the proposed response would be appropriate and effective, and this decision is recorded in the Risk Register.

PRIORITY	THREAT STRATEGY	OPPORTUNITY STRATEGY
1	Avoid	Exploit
2	Transfer	Share
3	Reduce	Enhance
4	Accept	

FIGURE 7-3: Priorities for Selecting Response Strategies

If there is no previously identified response, or if the initial response is rejected by the risk owner, they must select an appropriate response strategy for each risk. For opportunities, this is either exploit, share, enhance, or accept. Available threat strategies include avoid, transfer, reduce, or accept. It is recommended to consider strategies in the order shown in Figure 7-3, since the best option, if possible, is to avoid a threat or exploit an opportunity. This may be achieved by addressing the cause of the risk, as recorded in the description of the risk using the metalanguage. Where this is not feasible or cost-effective, alternative parties should be sought who are better able to manage the risk effectively, allowing a threat to be transferred or an opportunity to be shared. The third option is to modify the level of risk exposure by reducing a threat or enhancing an opportunity. The last option is to accept the risk, with possible development of a contingency plan, taking into account the effect of the risk as defined in the risk metalanguage.

Factors to be considered when deciding which strategy is appropriate include:

- Manageability

- Impact severity

- Resource availability

- Cost-effectiveness

For each risk, a single response strategy is selected that represents the current best choice for managing the risk effectively. This recognizes that a different strategy may be selected in the future if the one first chosen proves ineffective, but at this stage in the process each identified risk must have just one strategy.

Next, the risk owner determines specific actions that could be implemented to achieve the selected strategy. These are described in as much detail as possible, ideally including what is to be done, by whom, when, and at what cost, and with completion criteria. The aim is to define each action at the same level of detail as a normal activity in the project schedule. A particularly important step is to nominate suitable owners for each action (action owners) who have the necessary skills and experience to perform the action effectively.

After defining actions, the risk owner provides an assessment of the risk, assuming that the actions are completed successfully. Using the same P-I scales from the risk workshop, the post-response probability of occurrence and impacts on objectives for the risk are estimated. This gives an indication of how "risk-effective" the proposed actions are expected to be, and whether additional actions are required.

Finally, the risk owner considers whether the proposed actions will introduce secondary risks, defined as a risk that arises from implementation of an agreed response to another risk, as illustrated in Figure 7-4. Of course, a secondary risk can be either a threat or an opportunity. Where such secondary risks are identified, the risk owner and the risk champion together:

- Produce an agreed risk description for the secondary risk, using the metalanguage, with the action recorded as the cause of the secondary risk

- Assess the probability and impacts of the secondary risk against the agreed scales

- Select an appropriate response strategy for the secondary risk, and determine actions with nominated action owners

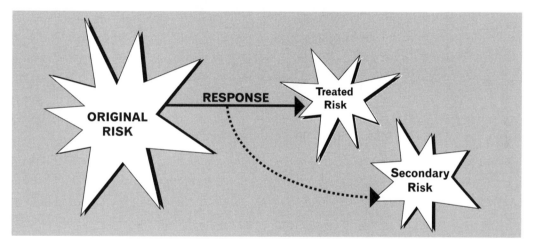

FIGURE 7-4: Secondary Risks

At this point the risk owner and risk champion may decide that the secondary risks associated with the proposed actions make them infeasible (particularly where significant additional threats would be introduced), in which case the proposed actions are rejected and new ones developed; in some cases this requires selection of an alternative response strategy. If, however, it is decided to proceed with the actions as originally planned, the associated secondary risks are recorded in the Risk Register and treated as any other risks.

After all risks have been considered, the risk champion asks whether the risk owner is aware of any additional risks in his or her area of responsibility that are not currently captured in the Risk Register. Any new risks are identified and assessed, and responses and actions developed.

The outcome from this discussion is captured by the risk champion during the interview, preferably directly into the risk tool being used to support the project risk process. Where direct data entry is not possible, the risk champion takes full notes during the interview and transfers them into the risk tool immediately following the interview.

Post-interview actions

After each interview is complete, the risk owner is responsible for liaising with nominated action owners to ensure that they agree with the proposed action and accept responsibility for its implementation. Risk owners and action owners together may decide to refine actions at this point, and the risk owner informs the risk champion of any agreed changes.

After feedback from risk owners that all action owners have accepted their proposed actions, the risk champion ensures that the Risk Register is updated to reflect the strategy and agreed actions. The risk champion also uses the information generated during risk interviews to update assessment results to reflect the post-response situation. This includes producing a post-response double P-I Matrix (Figure 7-5) to show the predicted position of each risk if

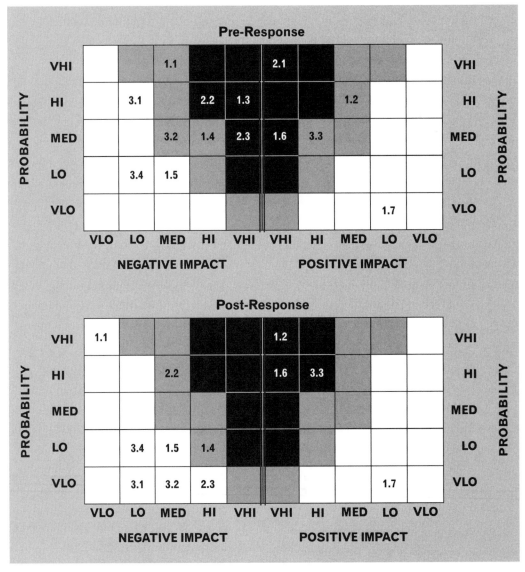

FIGURE 7-5: Pre- and Post-Response P-I Matrices

planned actions were fully effective (the risk tool might produce such an output automatically). For example, Figure 7-5 shows, among others, the result of avoiding threat 1.3, reducing threats 2.3 and 3.1, exploiting opportunity 2.1, and enhancing opportunity 1.2.

The risk champion also liaises with the project manager to raise new activities for inclusion in the project schedule to reflect agreed actions. Risk actions must be treated with the same degree of importance and attention as other project activities, and including them in the project schedule ensures this because they will then be subject to monitoring and control along with other activities. It is also essential to make appropriate funds and resources available to carry out risk actions, and to include them in the project budget.

Finally, the project manager considers the need for change control if it is required after modifying the project plan; in some cases contract changes may also be necessary.

Outputs

The main output from the Response Planning step is an updated Risk Register containing current information on selected responses, agreed actions with action owners, post-response assessments, and secondary risks (if any). This information forms an important part of the risk reports that are prepared in the next step of the ATOM risk process.

The risk champion also generates analysis outputs showing the predicted effect of planned actions on levels of risk exposure, such as the post-response P-I Matrix.

Another important output from this step is a set of updates to the project schedule and budget to include agreed actions. The project manager ensures that this is done with minimal delay.

One key factor in preparing outputs from Response Planning is timeliness. It is vital to communicate and implement response strategies and actions as quickly as possible after being identified. This is because risk is dynamic and fast-changing, and any delay in the risk process might result in the outputs becoming outdated. The risk champion should therefore aim to complete response planning within less than a week after the Identification/Assessment workshop.

Summary

The Response Planning step ensures that appropriate actions are identified for each identified risk. Implementation of these actions minimizes threats to the project and maximizes opportunities, optimizing the chances of project success. To complete this step, the following activities should be undertaken:

- Arrange interviews with all risk owners

- Consider all risks with their respective risk owners, and determine an appropriate response strategy, plus actions to implement the selected strategy, with a nominated action owner for each action

- Confirm and refine proposed actions with action owners

- Update the Risk Register with response strategies and agreed actions

- Update analysis outputs to reflect post-response expectations

- Modify the project schedule and budget to include agreed actions

When the Response Planning step of the First Risk Assessment is complete, the ATOM process continues with reporting current results and implementing agreed actions, as detailed in the next two chapters.

· ·

CHAPTER 8

Spread the Word (Reporting)

Risk management is about taking appropriate action in response to identified risks. Unfortunately the earlier steps of the risk process do not guarantee that those who must take such action possess the necessary information to do so. It is therefore important to include a step for communicating the results of the risk process to the people who need to know. In ATOM this step is called Reporting.

Following the First Risk Assessment on a medium-size project, Reporting simply combines the outputs from the previous steps into a single risk report. Extracts from this report can be distributed to different stakeholders; for example, the executive summary to senior management, or subsets of risks to individual risk owners. Additional reports may also be necessary, depending on the project reporting cycle or other organizational requirements.

The purpose of the Reporting step in ATOM is to:

- Document and communicate key results and conclusions from the risk process

- Inform project stakeholders of the current risk status of the project

- Ensure that each project stakeholder has the information required to fulfill his or her role in managing risk on the project

Reporting requires the following inputs:

- Risk Management Plan, defining the reporting requirements for this project

- Project communication plan, if available

- Risk Register containing full details of all identified risks, their assessment, responses, and current status

- Analysis results following the Assessment and Response Planning steps

Reporting requires the following activities:

- Produce the full risk report, first as a draft to be reviewed, then issued in final form

- Generate extracts and other reports as required

- Distribute reports to project stakeholders

The Reporting step produces the following output:

- Full risk report and extracts

These inputs, activities, and outputs are illustrated in Figure 8-1, and described in detail in the following sections.

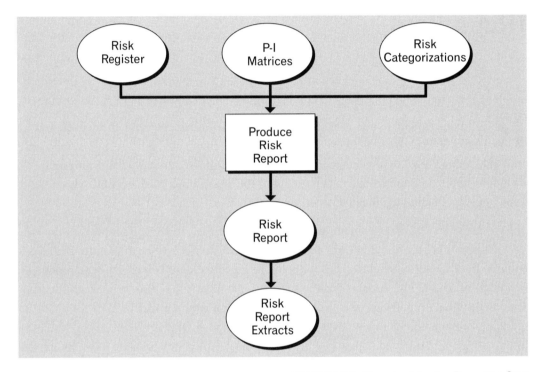

FIGURE 8-1: Flowchart for the Reporting Step

Inputs

The Risk Management Plan defines the project's reporting requirements. Where necessary, the risk champion refers to the Risk Management Plan to clarify these requirements. The project communication plan, if one exists, should also be consulted, because it may give more details on the precise information needs of project stakeholders.

The risk champion uses the results of the preceding steps in the risk process to generate the risk report and other reporting outputs. Most of these results are captured in the Risk Register, or may be produced directly from it (either manually or as outputs from the risk tool), though some additional analysis results may be documented elsewhere. Analysis outputs that are used in addition to the Risk Register to compile the risk report include Probability-Impact Matrices showing both pre-response and post-response assessments, prioritized lists of risks, and various groupings of risks (for example, sorting risks by priority in red, amber, green (RAG) groups, or mapped to RBS or WBS, etc.).

Activities

Based on the defined reporting requirements, the risk champion considers the inputs and compiles them into a full risk report. These inputs commonly include:

- The full Risk Register, which contains consolidated data on each identified risk, with a clear description of the risk, assessments of current probability and impacts, mapping against the RBS and WBS, an assigned risk owner, an agreed response strategy with actions and action owners, assessment of post-response probability and impacts, and the status of the progress of agreed actions

- A double Probability-Impact Matrix, which shows the current distribution of risks across the grid, allowing them to be prioritized for further attention, based on assessments of current probability and impacts

- Another double Probability-Impact Matrix, which shows predicted risk distribution based on post-response probability and impacts

- Two prioritized risk lists, one for threats and another for opportunities

- Analysis of risk causes, based on mapping identified risks to the various elements of the risk breakdown structure

- Analysis of risk effects from mapping risks to the work breakdown structure

If additional analysis is required to generate useful information from the risk data, the risk champion performs such analysis, seeking advice where necessary from other project stakeholders, technical specialists, or domain experts. In addition, the risk champion draws conclusions from the risk data concerning the overall risk exposure of the project, and particular areas where risk is concentrated (either common causes or "hot spots" of effects). Recommendations are also drafted that provide advice and guidance to project stakeholders on the course of action required to maintain effective management of risk, especially if the position has changed significantly since the last report.

Having drafted the risk report, the risk champion submits it to the project manager for review and comment, as well as to provide a "sanity check" that the conclusions are realistic and accurate, and that recommendations are feasible and appropriate. The project manager should not change any of the report data, but might be aware of additional factors in the project environment that influence the analysis, conclusions, or recommendations.

The risk champion and project manager together agree on any changes to the draft risk report; these changes are implemented by the risk champion, who then issues the report. It is recommended to distribute the full risk report to the project manager, project sponsor, key project team members, all risk owners, and other key stakeholders.

Depending on the reporting requirements for the project, as defined in the Risk Management Plan, the risk champion may also prepare extracts or subsets of the full risk report and distribute them to other project stakeholders, and may also produce specific report formats as required by the project or organizational reporting process. For example, the executive summary of the report may be extracted for senior management or clients, giving the highlights from the current risk assessment but excluding unnecessary detail. Risk owners may be offered a subset of the Risk Register that contains just those risks for which they are responsible. Risks falling within certain categories may be extracted for distribution to people with an interest in those areas; for example, sending legal risks to the contracts manager, or passing the subset of procurement risks to the commercial department.

Outputs

The main output from the Reporting step is a full risk report containing complete information on the results of the current major cycle in the risk process. Figure 8-2 gives a sample contents list for a full risk report, and its various items are outlined in the following paragraphs.

EXECUTIVE SUMMARY

SCOPE AND OBJECTIVES OF REPORT

PROJECT STATUS SUMMARY

OVERALL RISK STATUS

TOP RISKS, ACTIONS AND OWNERS

DETAILED RISK ASSESSMENT
   High/Medium/Low Risks
   Causal Analysis (Mapped To RBS)
   Effects Analysis (Mapped To WBS)

CONCLUSIONS AND RECOMMENDATIONS

APPENDICES
   COMPLETE RISK REGISTER
   PRIORITIZED RISK LIST
   (OTHER RESULTS AS REQUIRED)

FIGURE 8-2: Sample Contents List for a Full Risk Report

- *Executive summary.* This section summarizes the key findings, conclusions, and recommendations of the main body of the report, aiming for a maximum of a single page, and omitting unnecessary detail. It should be standalone and not dependent on reference to additional data in the body of the report. The executive summary should be written at a level suitable for senior management and key project stakeholders, since it may be extracted and distributed to this group.

- *Scope and objectives of report.* The main purpose of the report is described, highlighting its place in the risk process.

- *Project status summary.* This section briefly summarizes the current status of the project, including progress against the project schedule and budget, delivery of products, major issues that have arisen, etc. This summary sets the context within which the risk assessment was undertaken. Ideally, the summary of project status should be extracted directly from routine project progress reports.

- *Overall risk status.* A short summary is presented of the current level of risk exposure for the project. This summary highlights the main areas of risk, plus any significant individual risks together with planned responses. This section also highlights any concentrations of risk exposed during the categorization analysis, indicating any causes that give rise to a large number of threats or opportunities, as well as any areas of the project that could be affected by significant levels of threat or opportunity.

- *Top risks, actions, and owners.* In this section, lists of the top threats and opportunities are presented in priority order. Some projects prefer to use a combined list of "top risks," containing both threats and opportunities, and others like to see a "worst threats" list and a "best opportunities" list. These lists commonly present the "top ten," but a suitable number should be chosen to ensure that all the worst threats and best opportunities are included. These are discussed in turn in this section, detailing their causes and effects, planned actions with their owners, and expected changes. Significant groupings within the top-risk lists are noted, for example, if five of the top threats relate to requirements uncertainty, or if the best three opportunities all concern the same supplier.

- *Detailed risk assessment.* This is the main analysis section of the report, where the risk exposure is considered in detail. Discussion includes the numbers of risks in the red/amber/green categories, as well as distribution of risks within the RBS and WBS. Expected response effectiveness is discussed, based on the pre-response and post-response P-I matrices. The aim is to present all significant findings from the analysis, but not to swamp readers with unnecessary detail. This requires judgment by the risk champion to determine what is important to include and what can be omitted; the risk champion should draw on the experience of the project manager and other experienced project staff, if required.

- *Conclusions and recommendations.* Perhaps the most important part of any report is indicating what its contents actually mean and what action readers are expected to take as a result. This section draws conclusions based on the data within the main body of the report, without introducing any new facts, and presents findings at a summary level rather than simply repeating what is contained elsewhere in the report. Based on these conclusions, the report moves on to develop a series of focused and specific recommendations that respond to the level of risk currently faced by the project. Each recommendation should be written at a sufficient level of detail to be clearly understood and effectively implemented, following the SMART model (Specific, Measurable, Achievable, Realistic, Time-bound). Typically the number of recommendations should be limited to about ten, to avoid diluting the impact of the report.

- *Appendices.* Supporting information is presented in appendices. One of these contains the complete Risk Register, giving full details of every identified risk. It is also common to include a complete list of all risks in priority order. The content of other appendices is optional, depending on the information needs of the recipients.

Summary

The purpose of the Reporting step is to document the results of the First Risk Assessment and communicate these appropriately to project stakeholders, in order to make them aware of the project's current risk status and give them the information they need to take effective action.

Completing this step requires the following activities:

- Assemble all sources of information on current risk exposure, including the Risk Register and analysis outputs

- Perform any additional analysis required to understand the information

- Draft a full risk report presenting this information in a structured way

- Review the draft report for completeness and correctness, and modify as required

- Issue risk report to project sponsor, project manager, project team members, risk owners, and other key stakeholders

- Prepare and distribute extracts, subsets, and additional reports as required

The First Risk Assessment in the ATOM risk process is followed by the Reporting step, and also leads immediately to the start of Implementation, which is described in the next chapter.

....

CHAPTER 9

Just Do It
(Implementation)

The ATOM risk process for a typical medium-size project has so far set the scope and objectives (Initiation); then, using the First Risk Assessment, exposed and recorded uncertainties that could affect achievement of those objectives (Identification), prioritized and categorized them (Assessment), and developed appropriate responses and actions to deal with them (Response Planning). This is all-important and valuable, but it is not enough. In order for the risk exposure of the project to be changed, the agreed actions must be implemented. As a result, the first pass through the ATOM process cannot be considered complete until the Implementation step is under way. Of course, actions to address risks will be performed throughout the project, so in some ways Implementation does not have a distinct start and end. This chapter describes the activities that it contains.

Implementation starts immediately following the First Risk Assessment, but Major and Minor Reviews also produce actions that must be implemented. This chapter therefore describes how to ensure that all agreed actions are performed.

During the First Risk Assessment and subsequent reviews, risk owners select a response strategy for each risk and develop it into a series of actions, each of which has a nominated action owner. However, simply producing responses or actions does not in itself change risk exposure, although it does create the potential to do so. Without implementation of agreed actions, the risk process is all rhetoric or "hot air" and, in Shakespeare's words, what is required is "more matter with less art." Failing to implement the planned actions means that nothing will change, threats will not be minimized, opportunities will not be maximized, and the risk status quo will remain.

In ATOM the purpose of the Implementation step is to:

- Perform agreed actions and report on their progress

- Identify any additional secondary risks that arise as a result of implementing actions

- Identify any new risks that may arise between formal cycles of the ATOM risk process

- Keep the Risk Register up to date

- Raise any issues or problems that result from threats actually occurring

In order to do this, the following inputs are required:

- Risk Management Plan, which includes the agreed risk reporting process and project reporting cycle

- Risk Register, which contains details relating to each risk, including:

  - Risk owners

  - Agreed response strategies

  - Action owners

  - Agreed actions

- An updated project schedule showing all agreed risk actions as project activities

- Risk tool (spreadsheet, database, or proprietary software)

In the Implementation step, the following activities are performed:

- Implement agreed actions associated with the selected response strategy for each active risk

- Suggest further actions if those already implemented prove ineffective

- Identify secondary risks, raising new risks and issues or problems

- Report on the status of all risks and update the Risk Register

Implementation produces the following outputs:

- Updated Risk Register containing the latest information and status of all risks

- Inputs to risk reports and review meetings

- Inputs to the project issue log

These inputs, activities, and outputs are illustrated in Figure 9-1, and described in detail in the following sections.

Inputs

The Risk Management Plan defines the process that ensures that risk actions are implemented in order to give response strategies the greatest chance of success. Fundamental to this plan are the roles of the risk owner and action owner. The risk owner selects the response strategy that determines how the risk is to be managed; the action owner implements agreed actions in order to achieve the desired response strategy. The Risk Management Plan also defines the types of reports to be prepared and the project meetings at which risk will be discussed. This informs what information needs to be gathered as part of the Implementation step.

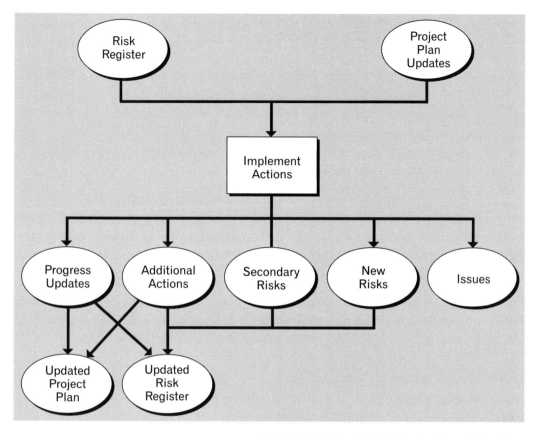

FIGURE 9-1: Flowchart for the Implementation Step

The Risk Register is also a key input to the Implementation step, and at this point in the ATOM process, it contains a complete set of data for each identified risk. This includes the name of the risk owner responsible for overall management of each risk, and the names of action owner(s) responsible for implementing those actions needed to realize the response strategy.

As in previous steps it is assumed that a risk tool is being used to support the ATOM risk process, and this is a key input to this step.

Activities

Implementation is a continuous process that takes place throughout the life of the project, which reflects the fact that many identified actions will not need to be carried out immediately, but will be scheduled to take place in the future. However, it is important that all in-progress actions are reviewed and their status reported as part of the normal reporting cycle of the project.

The risk champion oversees implementation of responses and actions, drawing on information provided by risk owners, and reports the status of each risk to the project manager and other key stakeholders. The risk champion also ensures that any new or secondary risks that are identified are properly described and assessed, and that they have a nominated risk owner with an agreed response strategy and actions.

The risk champion also ensures that any threats that have occurred are recorded as project issues or problems, and are reported and managed accordingly.

PERFORM AGREED ACTIONS

Each action owner implements the actions that were agreed with the risk owner and included in the project plan, making sure that they meet the agreed timelines, budgets, completion criteria, etc. As each agreed action is completed, the action owner reports this to the risk owner, and ensures that the status of the corresponding activity on the project plan is marked as complete. Progress reporting on completed actions is done either immediately upon completion, or periodically, as required by the risk owner.

Any problems encountered in implementing the actions as agreed are reported immediately by the action owner to the risk owner, who offers advice on how to proceed. This advice may include agreeing on additional actions aimed at implementing the existing response strategy, or the risk owner may consider a change in strategy. All agreed additional actions are recorded in the project plan.

The action owner might also discover previously unidentified secondary risks arising from implementation of agreed actions. All secondary risks must be reported immediately to the risk owner so that they can be brought into the risk process (see below).

IDENTIFYING ADDITIONAL SECONDARY RISKS

Secondary risks (which result from the response to another risk) should have been identified by the risk owner as part of planning responses, and action owners should be aware of these when they are implementing planned actions. However, it is unlikely that all secondary risks will have been identified, so action owners should consider the effects of their actions and whether they might introduce additional risks to the project. When action owners find such additional secondary risks, they should be raised immediately with the risk champion in the same way as other new risks (see below). The action owner should also inform the risk owner because new risks may influence other aspects of their selected response strategy.

RAISING NEW RISKS

New risks are likely to be identified during the normal course of the project outside of the formal workshops and review meetings of the risk process. At any time, any project stakeholder should be able to raise new risks. These might be risks that were previously unforeseen or missed by the earlier steps in the risk process, or they might be secondary risks arising from implementation of actions in response to other risks.

If someone believes that they have identified a new risk, they immediately inform the risk champion. The risk champion, in consultation with the project manager, nominates a risk owner to these risks as soon as possible, who ensures that each new risk allocated to them is described properly using the risk metalanguage (see Figure 5-4). The risk owner also assesses the probability and impacts of the risk, develops a response strategy and actions, and nominates action owners. The risk owner passes all of this additional data to the risk champion, who ensures that it is entered into the risk tool. In addition, the risk champion ensures that the project schedule and budget are updated to reflect the new agreed actions.

All new risks are then reviewed at the next risk review (Major or Minor—see Chapters 10 and 11), when the initial description, assessment, response, and actions proposed by the risk owner are validated and either confirmed or changed. Until the risks are reviewed, their status is set to draft.

RAISING ISSUES OR PROBLEMS

In the event that a threat has occurred, it is recorded as a project issue or problem and managed according to the standard project process. The risk champion ensures that this is done whenever a threat is reported as having occurred.

REPORTING ON RISK STATUS AND UPDATING THE RISK REGISTER

The Risk Register must be kept up to date to reflect the current status of each risk. Although the risk champion is responsible for the overall risk management process, risk owners ensure that all the data recorded for their respective risks is accurate and current. One important element of this is assigning a status to each risk, and ATOM provides the following eight possible status values (see Figure 9-2):

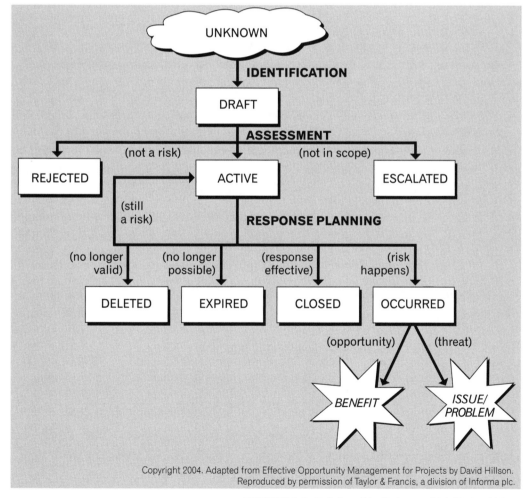

FIGURE 9-2: Relationship Between Risk Status Values

- **Draft:** A proposed risk that has not yet been validated

- **Rejected:** A proposed risk that the project manager has decided is not valid

- **Escalated:** A proposed risk that is outside the scope of the project. The project manager determines who should be notified about this proposed risk and communicates the details to that person or part of the organization.

- **Active:** A valid risk with a probability of occurrence greater than zero and that will impact one or more project objective if it occurs. An active threat can affect the project negatively, while an active opportunity has a potential positive effect.

- **Deleted:** Sometimes risks can just go away on their own, perhaps resulting from a change in the project's strategy, environment, objectives, or scope

- **Expired:** The time window in which the risk could have occurred has passed, therefore the risk no longer needs to be considered. An expired threat might be a source of relief for the project since it can no longer have a negative effect, whereas an expired opportunity would be a source of regret as the positive impact is no longer possible.

- **Closed:** This only applies to threats for which the response has been fully effective and can no longer affect the project. Opportunities cannot be marked as closed, because they will remain active until they have either occurred, expired, or been deleted.

- **Occurred:** The risk has happened and the impact is being experienced by the project. It is of course desirable for an opportunity to occur, and undesirable for a threat to occur. Occurred status might result if the response to a threat proved ineffective or the response to an opportunity was successful. (Note that when a threat has occurred, it is converted to an issue or problem and managed accordingly. When an opportunity has occurred, the additional benefits must be recognized and managed.)

In addition to the overall status of the risk, the risk owner considers all other information about the risk, and ensures that the Risk Register contains the latest information, including:

- The risk's current probability and impact (probabilities and impacts can go up or down)

- Progress on all agreed actions

- Changes to the risk owner or action owners

- Changes to the response strategy or new actions

Outputs

The main output from the Implementation step is an updated Risk Register, which contains the current status of each risk and progress on agreed actions. The updated Risk Register is a major input for risk reports and review meetings, as described in Chapters 8, 10, and 11.

If it is recognized during the Implementation step that a threat has occurred, the occurrence is recorded in the project issue log as appropriate.

Summary

The Implementation step is designed to make sure that what has been planned actually takes place. If the planned actions are not implemented, opportunities will not be maximized, threats will not be minimized, and the risk exposure of the project will remain unchanged. The implementation of actions cannot be left to chance, and therefore the following activities must be undertaken:

- Monitor each response strategy and its associated actions

- Ascertain the overall status of each risk

- Identify additional secondary risks and raise new risks

- Modify the project schedule and budget to include new actions or any replanned actions

- Raise any issues or problems

- Update the Risk Register with the current status of each risk and progress on agreed actions

- Produce information for risk reports and review meetings

The Implementation step is an ongoing part of the ATOM process and continues until the Post-Project Review takes place at the end of the project.

....

CHAPTER 10

Keeping It Alive
(Major Reviews)

Chapters 4 to 9 describe the steps required to undertake an initial assessment of risk for a medium-size project, but the ATOM process does not end when this first pass is complete. It is true that the first time a project team is involved in the risk process there is usually lots of enthusiasm, which can lead to an efficient process, which in turn increases effectiveness. However, doing the process once does not ensure that risk remains effectively managed on any project; indeed it is only the start. It is essential to maintain momentum throughout the project, and ATOM provides for this with a series of risk reviews. These are termed *major* and *minor* to reflect the required level of effort. Figure 10-1 illustrates the main differences between a Major and Minor Review.

Major Reviews usually take place at key points during the project, either at the beginning of a new phase or at significant milestones within a phase, but they do not happen often enough to ensure that the assessment of risk exposure remains current. To do this, ATOM uses a series of regular Minor Reviews that take place in line with the normal reporting regime of the project. In the typical medium-size project, the initial pass through the ATOM process is followed by one or more Minor Reviews, with a Major Review occurring some time later, as illustrated in Figure 10-2.

The remainder of this chapter describes the ATOM Major Review; Minor Reviews are covered in Chapter 11.

A Major Review essentially uses a single workshop to repeat all the steps that make up the First Risk Assessment, providing a full reassessment of the project's risk position. This workshop normally takes place at the beginning of a phase or at key milestones during the project, and at the frequency defined in the Risk Management Plan. However, there may be other times when an additional Major Review is justified (perhaps after a significant change to the project), and the project sponsor or project manager can initiate a Major Review at any time.

ACTIVITY	MAJOR REVIEW	MINOR REVIEW
Review existing risks	All risks plus secondary risks	Red risks (amber, if time)
Identify new risks	Brainstorming, assumptions/constraints, checklist	Facilitated team discussion
Assess new risks	Using P-I scales	Using P-I scales
Response planning– strategy and owners	Interviews	
Response planning actions	Post interview discussions	Post meeting discussions
Report	Full report	Summary report
Other activities	Process check	*None*
Duration	1 day	1/2 day
Attendees	Project manager, risk champion, key stakeholders	Project manager, risk champion, project team, risk owners

(Note: "Risk workshop" spans the Major Review column for rows "Review existing risks" through "Response planning–strategy and owners"; "Risk review meeting" spans the Minor Review column for rows "Review existing risks" through "Response planning–strategy and owners".)

FIGURE 10-1: Differences between Major and Minor Reviews

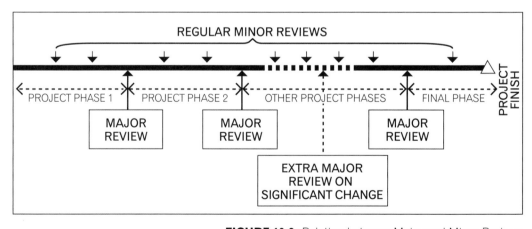

FIGURE 10-2: Relation between Major and Minor Reviews

The ATOM Major Review aims to:

- Review all current risks and any other risks raised since the last formal review

- Identify new risks (including secondary risks)

- Update the Risk Register

- Produce a full report and periodic reporting information for project progress reports and progress meetings

- Check the effectiveness of the current risk management process

In order to do this, the following inputs are required:

- Risk Management Plan outlining project objectives and scope of the risk process

- Risk breakdown structure (RBS)

- Work breakdown structure (WBS)

- The Risk Register, which contains full details of all risks (current and draft), including:

  - Risk owners and agreed upon response strategies

  - Action owners and agreed upon actions

  - Current status of each risk

- An overview of the current status of the project

- Risk tool (spreadsheet, database, or proprietary software)

A Major Review involves the following activities:

- Pre-workshop preparation

- Risk workshop, which includes:

  - Initial scene-setting

  - Reviewing all current and draft risks

  - Identifying, assessing, and categorizing new risks

  - Updating the Risk Register

  - Reviewing effectiveness of risk process

- Post-workshop actions:

  - Risk champion interviews risk owners to confirm new responses

  - Risk owners consider the need to modify existing responses

  - Risk owners liaise with risk action owners to refine existing actions and develop new actions

  - Risk owners liaise with risk champion to provide details of refined responses and new actions

  - Risk champion updates the Risk Register and produces a full risk report

- Risk champion liaises with the project manager to add any new activities to the project plan

- Project manager communicates escalated risks to the appropriate part of the organization or person, if known

- Project manager considers the need for change control as required

A Major Review produces the following outputs:

- Updated Risk Register containing the latest information and status of all risks

- Modified and new actions required to respond effectively to current risks

- Full risk report

- Inputs to project review meetings and periodic project reports

- Further activities in the project schedule that relate to risk actions

- A revised Risk Management Plan (if required)

These inputs, activities, and outputs are illustrated in Figure 10-3 and are described in detail in the sections that follow.

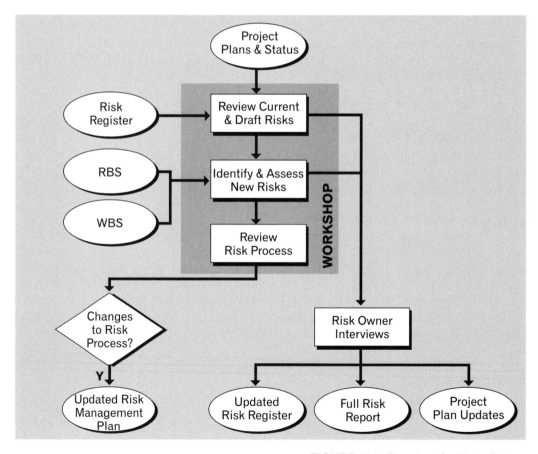

FIGURE 10-3: Flowchart for Major Review

Inputs

The Risk Management Plan defines when Major Reviews are planned, and also includes a list of key project stakeholders who may be invited to participate in the Major Review.

The RBS is used to structure risk identification techniques, and the WBS provides a structure for mapping the effects of risks.

The Risk Register is the prime input to the Major Review because it contains a complete set of data for each identified risk. This includes the name of the risk owner responsible for overall management of each risk, together with the agreed response strategy and the names of action owner(s) responsible for implementing those actions needed to implement the response strategy. In addition the Risk Register contains the current status of each risk (draft, active, expired, occurred, closed, or deleted). Draft risks are those that have been identified since the last risk review.

Another key input to the risk workshop is an overview of the current status of the project, which is provided by the project manager. It is important to know if anything in the project has changed, either internal or external, that could directly affect the assessment of an existing risk.

As in previous steps it is assumed that a risk tool is used to support the ATOM risk management process and that this tool will be available when required.

Activities

The activities in the Major Review are focused on a risk workshop, which for a medium-size project usually takes one day. Conducting the workshop properly requires a number of pre- and post-workshop activities. It is the risk champion's responsibility to ensure that all pre- and post-workshop activities are carried out, either by himself or others (e.g., risk owners). The risk champion is usually responsible for facilitating the risk workshop.

Many of the Major Review workshop tasks are identical to those that make up the initial risk identification and assessment workshop, and are summarized here (for detailed descriptions, see Chapters 5 and 6).

Pre-workshop preparation

This includes agreeing on attendees, preparing and distributing a workshop agenda (see Figure 10-4), and circulating pre-workshop briefing material—this material might include workshop objectives and current project status reports. Risk owners also receive a list, in priority order, of all the risks for which they are responsible. (The risk tool should produce these filtered and sorted lists automatically.) Risk owners should review their risks in advance of the meeting and be prepared to comment on the current status of each one.

The risk champion also prepares for himself and the project manager a prioritized list of all active risks, extracted from the Risk Register, showing key details for each risk such as the risk description, probability, and impacts, risk owner, and risk actions owners, agreed response strategy and associated actions, and last reported status. A list of all draft risks taken from the

TIME ALLOWANCE (hours)	CONTENT
½	1. Initial scene setting
3	2. Review current risks
1	3. Review draft risks
1	4. Consider new risks
—	5. Update risk register (done during steps 1-4)
½	6. Review risk process effectiveness
¼	7. Close workshop

FIGURE 10-4: Sample Agenda for a Major Review Workshop

Risk Register is also prepared for review at the meeting; this list may be either circulated in advance or handed out at the meeting.

The Major Review workshop

The Major Review workshop is usually facilitated by the risk champion, although it is possible to use a specialist facilitator, and includes the following elements.

INITIAL SCENE SETTING

If necessary, the workshop begins by introducing participants to one another, and confirming the project objectives. The risk champion also presents a brief summary of the risk management process, if required. These steps are not necessary when the project team is stable and participants have been involved in previous risk workshops.

The risk champion outlines the purpose, scope, and ground rules of the workshop, clarifying what is expected from the participants and what outputs should result. The project manager then presents a brief summary of the current status of the project, highlighting any current issues that workshop participants need to know when identifying risks.

REVIEW ALL CURRENT RISKS

The first main task during the Major Review workshop is to review existing risks. To ensure that effort is spent on the most important risks, all active risks are reviewed in priority order, taking threats before opportunities, as follows:

1. Red threats

2. Red opportunities

3. Amber threats

4. Amber opportunities

5. Green threats

6. Green opportunities

For each risk, the following must be reviewed:

- *Current status.* If a risk is no longer active, the risk owner explains its current status and why or how this status change has occurred.

- *Current probability and impact.* If the risk is still active, its probability and impacts are reassessed, taking into account the effects of any completed or in-progress actions, any changes to the internal or external environment of the project, and the overall status of the project.

- *Action status.* The risk owner will know the status of agreed actions for their risks, either from discussions with action owners or by checking progress as reported in the project plan. For actions that are either in-progress or recently completed, the risk owner reports to the meeting on their effectiveness in achieving the desired outcome. If completed actions are not addressing the risk in the expected way, the risk owner first considers whether an alternative response strategy is required, and then meets with allocated action owners immediately following the workshop to develop additional actions for either the existing or the new response strategy. If these actions also require the raising of new project activities, then that is done as well. Future or planned actions are considered and any adjustments to planned actions made.

REVIEW DRAFT RISKS

The meeting next considers all risks that have been raised since the last formal review (including proposed new risks and secondary risks arising from implementation of agreed actions). These are labeled with draft status in the Risk Register. Risk workshop participants either make these active if they are recognized as genuine risks, or mark them as rejected if they are not thought to be risks or if they are duplicates of existing risks. Rejected risks are marked in the Risk Register accordingly and not considered further. Risks with impacts outside the project are marked as escalated, and communicated by the project manager after the review to the appropriate part of the organization or person, if known.

Draft risks should have already been properly described using the risk metalanguage, had their probability and impacts assessed, a risk owner appointed, a response strategy developed, and action owners identified, as described in Chapter 9. When a draft risk is converted to active status, each element of this data is reviewed during the meeting and confirmed or amended as necessary.

IDENTIFY, ASSESS, AND CATEGORIZE NEW RISKS

Having reviewed all active and draft risks, the workshop moves on to identify new risks that have arisen since the last formal review. The risk champion or workshop facilitator chooses a suitable method, such as brainstorming, assumptions and constraints analysis, or a checklist (as previously described in Chapter 5), bearing in mind that a different technique might assist participants to expose risks not previously considered.

All newly identified risks are clearly and unambiguously described using the risk metalanguage, and given a unique risk identifier number. Participants should be careful to avoid raising risks that already exist in the Risk Register, and the facilitator should ensure that duplicates and nonrisks are removed at this stage.

The probability and impacts of each new risk are assessed, using the scales defined in the Risk Management Plan. New risks are also categorized using the RBS and WBS. Workshop participants agree on a response strategy for each new risk, and nominate a risk owner, who develops appropriate actions and appoints action owners after the workshop.

UPDATE RISK REGISTER

The Risk Register must be kept up to date to reflect the current status of each risk, and the risk champion is responsible for this, with input from risk owners. The Risk Register is updated during the Major Review workshop; otherwise the risk champion updates it immediately afterward.

All risks that are reviewed as part of the workshop, whether they existed beforehand or are newly raised, are assigned one of the five overall statuses: active (this applies to all new risks), expired, occurred, closed, or deleted.

In addition to the overall status, the risk owner records all other information about each risk, and ensures that the Risk Register holds the latest data, including:

- Current assessments of probability and impacts

- Progress on all agreed actions

- Changes to the risk owner or action owners

- Changes to the response strategy or new actions

REVIEW EFFECTIVENESS OF RISK PROCESS

The Major Review workshop ends by reviewing the risk process as currently implemented on the project, and considering whether it is appropriate to meet the risk challenge faced by the project. This includes the scope and objectives of the risk process, use of tools and techniques, frequency of updates, etc. The risk champion leads an open discussion on this, encouraging full feedback and expression of any concerns. It may be decided that the risk process as defined in the Risk Management Plan is either insufficiently robust or too detailed. In either case, the risk champion meets with the project manager and the project sponsor following the workshop to agree on process changes; significant changes result in revision and reissue of the Risk Management Plan.

CLOSE THE WORKSHOP

On completion, the risk champion summarizes the achievements of the workshop and lists any agreed actions. The schedule for the next planned review is also confirmed.

Post-workshop

Following the Major Review workshop, the risk champion interviews risk owners to refine any new responses generated in the workshop. In addition, risk owners in liaison with action owners refine existing actions and develop new ones. As part of this step, the post-response probability and impacts of each risk are assessed to determine the residual risk exposure, and to identify and record any secondary risks.

The risk champion liaises with the project manager to add any new activities to the project plan, and the project manager considers the need for change control as required.

If the Risk Register was not updated during the risk workshop, then the risk champion makes sure this is completed prior to producing the full risk report.

If the workshop suggests that a change is required to the risk process for the project, the risk champion, project manager, and project sponsor meet to agree on what modifications are necessary, and the risk champion then updates and reissues the Risk Management Plan. The project manager also communicates escalated risks to the appropriate part of the organization or person, if known.

Outputs

The two main outputs from a Major Review are an updated Risk Register that contains the current status of each risk and progress on agreed actions, and a full risk report. The contents of the full risk report match the report prepared after the First Risk Assessment, as detailed in Chapter 8, but with inclusion of an additional section focusing on changes since the last review, to communicate whether the risk exposure has improved or worsened. This section of the report highlights what has changed, including the numbers of threats closed or deleted, how many threats and opportunities have occurred, the number of new risks raised, etc. The project may develop simple metrics to provide indicators of changes in risk exposure, though this is not mandatory for the medium-size project. Examples of metrics are illustrated in Figure 10-5.

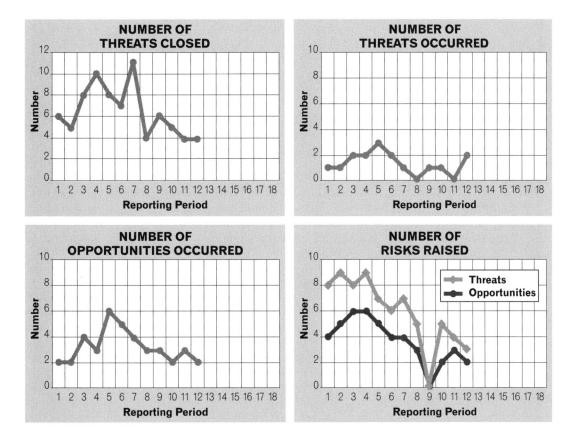

FIGURE 10-5: Sample Metrics to Measure Risk Exposure

If modified or new actions are identified during the Major Review, these feed into the Implementation step (see Chapter 9) to ensure that they are performed.

A Major Review also considers the effectiveness of the risk management process. If modifications are required to the current process, these will be reflected in a revised Risk Management Plan.

Summary

A Major Review ensures that the risk process is being carried out efficiently and effectively, updating the Risk Register to reflect the current risk exposure of the project. The Major Review contains the same steps as the First Risk Assessment but on a reduced scale and in a compressed timeframe. The following activities are required:

- Prepare for and facilitate a risk workshop

- Review all current risks and newly raised risks to determine their status

- Identify, describe, and assess new risks; appoint risk owners and develop responses

- Update the Risk Register

- Revise and define risk actions and appoint action owners

- Update the project plan to take into account risk actions

- Draft and distribute a full risk report and other information needed for project reporting

- Consider the efficiency and effectiveness of the risk management process

Major Reviews take place at the frequency set out in the Risk Management Plan, continuing until the Post-Project Review takes place as part of project closedown.

....

CHAPTER 11

Ongoing Updates
(Minor Reviews)

The ATOM process uses a series of reviews to ensure that the project team and key stake-holders have the latest current risk information to support effective management of the project. These reviews are conducted periodically throughout the lifetime of the project, with Major Reviews taking place at key points and significant milestones (as described in Chapter 10). It is usually insufficient, however, to rely just on the First Risk Assessment followed by periodic Major Reviews, so the ATOM Minor Review provides an opportunity to update the assessment of risk between Major Reviews. Minor Reviews are carried out at regular intervals throughout the project and in line with the project's normal progress review and reporting cycle, which occurs monthly on the typical medium-size project.

Since there is often a considerable period of time between the First Risk Assessment and the first Major Review, the First Risk Assessment is usually followed about a month later by a Minor Review.

A Minor Review is conducted in the context of a formal meeting that usually lasts about half a day. The meeting takes place either as part of a routine project progress meeting or as a stand-alone meeting. During a Minor Review most of the same tasks are performed as during a Major Review, though at a lower level of detail.

The aim of the ATOM Minor Review is to:

- Review the most significant current risks (all red risks, plus amber risks if time allows), and all draft risks raised since the last formal review

- Identify new risks

- Update the Risk Register

- Produce a summary risk report and periodic reporting information for project progress reports and progress meetings

To do this, the following inputs are required:

- The reporting cycle for the project, as set out in the project management plan

- The Risk Register containing details of all risks (current and draft), including:

  - Risk owners and agreed response strategies

  - Action owners and agreed actions

  - Current status of each risk

- An overview of the current status of the project

- Risk tool (spreadsheet, database, or proprietary software)

A Minor Review involves the following activities:

- Pre-meeting preparation

- Risk review meeting, the goal of which is to:

  - Review the most significant current risks

  - Review all draft risks

  - Identify and assess new risks

  - Update the Risk Register

- Post-meeting actions, which include:

  - Risk owners liaise with action owners to refine new responses and develop new actions

  - Risk owners liaise with risk champion to provide details of refined responses and new actions

  - Risk champion updates the Risk Register and produces a summary risk report

  - Risk champion liaises with the project manager to add any new activities to the project plan

  - Project manager considers the need for change control as required

  - Project manager communicates escalated risks to the appropriate part of the organization or person, if known

A Minor Review produces the following outputs:

- Updated Risk Register containing the latest information and status of all risks

- Modified and new actions to be implemented

- Summary risk report

- Inputs to project review meetings and periodic project reports

- Further activities in the project schedule that relate to risk actions

These inputs, activities, and outputs are illustrated in Figure 11-1, and detailed below.

Inputs

The project progress review and reporting cycle is usually described in the project management plan. Routine risk activities such as Minor Reviews are incorporated into this cycle to ensure that risk management is seen as an integral part of the overall project management process.

The Risk Register contains a complete set of data for each identified risk, including risk owners, action owners, and the current status of each risk. In addition, any risks identified since the last risk review will be included in the Risk Register with draft status.

A key input to the Minor Review is an overview of the current status of the project, which is provided by the project manager, indicating changes to the project that could directly affect existing risks.

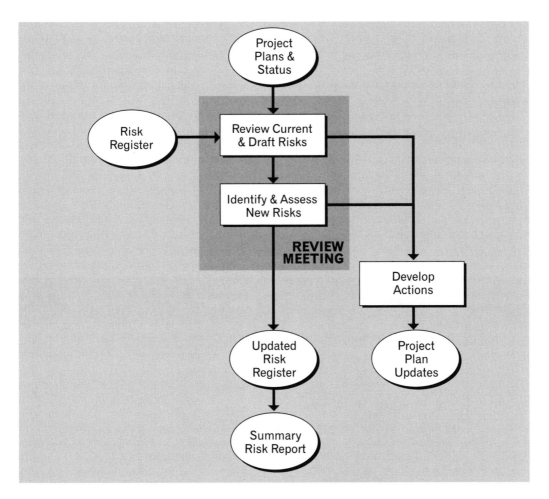

FIGURE 11-1: Flowchart for Minor Review

As in previous steps, it is assumed that a risk tool is used to support the ATOM risk management process and that this tool will be available when required.

Activities

The Minor Review is conducted through a risk review meeting, which requires a number of pre-meeting activities and post-meeting tasks. The risk champion is responsible for either performing these activities or ensuring that they are carried out by others (e.g., risk owners), and usually facilitates the risk review meeting.

Pre-meeting preparation

The project manager, risk champion, other members of the project core team (usually those who directly report to the project manager), and all risk owners attend the risk review meeting. The project sponsor is also invited, though his or her presence is not mandatory.

In preparation for the meeting, a formal agenda is prepared and circulated to all attendees; Figure 11-2 illustrates a typical agenda for a half-day risk review meeting. In addition to the meeting agenda, risk owners receive a prioritized list of all the active risks for which they are responsible, which should be automatically available from the risk tool. Risk owners should review their risks in advance of the meeting and be prepared to comment on the current status of each one.

The risk champion also prepares a prioritized list of all active and draft risks for review at the meeting.

The Risk Review Meeting

The risk champion facilitates the review meeting, and addresses the following topics.

INTRODUCTIONS

If the risk review meeting takes place as part of a routine project progress meeting, the risk champion will not need to set the scene because this will have been done by the project manager earlier in the meeting. If the risk review meeting is standalone, the project manager gives

TIME ALLOWANCE (hours)	CONTENT
¼	1. Introductions
2	2. Review red risks
½	3. Review draft risks
½	4. Consider new risks
	5. *Review amber risks if time permits*
—	6. Update Risk Register (done during earlier steps)
¼	7. Close meeting

FIGURE 11-2: Sample Agenda for a Half-day Risk Review Meeting

a short commentary on the current status of the project, highlighting progress to date and any current issues or problems.

REVIEW RED RISKS

The ideal Minor Review aims to review all active red and amber risks, but in many circumstances time constraints make this impossible. As a result, the risk champion uses the prioritized list to structure the review, starting with red threats and moving on to red opportunities. All red risks must be addressed during the meeting; amber risks may also be considered if time allows.

For each risk, the following must be reviewed:

- **Current status.** If a risk is no longer active, the risk owner explains its current status and why or how this has occurred.

- **Current probability and impact.** The probability and impacts of active risks is reassessed, taking into account the effects of any completed or in-progress actions, any changes to the project, and the overall project status.

- **Action status.** The risk owner reports on the effectiveness of planned actions in addressing each of their risks. If these actions are not affecting risk exposure in the expected way, the risk owner addresses them with action owners immediately after the risk review meeting.

REVIEW DRAFT RISKS

The meeting next considers all draft risks raised since the last formal review, as well as any secondary risks. These are confirmed as either active, rejected (if they are duplicates of existing risks), or nonrisks. Rejected risks are recorded in the Risk Register but not considered further. Risks with impacts outside the project scope are marked as escalated, and passed by the project manager to the appropriate part of the organization or person, if known.

For draft risks raised to active status, the meeting confirms the risk description and assessments of probability and impacts, appoints a risk owner, and agrees to a response strategy and initial actions with owners. Each element of this data is reviewed during the meeting and amended if necessary.

IDENTIFY NEW RISKS

Identifying new risks is an important part of the risk review meeting, although it is anticipated that relatively few new risks will actually be identified. The risk champion, as facilitator of the meeting, leads a discussion to identify new risks. For each new risk, the meeting will:

- Allocate a unique risk identifier based on the project risk breakdown structure

- Clearly and unambiguously describe the risk using the risk metalanguage

- Assess probability and impact using the scales defined in the Risk Management Plan

- Appoint a risk owner and agree on an initial risk response strategy with initial actions

- Determine the post-response assessment of probability and impacts

REVIEW AMBER RISKS

If time permits, amber risks are reviewed, concentrating on:

- Current status

- Current probability and impact

- Action status

UPDATE THE RISK REGISTER

The risk champion ensures that the Risk Register is updated with the current status of each risk. This can be done during the risk review meeting or immediately afterward.

CLOSE MEETING

The risk champion closes the meeting by summarizing the outputs and notifying attendees when the next risk review meeting will take place.

Post–Risk Review Meeting

Immediately following the risk meeting, risk owners liaise with action owners to refine any new responses, revise existing actions, and define new actions. The risk owner communicates these changes to the risk champion. The risk champion, in discussion with the project manager, ensures that new actions are added to the project schedule as planned activities, and resourced and budgeted for accordingly. The project manager considers the need for change control as a result of these additional project activities. The project manager also communicates escalated risks to the appropriate part of the organization or person, if known.

If the Risk Register was not updated during the risk review meeting, then the risk champion makes sure this is completed prior to producing the summary risk report.

Outputs

The main output from the Minor Review is an updated Risk Register containing full details of all risks, including current status and action progress. Actions arising from the Minor Review feed into the Implementation step (see Chapter 9).

A further output is a summary risk report, which is prepared by the risk champion and presents the results of the risk review meeting. Figure 11-3 gives a sample contents list for a summary risk report, and the various items are outlined below.

- *Executive summary.* A summary of the results of the Minor Review is given, in no more than one page.

- *Scope and objectives of report.* The purpose of the Minor Review is described, highlighting its place in both the risk process and the overall project reporting cycle.

- *Overall risk status.* A short summary is presented of the current level of risk exposure for this project.

- *Top risks, actions, and owners.* This section lists the top threats and top opportunities

EXECUTIVE SUMMARY

SCOPE AND OBJECTIVES OF REPORT

OVERALL RISK STATUS

TOP RISKS, ACTIONS AND OWNERS

CHANGES SINCE LAST REVIEW

CONCLUSIONS AND RECOMMENDATIONS

APPENDIX
    COMPLETE RISK REGISTER IN PRIORITY ORDER

FIGURE 11-3: Sample Contents List for a Summary Risk Report

in priority order, often as a "top ten," although all the worst threats and best opportunities are listed. These are discussed, including analysis of causes and effects, planned actions with owners, and expected changes.

• *Changes since last review.* It is important to communicate whether the risk exposure has improved or worsened since the last review. This section of the report highlights changes, presenting metrics such as the numbers of risks closed or deleted, how many threats have impacted, how many opportunities have been realized, the number of new risks raised, etc.

• *Conclusions and recommendations.* This section presents conclusions at a summary level, together with key recommendations.

• *Appendix.* The complete Risk Register is included, listing full details of every active risk in priority order.

Having drafted the summary risk report, the risk champion submits it to the project manager for review and comment to ensure that it is a true summary of the risk review meeting. The risk champion and project manager together agree on any changes required to the draft summary risk report; the risk champion implements these changes and then issues the report. The summary risk report is distributed to the project manager, project sponsor, key project team members, all risk owners, and other key stakeholders.

Additional outputs from the Minor Review include inputs to project review meetings and periodic project reports, most likely in the form of customized outputs from the Risk Register. The project manager, in consultation with the risk champion, determines exactly which reports are prepared. The use of an appropriate risk tool enables the production of information as and when required, and in the format required.

Summary

A Minor Review ensures that the risk process is maintained throughout the project, updating the Risk Register between Major Reviews to reflect the current risk exposure of the project. The Minor Review includes the following activities:

- Prepare for and facilitate a risk review meeting

- Review all current red risks and newly raised risks to determine their status. Amber risks will be reviewed if there is sufficient time

- Identify, describe, and assess new risks, appoint risk owners, and develop responses

- Update the Risk Register

- Revise and define risk actions and appoint action owners

- Update the project plan to take into account risk actions

- Draft and distribute a summary risk report and other information needed for project reporting

Minor Reviews are undertaken regularly between Major Reviews at the frequency set out in the Risk Management Plan. They are repeated until project closedown, at which time a Post-Project Review is undertaken, as described in next chapter.

CHAPTER 12

Learning from Experience (Post-Project Review)

Organizations conduct projects for at least two reasons. The first is to create the project deliverables that will be used, operated, or sold in order to create the stakeholder benefits and value defined in the business case or project charter. But each project also has a second purpose, which is to contribute to organizational learning. Project-based organizations should use completed projects to create a body of knowledge and experience on which they can draw in order to benefit future projects. Unfortunately, this second aspect is missing from many organizations, including those that regularly perform projects, and they are therefore denying themselves a major portion of the potential benefits that their completed projects offer.

Although each project is by definition unique, many areas of commonality exist between completed and new projects. As a result, the Post-Project Review offers a structured mechanism for capturing lessons from previous projects that can be applied to new ones. However, it is widely accepted that post-project reviews are one of the least well-performed parts of the project life cycle. There are at least three reasons for this:

- Organizations tend to disband project teams immediately on project completion, moving staff to new projects before capturing their knowledge and experience in a structured and usable way.

- In a cost-constrained environment, some view post-project reviews as an optional luxury. This is particularly true for contracting organizations that charge clients for project activities. Clients may be reluctant to pay for a task that does not directly benefit their own project, and the organization may not be willing to include post-project reviews in their overhead.

- Many organizations lack the knowledge management infrastructure to take advantage of previous experience, and feel that there is no point in recording information that is never used.

This last point is reflected in the term commonly used to describe outputs from the post-project review: "lessons learned." This term implies that simply identifying something during a post-project review ensures that future practice will take it into account. Unfortunately this is often not the case, because lessons are only truly learned when they have been implemented on a future project. As a result, it might be better to call these either "lessons identified" or "lessons to be learned."

Despite these weaknesses in current practice, the post-project review is an essential part of the project life cycle because it allows lessons to be drawn that can benefit future similar projects. This is particularly true of risk-related information, where organizations need to avoid making the same mistakes twice, either in terms of being hit by problems that could have been foreseen as threats, or in terms of missing benefits that could have been foreseen as opportunities.

This learning element is so important that it is included as a distinct step in the ATOM risk process. Even when an organization does not have its own formal post-project review process to address all aspects of the project, at least the risk elements are considered in a structured manner. Of course, when post-project reviews are implemented for projects, the requirements of the ATOM risk process can be met by including a risk element within the existing review meeting.

The Post-Project Review step in ATOM aims to:

- Capture and record risk-related knowledge and experience from a completed project in a form that can be used by future similar projects

This step requires the following inputs:

- Risk Register from the most recent risk review

- Risk report from the most recent risk review

- Risk breakdown structure (RBS)

- Issue log for the completed project (if this exists)

- Change log for the completed project

- Final project schedule and final outcome cost

- Existing risk checklist

The Post-Project Review step of ATOM involves either contributing to the main post-project review meeting for the project or conducting a separate risk-related meeting. In both cases the activities are the same, namely:

- Prepare risk information for consideration at the meeting

- Hold post-project review meeting

- Capture "lessons to be learned"

Post-Project Review produces the following outputs:

- When the project life cycle includes its own post-project review, ATOM contributes the risk section for the post-project report, capturing risk knowledge and experience in a structured way to benefit future similar projects. If there is no planned post-project review for the project, a separate risk lessons report is produced.

- Final Risk Register, showing the status of all identified risks at the end of the project.

These inputs, activities, and outputs are illustrated in Figure 12-1, and described in detail in the following sections.

Inputs

The main input to the Post-Project Review step is the Risk Register from the most recent risk review, since this contains full historical information on all identified risks, including those that were active at the last review, as well as those that were previously marked as expired, occurred, closed, or deleted (see Chapter 9 for a description of these status values). In addi-

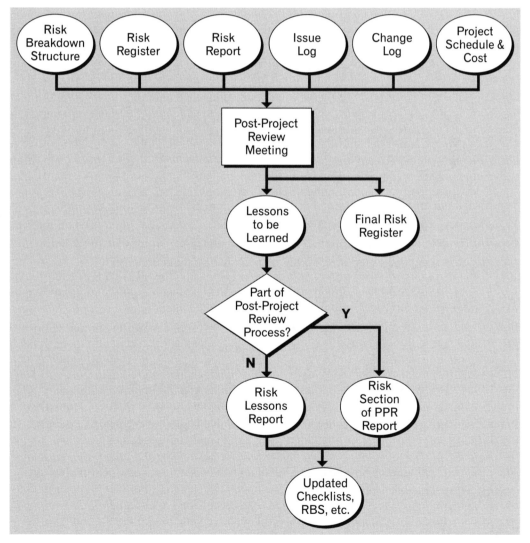

FIGURE 12-1: Flowchart for Post-Project Review Step

tion, for each identified risk the Risk Register includes details on changes during the project life cycle in assessments of probability and impacts, response strategies and actions, etc. This information forms the raw data for the risk element of the post-project review meeting.

The risk report from the most recent risk review is also an important input to the Post-Project Review step, since it provides a commentary on the risk exposure at the last review. The risk champion may decide to include the full risk report as an input, extract the executive summary, or provide a separate narrative summarizing the main risk highlights during the project life cycle.

The project risk breakdown structure is used as a framework for the risk elements of the post-project review, ensuring that all areas of risk to the project are considered.

If the project maintained an issue log of adverse events and circumstances that arose during the project, it is provided as input to the Post-Project Review step. This is because some issues occur when threats are not properly managed, so review of these can reveal potential generic threats that should be considered in future similar projects.

The project change log might also indicate areas where risks have occurred and resulted in a significant change to the project (either positive or negative). Reviewing the change log can therefore indicate both unmanaged threats that could be handled differently on another project, as well as captured opportunities that might be pursued again in similar circumstances.

The final project schedule and final outturn cost for the completed project are also reviewed as part of the Post-Project Review step. These show actual durations and costs against the original planned schedule and budget, and analysis might reveal areas of time or cost risk exposure that could affect similar projects.

The final input to the Post-Project Review step is the risk checklist that was used for the Identification step. Because the main aim of Post-Project Review is to carry forward learning from this project to benefit future projects, it is important to ensure that the standard risk checklist includes all risks identified on this project that might affect others.

Activities

Conducting a formal post-project review meeting at the end of a project should be normal practice on a medium-size project. This is typically chaired by the project manager, or in some cases a third-party facilitator, and attended by the project sponsor, key members of the project team, and other stakeholders. The ATOM Post-Project Review step is incorporated within this meeting, with the risk champion providing risk-related information for consideration. In the absence of a post-project review meeting for the whole project, the project manager calls a separate meeting dedicated to addressing risk management on the project.

The following activities apply equally to a risk section within a project post-project review meeting, or to a specific risk meeting.

Prepare meeting inputs

The risk champion prepares an information pack for meeting attendees, and circulates it in advance of the meeting along with an agenda (see Figure 12-2 for a sample agenda). The most important item in this pack is the latest Risk Register, but it should also include the RBS and risk checklist used during the risk process. In addition to this raw data, the risk champion may wish to include the most recent risk report or its executive summary, or a separate narrative as described above.

TIME ALLOWANCE (hours)	CONTENT
¼	1. Introductions
½	2. Review final Risk Register
2	3. Identify risk-related "lessons to be learned"
½	4. Summarize "lessons to be learned"
¼	5. Close the meeting

FIGURE 12-2: Typical Agenda for a Post-Project Review Meeting

If the project is conducting its own post-project review, other items for review include:

- Issue log for the completed project, if it exists

- Change log for the completed project

- Final project schedule and final outturn cost

If these are not supplied, or if a separate risk meeting is being held, the risk champion obtains them for inclusion in the pre-meeting briefing pack.

Hold post-project review meeting

INTRODUCTIONS

The project manager (or an external third-party facilitator) chairs the post-project review meeting, following the usual meeting ground rules and etiquette. During the risk section of the meeting, the risk champion presents the main points from the risk information supplied in the pre-meeting briefing pack, assuming that all attendees have read the information.

REVIEW FINAL RISK REGISTER

At this point in the project no risks can remain active, so the first step in the risk section of the meeting is to review the most recent Risk Register and update it to show the final status of all risks as expired, occurred, closed, or deleted.

IDENTIFY RISK-RELATED "LESSONS TO BE LEARNED"

It is recommended that the risk element of the post-project review be structured using the RBS as a framework, to ensure that all sources of risk are considered and to provide a comparative structure for transferring lessons between projects. The review addresses the following questions for each Level 1 or Level 2 element of the RBS in turn, referring to the most recent Risk

Register, project issue and change logs, and final project schedule and costs as appropriate:

• What were the main risks identified on this project (both threats and opportunities)? Do any of these represent generic risks that might affect similar projects?

• Which foreseeable threats actually occurred, and why? Which opportunities that could have been captured were missed, and why?

• Which issues or problems occurred that should have been foreseen as threats? Which unplanned benefits arose that should have been identified as opportunities?

• What preventative actions could have been taken to minimize or avoid threats? What proactive actions could have been taken to maximize or exploit opportunities?

• Which responses were effective in managing risks, and which were ineffective?

• How much effort was spent on the risk process, both to execute the process and to implement responses?

• Can any specific benefits be attributed to the risk process, for example, reduced project duration or cost, increased business benefits or client satisfaction, etc.?

SUMMARIZE "LESSONS TO BE LEARNED"

The aim in answering the previous questions is to identify lessons from this project that could be useful to future similar projects. During the discussion, the risk champion records the following items:

• Generic risks (both threats and opportunities) that could affect future projects

• Responses and actions that have proved effective and should be actively considered for future projects

• Responses and actions that were tried but were ineffective, and which therefore might be excluded from future projects

• Elements of the risk process that were particularly effective or ineffective, and ways in which these could have been overcome or improved, including tips and hints on using the various tools and techniques

If possible, during this part of the meeting the risk champion summarizes these items into discrete statements of "lessons to be learned," which are presented to the meeting attendees for their comment and agreement.

CLOSE THE MEETING

On completion, the risk champion summarizes the results of the post-project review meeting and lists any agreed actions. It is also important for all participants to be given the opportunity to raise any unmet objectives or remaining concerns, so the risk champion makes time for this before the meeting concludes.

Outputs

After the post-project review meeting is complete, the risk champion writes up the findings and conclusions of the risk part of the meeting. This might be issued as part of a larger post-project review report, or it might form a separate risk lessons report, depending on the reporting requirements of the project. The report is approved by the project manager and issued to all attendees of the post-project review meeting, as well as any key stakeholders who were absent from the meeting.

The report includes recommendations for the following:

- Risks to be added to the organization's risk checklist for consideration during the risk identification step of future similar projects

- Modifications to the organization's risk breakdown structure(s), if risks were identified that did not map into the existing RBS framework

- Proactive and preventative actions to be included in the strategy of future similar projects to address the types of risks likely to be encountered

- Changes to the risk process to improve effectiveness, either in use of tools or techniques, or in development of standard templates to support the process

In addition it may be possible to calculate the return on investment (ROI) of the risk process, based on the cost of undertaking the risk process for this project, compared with an indication of the additional benefit obtained through avoided threats and exploited opportunities.

A final Risk Register is also issued, showing the status of all identified risks at the close of the project. Since no project risks can remain after the project has ended (as it is no longer possible for uncertainty to affect project objectives), the closing status of all risks must be set to either expired, occurred, closed, or deleted. In addition, any risks remaining at the end of the project that might affect other projects or other parts of the organization are escalated by the project manager to the appropriate part of the organization or person, if known, and their status is set to escalated.

Following issue of the post-project review report or risk lessons report, the risk champion liaises with the person in the wider organization responsible for maintaining the risk checklist and risk breakdown structures to ensure that recommendations arising from the post-project review are considered and implemented where appropriate. If the organization has a structured knowledge management system, the risk champion also ensures that all lessons to be learned are entered into the system for future use.

Summary

The purpose of the Post-Project Review step is to capture and record risk-related knowledge and experience from a completed project in a form that can be used on future similar projects. This is achieved either by ensuring that the project's post-project review addresses risk explicitly, or by holding a separate risk-related meeting, recording lessons to be learned in a post-project report or risk lessons report.

Post-Project Review is the final step in the ATOM risk process; it ensures that reusable knowledge and experience are not lost to the organization. Projects are undertaken for two reasons (creating project deliverables and increasing organizational learning), and the Post-Project Review step is an essential contributor to meeting the second aim.

PART III

Variations on a Theme

CHAPTER 13

ATOM
for Small Projects

Everyone involved with projects agrees that they are risky endeavors subject to a wide range of sources of uncertainty. If all projects are risky, it follows that all projects need risk management, at least to some degree. However, it is also abundantly clear that not all projects are the same, either in scope or risk exposure. The risk level is vastly different for a project to move an office and for a project to launch a space shuttle. So although all projects need to address risk management somehow, the level of treatment can and should vary.

Although risk management can be undertaken at a variety of levels, the standard risk process still applies to every project, because there is always a need to clarify scope and objectives (Initiation), find the risks that could affect the project (Identification), prioritize those risks for further attention (Assessment), decide how to deal with them (Response Planning), take appropriate action (Implementation), communicate results (Reporting), keep it up to date (Reviews), as well as identify lessons to be learned at the end of the project (Post-Project Review). Therefore, the standard ATOM risk process as described in earlier chapters can be applied to every project. However, the fact that different projects face different risk challenges is reflected in the scalable nature of the ATOM process.

Chapter 3 discussed how projects could be divided into three notional groups using a project sizing tool. Within the typical organization, most projects fall into the medium-size category; the standard ATOM risk process detailed in Part II (Chapters 4 through 12) provides an approach for these types of projects. Because ATOM is scalable, it can also be applied to small and large projects, following the same process framework but with varying levels of detail. This chapter describes how to modify the standard ATOM risk process to make it suitable for small projects; Chapter 14 addresses process modifications for large projects.

Less Is More

Small projects lack some of the characteristics that result in higher risk exposure, though, like all projects, they involve uncertainty. Their lower level of risk, however, allows the ATOM risk process to be simplified while retaining the essential elements for effective management of risk.

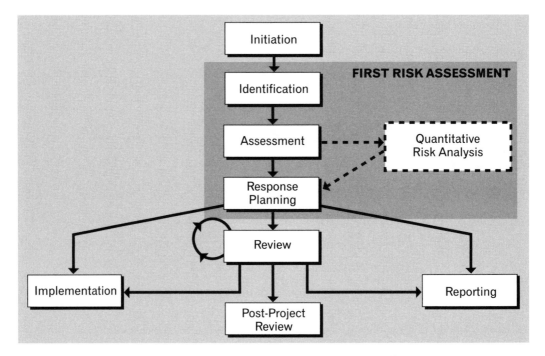

FIGURE 13-1: Steps in the ATOM Process

The challenge is to reduce process complexity without making the resulting process inadequate for the task—to simplify without becoming simplistic.

ATOM for small projects follows the same generic risk process (see Figure 13-1), but each step is reduced to minimize the time and effort required without cutting important tasks. This chapter works through the steps in the ATOM risk process and presents changes to the standard approach previously described for medium projects. (For further details of the standard approach, refer to the appropriate chapter in Part II.)

As for medium projects, the ATOM process for small projects is iterative, starting with the Initiation step, followed by the First Risk Assessment, with regular reviews throughout the project life cycle, and ending with the Post-Project Review step, as illustrated in Figure 13-2.

Initiation

The purpose of the Initiation step is to define the scope and objectives of the risk process as it will be applied to this project, and to allocate roles and responsibilities for risk management. Decisions made during the Initiation step are documented in a Risk Management Plan, so all project stakeholders know how risk will be managed for their project.

The Initiation step for the small project is reduced in several ways from the requirements for a medium project (see Chapter 4). The main difference is in the method used to produce the information contained in the Risk Management Plan. For medium projects an Initiation meeting is held, attended by key stakeholders and facilitated by the risk champion. This meeting is not required for a small project, and the project manager produces the Risk Management Plan in liaison with key stakeholders. Nor is there a need for a formal stakeholder

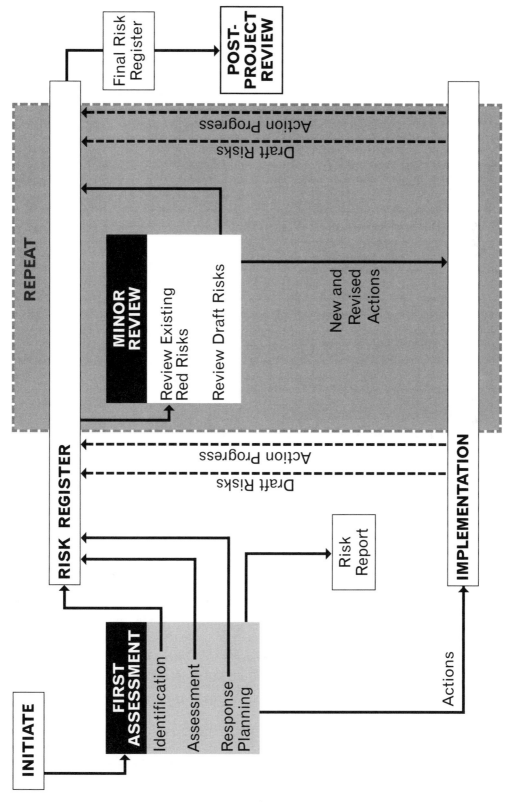

FIGURE 13-2: The ATOM Process for Small Projects

analysis during the Initiation step for a small project, because the project manager is likely to be aware of the stakeholders and their needs, and is able to reflect these in the Risk Management Plan without conducting a stakeholder analysis.

The Risk Management Plan itself is also simpler than the version required for a medium project, and is usually produced from a template following the sample contents list in Figure 13-3. The contents for a small project Risk Management Plan mirror those for medium projects (see Figure 13-3), but with less detail. One particular area where detail is reduced is in the definition of roles and responsibilities, where a RACI chart (Figure 4-6) is not required.

INTRODUCTION

PROJECT DESCRIPTION AND OBJECTIVES

AIMS, SCOPE, AND OBJECTIVES OF RISK PROCESS

APPLICATION OF THE ATOM PROCESS

RISK TOOLS AND TECHNIQUES

ORGANIZATION, ROLES AND RESPONSIBILITIES FOR RISK MANAGEMENT

RISK REVIEWS AND REPORTING

APPENDICES

    PROJECT-SPECIFIC DEFINITIONS OF PROBABILITY AND IMPACTS

    PROJECT-SPECIFIC SOURCES OF RISK (RISK BREAKDOWN STRUCTURE)

FIGURE 13-3:
Sample Contents List for a Risk Management Plan for a Small Project

Another key difference is in the allocation of staff to risk roles. A small project rarely has a full-time risk champion. This role can either be provided as part-time support from a central resource pool such as a project office, or, more typically, the responsibilities of the risk champion are undertaken directly by the project manager. However, even the small project needs to nominate risk owners and action owners who are responsible for managing individual risks, because the project manager cannot be expected to manage all identified risks.

The Risk Management Plan defines the assessment framework to be used during the risk process, which can be simplified for the small project. The framework for a medium project usually has five-point scales (VLO, LO, MED, HI, VHI) for both probability and impacts (see Figure 4-8) to provide the necessary granularity to discriminate between risks. For a small project, the project manager should consider using a simpler risk assessment framework, perhaps with three-point scales (LO, MED, HI) or four-point scales (VLO, LO, MED, HI). Figures 13-4 and 13-5 give examples of such scales; the project manager should agree with the project sponsor on the assessment framework to be used and document this decision in the Risk Management Plan.

SCALE	PROBABILITY	+/- IMPACT ON PROJECT OBJECTIVES		
		TIME	COST	QUALITY
HI	67–99%	>20 days	>$20K	Major impact on overall functionality
MED	34–66%	10–20 days	$10K–$20K	Significant impact in key functional areas
LO	1–33%	<10 days	<$10K	Minor impact on overall functionality
NIL	<1%	No change	No change	No change in functionality

FIGURE 13-4: Three-Point Project Specific Probability-Impact Scales

SCALE	PROBABILITY	+/- IMPACT ON PROJECT OBJECTIONS		
		TIME	COST	QUALITY
HI	71–99%	>20 days	>$20K	Major impact on overall functionality
MED	41–70%	11–20 days	$11K–$20K	Significant impact in key functional areas
LO	11–40%	3–10 days	$3K–$10K	Minor impact on overall functionality
VLO	1–10%	<3 days	<$3K	Minor impact on secondary functions
NIL	<1%	No change	No change	No change in functionality

FIGURE 13-5: Four-Point Project-Specific Probability-Impact Scales

The Risk Management Plan also describes the tools to be used to support the risk process; the small project typically uses simple spreadsheets or databases rather than a proprietary risk tool. The exception is when the organization uses a standard risk toolset for all projects, or an enterprise-wide risk system containing data for every project undertaken by the business, in which case even small projects are required to use the standard tools or hold their risk data on the standard system.

The tasks required to perform the Initiation step for a small project are summarized as follows:

- Project manager confirms project objectives and risk assessment framework with project sponsor

- Project manager drafts Risk Management Plan for approval by project sponsor

- Project manager issues Risk Management Plan to project team and key stakeholders

Identification

The Identification step aims to expose and document all knowable risks to project objectives. In reality this is a never-ending task; it is therefore important to place boundaries on the effort spent on this step. However, it is also essential to not skip this step or pay too little attention to risk identification, since risks that are not identified cannot be managed, and the project will experience unexpected problems as well as miss potential benefits.

For the Identification element of the First Risk Assessment on a small project, two reductions are made from the Identification step as implemented on the medium project (see Chapter 5). These are:

1. Perform risk identification (as well as assessment and response development) in an existing project team meeting rather than hold a specific risk identification workshop

2. Limit the risk identification techniques used

The project manager leads the project team in the risk process, and sets aside time for this in regular project team meetings. The project team should expect to spend more time on the risk process during the First Risk Assessment than later in the project; typically two to three hours should be allocated to this activity (to include risk identification, assessment, and response development). It is recommended to include the risk element of the project team meeting as the first agenda item, when people are fresh for the task. The project manager facilitates the risk identification process, unless a part-time risk champion is available to lead this part of the project meeting. Figure 13-6 outlines the risk identification steps included in this part of the meeting.

1. Confirm scope and objectives of risk process

2. Identify risks using:
        Assumptions and constraints analysis
        Standard risk checklist
        Open discussion/brainstorm (if necessary)

3. Rationalize risks
4. Assess probabilities and impacts, plot P-I matrix
5. Assign risk owners
6. Prioritize risks
7. Determine response strategy and initial actions
8. Record risk data (after meeting)

FIGURE 13-6: Risk Steps During Project Team Meeting for Small Projects

Two risk identification techniques are used for the small project that provide results quickly and with minimum effort, but without compromising the data quality or shortcutting the process. It is important to have sufficient time for risk identification, otherwise key risks are likely to be missed and go unmanaged. The two techniques are:

1. Analysis of assumptions and constraints

2. Risk identification checklist

These techniques are detailed in Chapter 5, and summarized below.

- **Analysis of assumptions and constraints.** The project assumptions and constraints should already be documented in the project business case, project charter, or other statement of work. If not, the project manager arranges a short meeting with the project sponsor before the project team meeting in order to identify and document them, and to ensure that hidden or implicit/tacit assumptions and constraints—as well as the explicit or more evident ones—are exposed as much as possible. The list of assumptions and constraints from this meeting or from the existing project documentation is then discussed at the project team meeting. Team members review each assumption and constraint in turn, asking two questions:

  - Could this assumption or constraint be false?

  - If it is false, how will project objectives be affected?

If an assumption or constraint could be false and would matter to the project, team members should raise a risk.

- **Risk identification checklist.** If the organization has a standard risk checklist, it is considered during the team meeting. Each item on the checklist is reviewed, asking whether the risk could be relevant to the project, and raising a risk when the answer is yes or don't know. If there is no existing risk checklist, the project manager may lead a short open discussion with the project team to identify any risks not raised during the assumptions and constraints analysis.

Following use of these two structured risk identification techniques, the project manager invites team members to raise any risks not yet mentioned, perhaps by leading a short brainstorming session. This need not take long since the two main techniques should have exposed most of the risks, but it allows each team member to have his say.

The project manager encourages the team to identify both threats and opportunities, and ensures that all risks raised during the meeting are properly described and distinguished from causes and effects using risk metalanguage. Risks raised during the team meeting are recorded by the project manager or meeting scribe, and entered into the risk tool immediately after the meeting. The project manager then reviews each risk to ensure that the risk description is accurate and clear, and that there are no duplications, making amendments as required.

Identification during the First Risk Assessment for the small project requires the following tasks:

- Project manager clarifies project assumptions and constraints, and generates list if necessary

- Identify risks during project team meeting, using assumptions and constraints analysis; then consider the risk identification checklist, followed by a short discussion or brainstorm

- Record all identified risks and enter into risk tool after project team meeting

Assessment

After the list of risks is generated, these risks are prioritized for further attention and action, which is the purpose of the Assessment part of the First Risk Assessment. Assessment is described for the medium project in Chapter 6. For small projects, risk assessment is performed in the same project team meeting immediately following risk identification. A simple prioritization is achieved by assessing the two key dimensions for each risk: the probability of occurrence and the impacts on project objectives.

The project manager presents the risk assessment framework agreed on with the project sponsor and documented in the Risk Management Plan to be used when assessing identified risks. For each risk in turn, the project manager leads a discussion among project team members, covering the following topics:

- The project manager first asks for opinions and estimates of how likely it is that the risk will occur, seeking consensus on one of the values in the assessment framework.

- Next, the team considers how each risk might affect project objectives, using the assessment framework, again seeking consensus among team members.

- Each risk is plotted onto a double P-I Matrix during the meeting, reflecting the assessments of probability and impact.

- Next, each risk is assigned a risk owner, who selects an appropriate strategy and develops an initial set of actions to address the risk. Typically, project team members present at the meeting are allocated as risk owners, though others might be nominated if necessary. If people outside the meeting are assigned as risk owners, the project manager informs them and obtains their consent immediately after the meeting.

Agreed estimates of probability and impacts, as well as agreed risk owners, are recorded for each risk and entered into the risk tool immediately after the meeting. These steps are also included in Figure 13-6.

After the discussion in the meeting to assess if each risk is complete, the project manager produces a prioritized list of threats and opportunities, based on the assessed probability and impacts and the position of the risk on the P-I Matrix. Figures 13-7 and 13-8 give prioritization schemes for a double three-by-three P-I Matrix and a double four-by-four version, respectively. It may be prudent to arrange a short break in the team meeting while this is done.

The Assessment step for small projects differs from that used for medium projects by not progressing to categorize risks by source (using the risk breakdown structure) or by area of the project affected (using the work breakdown structure), because this level of detail is usually not required for effective management of risks on small projects.

Undertaking Assessment for small projects involves the following:

- Assess risks during the project team meeting, using the definitions of probability and impacts detailed in the Risk Management Plan

- Nominate a risk owner for each risk

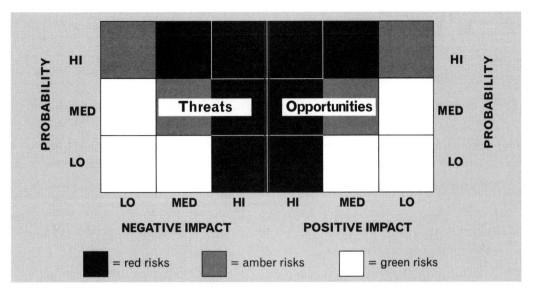

FIGURE 13-7: Double Three-by-Three Probability-Impact Matrix

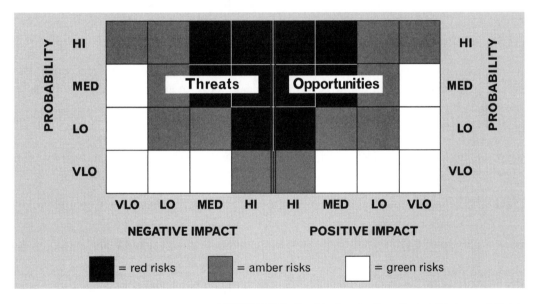

FIGURE 13-8: Double Four-by-Four Probability-Impact Matrix

• Produce a prioritized list of threats and opportunities, based on assessments of probability and impact

• Record assessments of probability and impacts, as well as agreed risk owners, for all identified risks, and enter into risk tool after project team meeting

Response Planning

This part of the First Risk Assessment step in the ATOM risk process is also undertaken during a project team meeting for a small project, but without the interviews employed for medium projects (see Chapter 7). The required steps are included in Figure 13-6. There is also no requirement to formally consider secondary risks when developing risk responses on a small project, though these should be recorded and included in the risk process if they arise during the discussion of risk responses.

The Assessment step results in choosing a risk owner for each identified risk, usually one of the project team members present in the team meeting. During the Response Planning part of the project team meeting, the project manager leads a short, focused discussion with each nominated risk owner, dealing first with threats and then with opportunities, and taking them in priority order. For each risk, this discussion has two steps:

- The risk owner is first asked to select an appropriate strategy for each risk, in agreement with the project manager. Threat strategies include avoid, transfer, reduce, or accept; opportunity strategies include exploit, share, enhance, or accept.

- Having selected a strategy, the risk owner develops an initial set of actions, with at least one action per risk, and suggested action owners. Actions should be properly defined, with completion criteria, timelines, and budgets, providing sufficient information that the action can be unambiguously understood by the action owner and monitored by the project manager.

The Response Planning step is done during the team meeting so that other team members can contribute to the discussion with risk owners and add ideas for appropriate ways to tackle an identified risk. Team members are also likely to be nominated as action owners, so their agreement to perform actions can be obtained during the meeting.

Agreed responses and actions for each risk, as well as agreed risk owners, are recorded during the meeting; this data is also entered into the risk tool immediately after the meeting.

If the risk owner of a particular risk is not present at the project team meeting, the project manager arranges a meeting with that risk owner as soon as possible to develop responses and actions. The project manager then ensures that this data is entered into the risk tool.

The project manager also ensures that all agreed actions are incorporated into the project plan immediately after the meeting, so that they can be monitored alongside other project tasks as part of the normal project management effort.

The following tasks are required when performing Response Planning during the First Risk Assessment for a small project:

- Develop responses in the project team meeting

- Risk owners for each risk select an appropriate strategy and determine actions with agreed action owners, and enter data into risk tool after project team meeting

- Project manager includes agreed actions in the project plan

Reporting

The reporting requirement for a small project is considerably reduced from that of a medium project (as detailed in Chapter 8). The nature, content, frequency, and distribution of risk reports is defined in the Risk Management Plan, and the project manager is responsible for producing these. For the small project, the main reporting output is the Risk Register, usually generated directly from the risk tool. It is also common to produce a short risk report highlighting the current risk status of the project. A typical contents list for such a report is presented in Figure 13-9. An acceptable alternative to a standalone risk report is to include a risk section in the regular project progress report, which should include the same content.

EXECUTIVE SUMMARY

SCOPE AND OBJECTIVES OF REPORT

OVERALL RISK STATUS

TOP RISKS, ACTIONS AND OWNERS

CONCLUSIONS AND RECOMMENDATIONS

APPENDIX
    COMPLETE RISK REGISTER IN PRIORITY ORDER

FIGURE 13-9: Sample Contents List for a Small Project Risk Report

Completion of the Reporting step at the end of the First Risk Assessment for a small project involves these tasks:

- Project manager compiles data from the earlier steps in the risk process

- Project manager produces a Risk Register and draft risk report (or risk section in regular project progress report), for approval by project sponsor

- Project manager issues and distributes the Risk Register and report

Implementation

The Response Planning step of the ATOM process results in nomination of a risk owner for each identified risk, who selects an appropriate strategy and develops suitable actions, each of which has an action owner. The final step in the First Risk Assessment is to implement agreed actions, which is as important for small projects as it is for medium projects. Consequently, there is no difference in how the Implementation step is performed for small projects compared with medium projects (see Chapter 9).

During this step, action owners perform agreed actions and report on their progress to the risk owner. This progress is then entered into the project plan as part of the normal project monitoring process, so that the plan includes the current status of all actions.

It is also important during the Implementation step for all project team members to remain alert to the possibility of new risks. Whenever a new risk is identified, the project manager should be notified immediately. The project manager then enters it, noting the status as draft, into the risk tool, for review during the risk section of the next project team meeting.

Though it appears simple, the Implementation step is in some ways the most important of all in the ATOM risk process, because failure to implement agreed actions means that risks remain unmanaged, some threats will turn into problems that should have been avoided or minimized, and some opportunities that could have been captured will be missed. It is therefore crucial to pay proper attention to this step, even for the small project.

The Implementation step for the small project involves the following tasks:

- Action owners perform agreed actions and report to risk owners

- Risk owners update the project plan with the status of all actions

- All project team members raise new risks as they become visible

- Project manager enters newly raised risks, with draft status, into the risk tool

Review

As with any project, risk exposure changes throughout the life of a small project. It is therefore important to keep the assessment of risk current, which requires undertaking risk-related actions in addition to the First Risk Assessment. The ATOM risk process includes reviews to keep the assessment of risk up to date; the medium project uses a series of Major and Minor Reviews (see Chapters 10 and 11). The Major Review essentially repeats all the steps of the First Risk Assessment, using a dedicated workshop, whereas the Minor Review is performed at a lower level of detail.

The small project is unlikely to require the full rigor of a Major Review, so the ATOM risk process includes only Minor Reviews for small projects. These are incorporated into regular project team meetings, and do not require a separate risk review meeting.

During the risk portion of the project team meeting, all active red risks are reviewed in priority order, dealing first with threats, then opportunities, in a discussion led by the project manager. For each risk, the risk owner reports on progress with agreed actions, and allocates a status value to the risk (active, expired, occurred, closed, or deleted). If a risk remains active, the risk owner assesses its current probability and impacts, and, in discussion with the project team, determines whether new actions and action owners are required.

After all red risks have been discussed, the project manager leads a review of draft risks raised since the last meeting. These are either discarded, in which case they are marked in the risk tool with a status of rejected, or they are accepted, in which case their status is set to active. For new active risks, the team agrees on probability and impacts, and chooses a risk owner who selects a response strategy and agrees on actions with action owners.

If time remains in this section of the project team meeting, the project manager might discuss amber risks, but this is optional. The team should also be allowed to discuss other active risks by exception; report changes in status; or suggest changes in response strategy, action, or action owners.

All changes in risk data agreed during the meeting must be recorded and entered into the risk tool. An updated Risk Register is produced after the meeting and made available to project team members and other key stakeholders; however, a risk report is not usually required.

The Review step of the ATOM process for a small project involves the following tasks:

- Review existing active risks and newly raised draft risks in the project team meeting

- Review all red risks, and others by exception

- Review draft risks and either reject or accept them

- Project manager enters updated risk data into the risk tool

- Project manager reissues the Risk Register

Following a review, if the project manager wishes to communicate the latest project risk status to stakeholders, a risk section is incorporated into the regular project status report; the current Risk Register can also be distributed.

Post-Project Review

Even small projects can generate valuable lessons for future projects, so a post-project review should form part of the normal project life cycle, though this is often not the case. For medium projects, ATOM recommends including a risk element in the post-project review meeting, if one is held, or holding a separate risk-related meeting (as described in Chapter 12). The same process is also recommended for small projects, with the following tasks:

- Project manager prepares risk data for the meeting, including the final issue of the Risk Register

- Hold post-project review meeting (or a separate risk meeting)

- Capture "lessons to be learned," including generic risks, effective responses, and process improvements

Conclusion

The ATOM risk process is designed to apply to all projects, including those with characteristics that suggest they are less risky. Even on these small projects, however, it is important to identify threats and opportunities, and to ensure that they are managed proactively and effectively.

There is no excuse for managers or teams of small projects to say that they have insufficient time or inadequate resources for risk management, because the simplified process described here maximizes the results while minimizing the overhead. Existing project team meetings are used instead of special risk workshops or risk interviews, and the reporting requirement is kept to a minimum. The reduced ATOM risk process for small projects described in this chapter and summarized in Figure 13-10 provides all the benefits of the more detailed process required for the medium project, but in a way that is affordable and appropriate.

Initiation:
- Confirm project objectives and risk assessment framework
- Draft and issue Risk Management Plan

Identification:
- Clarify project assumptions and constraints
- Identify risks in project team meeting

Assessment:
- Assess probability and impacts of identified risks during project team meeting
- Nominate a risk owner for each risk
- Produce a prioritized list of threats and opportunities

Response Planning:
- Develop appropriate responses and actions during project team meeting
- Record all risk data into risk tool after project team meeting
- Include agreed actions in the project plan

Reporting:
- Produce and issue the Risk Register
- Draft and issue risk report (or risk section in regular project progress report)

Implementation:
- Perform agreed actions and report to risk owners
- Update the project plan with action status
- Raise new risks as they become visible and enter into risk tool

Review:
- Review existing red risks and all draft risks in project team meeting
- Enter updated risk data into risk tool
- Reissue Risk Register

Post-Project Review:
- Prepare risk data for the meeting
- Consider risks during post-project review meeting (or hold a separate risk meeting)
- Capture "lessons to be learned," including generic risks, effective responses, and process improvements

FIGURE 13-10: ATOM Activities for a Small Project

CHAPTER 14

....

ATOM
for Large Projects

A key feature of the ATOM approach is scalability. ATOM is designed to be applicable to any project in any industry, offering a generic process that is suitable for all. However, some projects are undeniably more risky than others. Attempting to send a manned mission to Mars is on a different scale from moving an office from the first floor to the second, though both are projects, and both need some sort of risk management process.

The ATOM project sizing tool, discussed in Chapter 3 (with an example in Figure 3-4), allows an organization to classify its projects by size into three groups: small, medium, and large. Of course, size is relative—a project with a $1M budget may be considered enormous for one organization but tiny for another—and has many dimensions (e.g., complexity, value, duration, strategic importance, etc.), so the project sizing tool must reflect what is important to the organization. Once projects are categorized, the risk process can be tailored according-ly. The ATOM process for a typical medium-size project is described in Part II (Chapters 4 through 12); Chapter 13 discusses how to modify it for a small project. This chapter covers how to apply ATOM to a large project, which might be expected to be riskier and therefore require a more rigorous approach to risk management.

The process described here assumes that a large project will be treated as a whole, and not divided into subprojects. Sometimes, however, very large projects can be broken down into smaller components. In these cases it may be beneficial to apply the ATOM process at mul-tiple levels across the large project. A hierarchy of risk assessments could be performed, with a whole project risk assessment at the highest level and lower-level assessments of subprojects. Multiple Risk Registers might be produced, describing risks at different levels within the large project. (This approach is also suitable for managing risk on a program or portfolio, but managing risk at this level is outside the scope of ATOM, which is designed for projects.)

The remainder of this chapter describes ATOM as it should be applied to a single unitary large project.

Bigger Is Better

Many characteristics might result in categorizing a project as large. Using the example project sizing tool in Figure 3-4, a large project would have several of the following features:

- Strategic importance: the project is critical to business success

- Commercial/contractual complexity: groundbreaking commercial practices with unresolved issues

- External constraints and dependencies: overall project success depends on uncontrollable external factors

- Requirement stability: requirements are not finalized and are subject to negotiation

- Technical complexity: groundbreaking product/project with high innovation

- Market sector regulatory characteristics: highly regulated or novel sector

- Project value: large project value compared with other projects in the organization

- Project duration: long duration compared with other projects in the organization

- Project resources: international project team or joint venture

- Post-project liabilities: punitive exposure

Clearly a large project poses a significant risk challenge to any organization, and the standard ATOM risk process might not prove adequate. The process modifications described here are designed to provide a robust risk process while retaining a simple framework that does not present an unacceptable overhead burden to the project team.

The generic ATOM risk process applied to both small and medium projects is also applicable for large projects (see Figure 14-1), but for a large project each step is reinforced to ensure the necessary rigor. As for all projects, the ATOM process for large projects is iterative, starting with the Initiation step, followed by the First Risk Assessment, with regular reviews throughout the project life cycle, and ending with the Post-Project Review, as illustrated in Figure 14-2.

The rest of this chapter works through the ATOM risk process steps and presents changes to the standard approach previously described for medium projects. (For further details of the standard approach, refer to the appropriate chapters in Part II.)

Initiation

This important set-up step ensures that the risk process is properly targeted to meet the specific needs of the project. During this step, key decisions are made about the risk process, including:

- Scope and objectives of the risk management process

- The degree to which ATOM should be applied

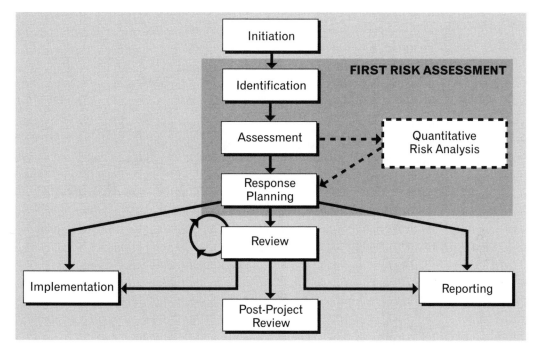

FIGURE 14-1: Steps in the ATOM Process

- Tools and techniques to be used

- Roles and responsibilities for risk management

- Reporting and review requirements

- Definitions of probability and impact scales for qualitative assessment

For a large project, these decisions must reflect the increased attention and effort required for risk management. Decisions must be recorded in the Risk Management Plan, which might be a more substantial document than is required for a medium project, though the content headings are the same. Figure 14-3 provides a sample contents list for a Risk Management Plan suitable for use on a large project.

Initiation for a large project is still done in a dedicated Initiation meeting, attended by key stakeholders and facilitated by the risk champion. The Initiation meeting for medium projects is described in Chapter 4, and does not require significant modification for large projects. The Initiation meeting agenda is the same (see Figure 4-5), and the attendees and duration are also similar.

One key decision for a large project is whether it justifies use of quantitative risk analysis techniques such as Monte Carlo. These techniques reveal the predicted effect of identified risks on overall project outcome, and can be applied to both cost and schedule risk. The Initiation meeting also determines the scope of required quantitative risk analysis, and whether it should be applied to cost, schedule, or both. ATOM recommends using these techniques on most large projects, but they are not required for all. Chapter 15 describes how to use Monte

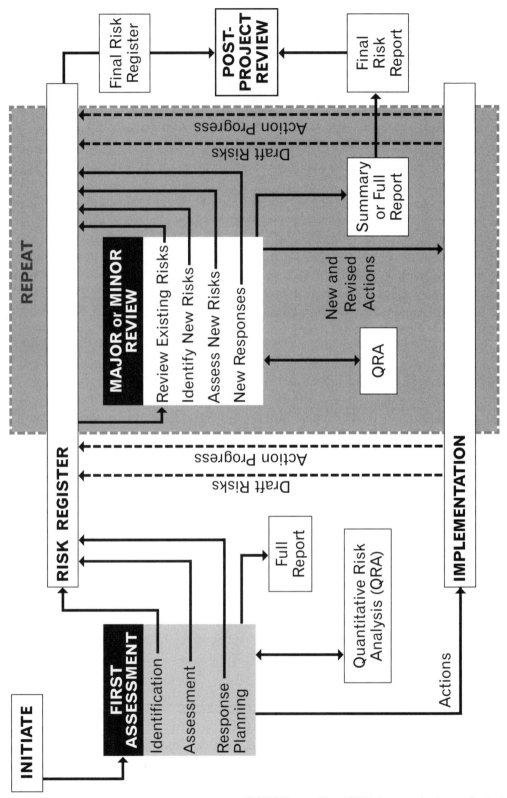

FIGURE 14-2: The ATOM Process for Large Projects

INTRODUCTION

PROJECT DESCRIPTION AND OBJECTIVES

AIMS, SCOPE AND OBJECTIVES OF RISK PROCESS

APPLICATION OF THE ATOM PROCESS

RISK TOOLS AND TECHNIQUES

ORGANIZATION, ROLES, AND RESPONSIBILITIES FOR RISK MANAGEMENT

RISK REVIEWS AND REPORTING

APPENDICES

    PROJECT-SPECIFIC DEFINITIONS OF PROBABILITY AND IMPACTS

    PROJECT-SPECIFIC SOURCES OF RISK (RISK BREAKDOWN STRUCTURE)

FIGURE 14-3: Sample Contents List of a Risk Management Plan for a Large Project

---

DAY 1

Morning
1. Introductions
2. Confirm project objectives
3. Confirm scope of risk process for this workshop
4. Workshop ground rules
5. Risk management briefing (if required)
6. Expectations and results
7. Identify risks
   Brainstorm risks using the risk breakdown structure

Afternoon
   Analyze assumptions and constraints to generate further risks
   Standard risk checklist to identify any further/final risks
8. Rationalize risks
9. Describe risks using risk metalanguage
10. Record identified risks (during workshop or after meeting)

DAY 2

Morning
11. Explanation of assessment scheme (recap)
12. Assessment of probability and impacts
13. Risk categorization

Afternoon
14. Nomination of risk owners
15. *If time, develop initial responses to priority risks*
16. Close the workshop

FIGURE 14-4: Sample Agenda for a First Risk Assessment/
Two-Day Risk Workshop for Large Projects

Carlo quantitative risk analysis techniques, and includes criteria for deciding when they are applicable. During the Initiation meeting key stakeholders should consider the potential benefits of using Monte Carlo techniques on the project, and compare them with the associated costs in terms of specialized tools, the need for expert analytical skills, and the time and effort required for the analysis (especially for data generation). The ATOM process assumes that quantitative risk analysis techniques are appropriate for most large projects, so the emphasis of the discussion should be to question whether their use might not be justified for this particular project.

ATOM for large projects also differs from medium projects in the requirement for a more rigorous review cycle, which is considered and decided on during the Initiation meeting. Whereas an alternating series of Major and Minor Reviews is done for the typical medium project, on large projects doing the Major Review more frequently may be appropriate. Indeed in some cases it may be decided that all risk reviews will be Major, perhaps to respond to high risk exposure, or where the pace of change on the project is fast.

Project-specific scales for probability and impact are also determined and agreed on during the Initiation meeting. Five-point scales (VLO, LO, MED, HI, VHI) are usually considered adequate for large projects, using the same framework as recommended for medium projects (see Figure 4-8), though in some cases considering additional scale points. However, the trade-off between additional granularity and increased complexity should be considered carefully; five-by-five scales are recommended even for large projects.

Finally, consider the choice and use of a software tool to support the risk process. For medium projects, ATOM leaves open the option of using either a proprietary risk tool or bespoke methods for recording and reporting risk data. A large project will likely generate sufficient data to justify use of a proprietary risk tool; this tool should be fully integrated with the project management toolkit and the wider business infrastructure. The ATOM process for large projects does not depend on any particular software package, but the sheer volume of risk data handled in a large project will likely justify the investment in professional risk software that will facilitate the analysis and reporting process.

To complete the Initiation step for a large project, the following activities are required:

- Determine key stakeholders who will provide input to this step

- Hold an Initiation meeting with key stakeholders in order to:

  - Confirm project size

  - Clarify project objectives

  - Set the scope and objectives for the risk process

  - Confirm the tools and techniques to be used, and decide whether to use quantitative risk analysis

  - Allocate roles and responsibilities for risk management tasks

- Agree on reporting and review requirements

- Define scales for probability and impacts

- Identify potential sources of risk to the project

- Document the decisions from the Initiation meeting in the Risk Management Plan, and distribute to key stakeholders

Identification

Many believe that risk identification is the most important step in the risk process, because unidentified risks remain unmanaged, exposing the project to unnecessary threats and losing potential opportunities. For a large project this is particularly true because the higher level of inherent risk presents a greater level of uncertainty. Indeed, while an organization might be able to cope with the failure of a small- or medium-size project, problems with a large project might spell disaster. For this reason, particular care must be given to the risk identification step in the ATOM process for large projects.

Identification for medium projects (see Chapter 5) forms the initial part of the First Risk Assessment, and is a structured approach involving key stakeholders with the aim of exposing all knowable risks. ATOM recommends three basic techniques to identify risks on medium projects, namely brainstorming, assumptions and constraints analysis, and a risk identification checklist. Each of these techniques is also useful during the Identification part of the First Risk Assessment for a large project, and can be expected to reveal a significant number of risks. However, the increased complexity and importance of a large project justifies use of additional risk identification techniques as part of this step. In particular, the following three methods are recommended for inclusion:

- SWOT analysis

- Structured interviews

- Review of past projects

The forum for risk identification on large projects is the same as for medium projects, namely a risk workshop attended by key stakeholders and facilitated by the risk champion. The typical risk workshop is expected to last for two days and covers both Identification and Assessment steps, although more time may be required for some large projects. The content of the risk workshop is the same as is described in Chapter 5 for a medium project. The risk champion might either replace the standard brainstorm session with a SWOT analysis or include it in the workshop as an extra element. The workshop is preceded by the same set of pre-workshop preparatory activities, including circulating a workshop agenda (see Figure 14-4 for an example) and other supporting material. In addition to the risk workshop, large-project risks are identified using a series of structured interviews, as well as a structured review of past projects.

The three additional risk identification techniques recommended for large projects are summarized below.

SWOT analysis

The four elements of a SWOT analysis when used for risk identification are:

- **Strength:** a characteristic, resource, or capacity the organization can use effectively to achieve its objectives

- **Weakness:** a limitation, fault, or defect in the organization that might keep it from achieving its objectives

- **Opportunity:** an uncertain beneficial event or condition that, if it occurs, results in favorable outcomes on the project

- **Threat:** an uncertain adverse event or condition that, if it occurs, results in unfavorable outcomes on the project

SWOT analysis for project risk identification within ATOM has a different focus from use of this technique for strategic decision-making. The first element of this version of SWOT analysis is a facilitated brainstorming process that identifies organizational strengths and weaknesses as they relate to the project, usually limiting this to about ten. The second element is identifying opportunities and threats that might affect achievement of the objectives, using the identified strengths and weaknesses as a starting point, as illustrated in Figure 14-5. Risk metalanguage offers a mechanism for deriving opportunities from organizational strengths, and for finding threats that arise from weaknesses, using structured risk statements such as:

- As a result of <strength>, <opportunity> may occur, which would lead to <benefit>

- As a result of <weakness>, <threat> may occur, which would lead to <problem>

Several opportunities often arise from a single strength, and several threats might come from one weakness, so the risk champion ensures that all options are considered during the workshop.

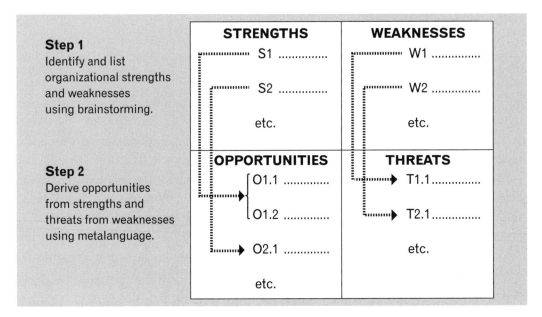

FIGURE 14-5: Identifying Opportunities and Threats Using SWOT Analysis

Interviews

Short, focused risk identification interviews are conducted by the risk champion immediately after the risk workshop, and can be conducted with either individuals or small groups of stakeholders.

- When interviewing individuals, it is important to decide who to include. Conducting too many interviews can waste time through repetition, so the aim is to interview only as many key stakeholders as are required to cover all the major areas of the project.

- If risk interviews are conducted with groups instead of individuals, the interviewer must take additional care to manage the group dynamics, ensuring that each participant is heard and that no individual dominates. Group interviews should be kept small, say three to five people, with all participants from the same area of expertise. It is also best if they share the same level of seniority, to encourage openness and avoid reluctance to speak honestly in front of superiors.

Structure is a valuable aid to the risk interview; ATOM uses a framework based on a work breakdown structure (WBS) or risk breakdown structure (RBS). Other factors required for a successful risk identification interview include:

- **Preparation.** To make the best use of the time available for the interview, both interviewer and interviewees need to have reviewed and be familiar with the project objectives and current status, and should have spent some time prior to the interview considering possible risks.

- **Trust.** The interview should be kept confidential so interviewees can express their concerns honestly and without fear of reprisal or blame. Asking open-ended questions, avoiding a judgmental or critical attitude, demonstrating respect, and acknowledging confidentiality can encourage this trust.

- **Interview skills.** These include active listening and selective questioning. Active listening means paying attention, encouraging openness, demonstrating empathy, etc. Selective questioning means using different question types appropriately, including open, probing, hypothetical, reflective, and closed questions.

- **Recording and follow up.** Many items discussed in the interview might not be well-described risks, so the risk champion must take good notes during the interview and use them later to filter out nonrisks, merge duplications, and record properly described risks. Additional clarification from the interviewee might be required after the interview to ensure that the final output fairly reflects the interviewee's views.

Review past projects

Although each project is unique, many areas of commonality exist between completed and new projects. As a result, the post-project review offers a structured mechanism for capturing lessons to be learned from previous projects and applied to new ones.

The post-project review addresses all aspects of completed projects, including the management of risk. The risk element of the post-project review should be structured using the RBS as a framework, to ensure that all sources of risk are considered and to provide a comparative structure for transferring lessons between projects. The results from the post-project review are usually captured in a post-project review report, and can be used to update risk identification tools such as checklists, to incorporate proactive risk response strategies into future projects, and to improve the effectiveness of the risk analysis and management process.

The risk champion, in discussion with the project manager, usually undertakes the post-project review analysis as a mechanism for risk identification, though it can also be conducted in a group that includes the risk champion, project manager, and other key stakeholders. The following steps are required:

1. Identify relevant comparable projects that have been completed and have similar characteristics to the current project

2. Review the post-project review reports for these projects, noting generic risks and effective responses

3. Consider the extent to which the risks and responses might apply to the current project

It is vital for the success of the ATOM risk process that all knowable risks are identified and recorded. For large projects, this requires performing the following activities as part of the First Risk Assessment:

• Determine workshop attendees; prepare a workshop agenda and workshop prebrief

• Facilitate a risk workshop to identify all knowable risks, which are then properly described using risk metalanguage

• Consolidate risks to remove duplicates and nonrisks

• Conduct post-workshop risk identification interviews and post-project review analysis

• Record all identified risks in the risk tool

Assessment

For large projects, the major change in the Assessment step is inclusion of quantitative risk analysis techniques, usually Monte Carlo analysis. This is described in detail in Chapter 15, which outlines how to build a risk model, perform the analysis, and interpret outputs. One key element in producing a realistic risk model is to use data from the qualitative Assessment step as a basis for determining risk model parameters. It is also valuable to use Monte Carlo analysis both before and after developing suitable responses to identified risks in order to evaluate the effect of planned responses on the risk exposure of the project.

Since qualitative assessment is a prerequisite for quantitative analysis, on large projects the qualitative part of the Assessment step must be performed first, as part of the First Risk Assessment.

The activities in the Assessment step for a large project mirror those used for medium projects (as described in Chapter 6), and are conducted during the latter part of a risk workshop.

Each identified risk is assessed against the agreed scales for probability and impacts to allow risks to be prioritized, using both the red/amber/green zones of the double P-I Matrix (as in Figure 6-3), and using P-I scores (see Figures 6-4 and 6-5). Risks are also categorized using the project's WBS and RBS to identify hot spots arising from common risk sources and areas of the project particularly exposed to risk. For the large project, RBS and WBS categorizations can be merged into a two-dimensional matrix (see Figure 14-6) to show particular combinations of source and area affected, allowing risk response development to be more closely targeted.

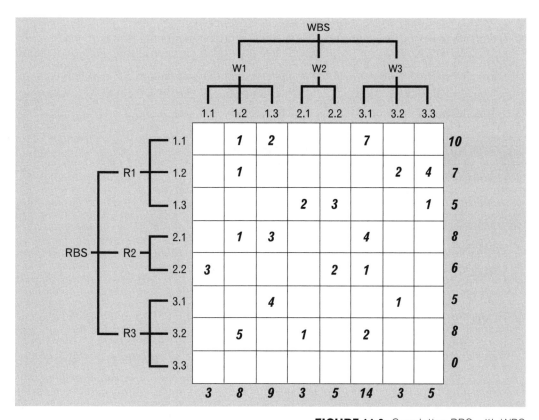

FIGURE 14-6: Correlating RBS with WBS

In addition to these main risk characteristics (probability, impacts, WBS category, RBS category), assessment of risks for a large project considers a number of other factors for each risk:

•   **Strategic impact.** Some risks may have potential impacts outside the project, perhaps affecting other projects, a higher-level program, business-as-usual activities, or even the wider organization. These nonproject impacts are also considered; an example scale is presented in Figure 14-7.

•   **Manageability.** Some risks are easier to address than others, and this should be taken into account when prioritizing risks. For example, a high-probability/high-impact threat that can be easily managed might be prioritized above one with a medium probability/medium impact but that cannot be influenced. A scale such as the one in Figure 14-8 can be used for this assessment, with results ranging from unmanageable to controllable by normal activities.

• **Impact window.** Assessing when a risk impact might occur can affect its overall prioritization, since risks that could happen soon should receive higher priority than those further off. (This is sometimes referred to as proximity.)

• **Action window.** The period of time when effective action can be taken is another important factor when assessing a risk. (This is sometimes called urgency.) If addressing a risk is only possible in the next few days, that risk receives higher priority than one where the ability to act is less immediate. Impact and action windows are often presented using an overlay chart (Figure 14-9), indicating risks with high proximity and urgency. This chart also shows potential problem areas where the action window is later than the impact window—i.e., the risk is expected to occur before the project has a chance to take action. In this case new action strategies should be sought or contingency plans developed.

SCALE	+/– IMPACT ON NON-PROJECT OBJECTIVES*
VHI	Critical
HI	Major
MED	Significant
LO	Minor
VLO	Insignificant
NIL	None

* For example, strategic goals, program benefits, or company reputation

FIGURE 14-7: Example Scale for Non-Project Impacts

SCALE	MANAGEABILITY
VHI	Can be controlled by normal activities
HI	Suitable responses are available if needed
MED	Requires significant effort to address
LO	Requires innovation or research
VLO	Unmanageable

FIGURE 14-8: Example Scale for Manageability

The overlay chart below illustrates a different picture for each of the six risks shown. The action window for Risk 1 starts now, and the action must be in place within three weeks or it is too late to take action. Risk 2 has a longer action window, and action cannot start for two weeks. Risk 3 action must take place in three weeks' time and there is no room for maneuver. The action window for Risk 4 overlaps the impact window, so although the action could take longer to implement, delaying action might be foolish. The planned action for Risk 5 can only take place three weeks after the impact window for the risk opens. In this case new action strategies should be sought or contingency plans developed. Risk 6 has a long action window, so there should be no reason why the action cannot be successfully implemented.

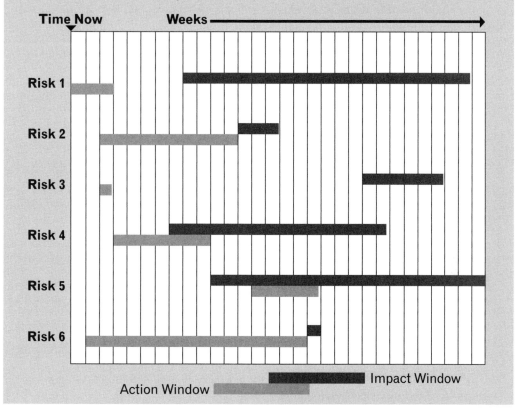

FIGURE 14-9: Impact and Action Windows Overlay Chart

Chapter 6 lists a standard set of assessment outputs usually produced following the risk workshop for a medium project, as follows:

- Initial Risk Register

- Prioritized risk list

- List of top threats and top opportunities

- Categorization of risks by RBS element

- Categorization of risks by WBS element

- Double P-I Matrix

These are also produced for the large project, with the addition of some other assessment outputs:

- RBS x WBS cross-categorization analysis

- Prioritization by other factors (strategic impact, manageability, impact and action windows)

- Risk metrics

A number of risk metrics can be established at this stage of the First Risk Assessment to form a baseline for later trend analysis. These include:

- Number of active risks (separated into threats and opportunities)

- Number of expired/occurred/closed/deleted risks (initially this will be zero)

- Total P-I score for active threats and opportunities

- Average P-I score for active threats and opportunities

After completing the qualitative assessment of all identified risks, a quantitative risk analysis is performed using the assessment data, following the guidance outlined in Chapter 15. This analysis demonstrates the predicted effect of identified risks on the overall project outcome (either cost or schedule or both), and informs the Response Planning step.

The Assessment step conducted as part of the First Risk Assessment for a large project requires the following activities:

- Assess probability and impacts for each risk, plot the risk on the P-I Matrix, and calculate P-I scores

- Categorize risks using the RBS (causes) and WBS (effects) to determine hot spots

- Assess other key characteristics of identified risks, including strategic impact, manageability, proximity, and urgency

- Nominate risk owners

- Generate baseline risk metrics

- Develop a Monte Carlo risk model based on qualitative risk data, and perform an initial analysis to demonstrate the predicted effect of risk on overall project outcome

- Record all additional risk data in the risk tool

- Prepare a set of outputs that will inform the continued risk management process as well as the overall project management process

Response Planning

During the First Risk Assessment of a medium project, Response Planning occurs during a series of interviews with risk owners (as described in Chapter 7). This step is essentially identical for large projects, using the expertise and experience of risk owners to determine appropriate response strategies and effective actions, as well as nominating action owners to implement agreed actions. Scenario planning may be used to develop response strategies or fallback plans and to determine what type of response is appropriate. Because Response Planning is so important for a large, risky project, it deserves the same level of detailed planning as the production of the project plan itself.

The Response Planning step for large projects, however, requires one additional step, which is to update the Monte Carlo quantitative risk analysis to take account of planned responses, as described in Chapter 15. The data in the risk model is adjusted through a series of data-gathering interviews with risk owners, indicating where values for individual model activities and other parameters have changed as a result of the actions that are to be implemented. Repeating the analysis with this revised data predicts the expected effectiveness of planned responses in improving the overall risk exposure of the project. One key output here is the "onion ring diagram" (Figure 14-10), which overlays the S-curve for the "all risks/no responses" position with an S-curve showing the effect of all planned responses. It is also possible to build up a series of intermediate S-curves to show the cumulative effect of different responses, indicating which have the greatest influence on overall project outcome. This analysis can suggest whether currently planned responses are adequate to meet the risk challenge or whether additional response planning is required. Holding additional interviews with risk owners to develop new responses might be necessary if the Monte Carlo analysis shows insufficient expected improvement.

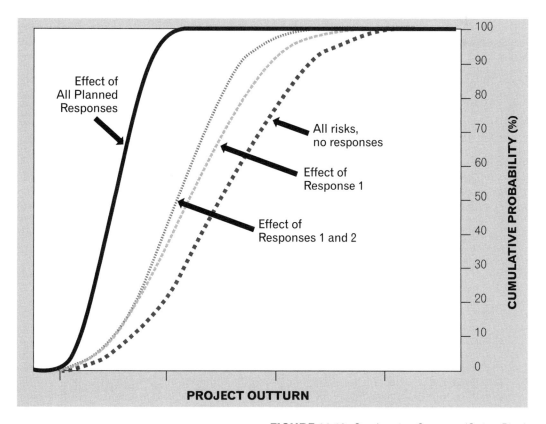

FIGURE 14-10: Overlapping S-curves (Onion Ring)

To complete Response Planning for a large project, the following activities should be undertaken:

- Conduct interviews with risk owners to determine appropriate response strategies and actions with nominated action owners

- Confirm and refine proposed actions with action owners

- Update the Risk Register with response strategies and agreed actions

- Update quantitative risk analysis to reflect post-response expectations

- Conduct additional response development interviews if required

- Modify the project schedule and budget to include agreed actions

Reporting

Risk reporting is an essential element of the ATOM process because it communicates results to stakeholders in a way that enables effective decision-making and management action. As might be expected, the reporting requirement for a large project is more detailed than for a medium project (see Chapter 8), though the main output is still the full risk report. However, the content of this report includes other elements arising from the additional data generated during the enhanced ATOM risk process; Figure 14-11 gives a sample contents list.

EXECUTIVE SUMMARY

SCOPE AND OBJECTIVES OF REPORT

PROJECT STATUS SUMMARY

OVERALL RISK STATUS

TOP RISKS, ACTIONS AND OWNERS

DETAILED QUALITATIVE RISK ASSESSMENT
    High/medium/low risks
    Causal analysis (mapped to RBS)
    Effects analysis (mapped to WBS)

QUANTITATIVE RISK ANALYSIS RESULTS
    Overall project risk
    Expected values
    Main risk drivers and key risks

CONCLUSIONS AND RECOMMENDATIONS

APPENDICES
    COMPLETE RISK REGISTER
    PRIORITIZED RISK LIST
    INPUT DATA FOR RISK MODEL
    DETAILED QUANTITATIVE ANALYSIS OUTPUTS
    (OTHER RESULTS AS REQUIRED)

FIGURE 14-11: Sample Contents List for a Full Risk Report

For a large project, the full risk report produced at the end of the First Risk Assessment includes the sections listed below:

- **Executive summary.** This summarizes key findings, conclusions, and recommendations at a level suitable for senior management and key project stakeholders.

- **Scope and objectives of report.** The purpose of the report is described, highlighting its place in the risk process.

- **Project status summary.** This summarizes project status to set the context for the report.

- **Overall risk status.** A summary is presented of the current level of risk exposure, highlighting main areas of risk, plus any significant individual risks together with planned responses. Any concentrations of risk exposed during the categorization analysis are detailed, including common causes and areas of the project particularly affected.

- **Top risks, actions, and owners.** This lists top threats and opportunities in priority order, and discusses each in turn, detailing causes and effects, planned actions with owners, and expected changes. Significant patterns within the top risk lists are discussed.

- **Detailed qualitative risk assessment.** This is the main analysis section of the report, where the risk exposure is considered in detail. The number of risks in each red/amber/green category is presented, as well as categorization by RBS and WBS, plus the RBS x WBS cross-analysis. Expected response effectiveness is discussed, based on the pre-response and post-response P-I matrices.

- **Quantitative risk analysis results.** Findings from the Monte Carlo analysis are presented here, concentrating on the overall results rather than details of the risk model or particular outputs (these details are presented in appendices). The degree of uncertainty in project outcome is presented, and expected values from the calculation are given and discussed. The main risk drivers are identified, together with key risks, and the predicted effectiveness of planned responses is also covered.

- **Conclusions and recommendations.** Key findings are presented at a summary level, and conclusions are drawn based on the data within the main body of the report. Based on these conclusions, a series of focused and specific recommendations are presented that respond to the level of risk currently faced by the project.

- **Appendices.** Supporting information is presented in appendices. One of these should contain the complete Risk Register with full details of every identified risk. It is also common to include a complete list of all risks in priority order. Input data for the risk model may be included; detailed quantitative risk analysis outputs can also be presented in an appendix. The content of other appendices is optional, depending on the information needs of the recipients.

Reporting at the conclusion of the First Risk Assessment for a large project involves the following activities:

- Assemble all sources of information on current risk exposure, including the Risk Register and quantitative risk analysis outputs

- Perform any additional analysis required to understand the information

- Draft a full risk report presenting this information in a structured way

- Review the draft report for completeness and correctness, and modify as required

- Issue risk report to project sponsor, project manager, project team members, risk owners, and other key stakeholders

- Prepare and distribute extracts, subsets, and additional reports as required

Implementation

Not everyone agrees that risk identification is the most important step in the risk process. Some would say that this is Implementation, since the best risk responses are useless if they are not put into practice. For this reason, ATOM places considerable emphasis on the Implementation step, whether the project is small, medium, or large. In fact, Implementation activities for large projects are exactly the same as those already described for medium projects (see Chapter 9), and for small projects (see Chapter 13).

So although Implementation is extremely important, there is not much different or extra to say about it for large projects; it requires the same level of attention and effort for all projects, and involves the following activities:

- Complete agreed actions and report progress

- Monitor each response strategy and its associated actions

- Ascertain the overall status of each risk

- Identify additional secondary risks and raise new risks

- Modify the project schedule and budget to include new actions or any replanned actions

- Raise any issues or problems

- Update the Risk Register with the current status of each risk and progress on agreed actions

- Produce information for risk reports and review meetings

Review

As for Implementation, the Review step of the ATOM process is essential to keeping the process alive. This is especially true for large projects, which have characteristics that introduce significant risk exposure. They are likely to involve substantial innovation or technical complexity and take place over long durations, which is a recipe for a high degree of change in the level of risk exposure. As a result the ATOM process needs an effective Review step to ensure that project stakeholders have correct and timely information to support good decision-making.

For the medium project, ATOM keeps up to date with a combination of Major and Minor Reviews, as described in Chapters 10 and 11. The expected high degree of change on a large project means that more reliance is placed on Major Reviews, where a comprehensive reevaluation of risk exposure is undertaken. The review cycle for the project is determined and agreed during the Initiation step, and documented in the Risk Management Plan, and large projects commonly use Major Reviews more often during the project life cycle than do medium projects. However, even on the largest project, there are unlikely to be sufficient resources and effort available to perform a full Major Review every time, especially when the review cycle is monthly. Consequently, large projects also make use of alternating Major/Minor Reviews.

The large-project Minor Review matches that used for medium projects exactly (see Chapter 11), and does not include revision of the quantitative risk analysis model. The review requires the following activities:

- Hold a facilitated risk review meeting to review all current red risks and newly raised risks, plus amber risks if time allows

- Identify, describe, and assess new risks; appoint risk owners; and develop responses

- Update the Risk Register

- Revise and define risk actions and appoint action owners

- Update the project plan to take into account risk actions

- Draft and distribute a summary risk report and other information needed for project reporting

For the Major Review, however, Monte Carlo analysis is repeated in addition to the activities used for a medium project: updating the model parameters to reflect project progress, changes in individual risks, the effect of implemented risk response actions, the identification of new risks, and the predicted effect of remaining actions. As in the First Risk Assessment, Monte Carlo analysis is performed both before and after development of risk responses—the first time to assist in response development, the second time to model the post-response situation. In addition, the large project Major Review includes calculation of risk metrics to compare against the baseline that was established during the First Risk Assessment; this enables trend analysis. The activities required for a large project Major Review are therefore:

- Facilitate a risk workshop to review all current risks and newly raised risks

- Identify, describe, and assess new risks; appoint risk owners; and develop responses

- Update the Risk Register

- Revise and define risk actions, and appoint action owners

- Update the quantitative risk analysis model to determine predicted project outcomes both pre-response and post-response

- Update the project plan to take into account risk actions

- Update risk metrics to allow trend analysis

- Draft and distribute a full risk report and other information needed for project reporting

- Consider the efficiency and effectiveness of the risk management process

Post-Project Review

The ATOM risk process emphasizes learning from experience by concluding with a Post-Project Review step at the completion of the project. Organizations perform projects for two main reasons: to create the specific project deliverables that enable achievement of benefits, and to gain experience that can be used on future similar projects. Even the smallest project can generate useful lessons for future projects. Therefore, the ATOM Post-Project Review is required for small, medium, and large projects.

Like other parts of ATOM, the Post-Project Review step is scalable. For small projects, this activity forms part of the wider post-project review meeting, as described in Chapter 13. Medium projects might also perform ATOM Post-Project Review tasks during the post-project review meeting, or may elect to hold a separate risk-related meeting, as described in Chapter 12. However, for large projects the scope of lessons that can be learned is likely to be greater, and consequently more effort is justified for the Post-Project Review step. As a result, Post-Project Review for large projects is always undertaken in a separate dedicated risk lessons learned meeting, held prior to the main post-project review meeting.

The risk lessons learned meeting is chaired by the project manager, supported by the risk champion, and attended by all key stakeholders. A sample agenda is provided in Figure 14-12. Discussion at this meeting is structured around the project's RBS to ensure consideration of all sources of risk, and to provide a consistent framework for transferring lessons to future projects. The risk champion captures lessons to be learned during the meeting, and

TIME ALLOWANCE (hours)	CONTENT
¼	1. Introductions
¼	2. Confirm original project objectives
¼	3. Confirm meeting objectives
1	4. Review final Risk Register and risk reports
2	5. Identify risk-related "lessons to be learned"
½	6. Summarize "lessons to be learned"
¼	7. Close the meeting

FIGURE 14-12: Typical Agenda for a Risk Lessons Learned Meeting

produces a risk lessons report to communicate lessons learned to key stakeholders and the wider organization.

The activities required to perform the Post-Project Review step for a large project are:

- Prepare risk information for consideration at the meeting

- Hold risk lessons learned meeting

- Capture conclusions in risk lessons report as input to the main post-project review process

Conclusion

The scalable nature of ATOM makes it applicable to all projects, including those that are significantly risky. For these large projects, it is particularly important that all risks are managed proactively and effectively, in order to maximize the benefits delivered to clients, the organization, and other stakeholders, and to minimize the potential for disastrous adverse outcomes.

The key is to provide a risk management process that is sufficiently robust to meet the risk challenge of a major project, but that does not impose an unacceptable bureaucratic overhead on the project team. By building on the ATOM process for medium projects, ATOM for large projects only adds effort and complexity where there is a clear need to do so. The enhanced ATOM risk process for large projects described in this chapter is summarized in Figure 14-13, and offers a process that provides the required benefits cost-effectively.

Initiation:
- Determine key stakeholders and hold Initiation meeting
- Draft and issue Risk Management Plan

Identification:
- Identify risks through facilitated risk workshop, risk identification interviews, and post-project review analysis
- Record all identified risks in risk tool

Assessment:
- Assess identified risks during facilitated risk workshop (probability, impacts, other key characteristics)
- Categorize risks using the risk breakdown structure and work breakdown structure
- Nominate a risk owner for each risk
- Generate baseline risk metrics
- Develop a Monte Carlo risk model and perform initial analysis
- Record all additional risk data in the risk tool
- Produce assessment and analysis outputs

Response Planning:
- Determine response strategies and action owners during interviews with risk owners
- Confirm and refine proposed actions with action owners, and include in project plan
- Update the Risk Register with response strategies and agreed actions
- Update quantitative risk analysis to reflect post-response expectations

Reporting:
- Analyze current risk exposure, and draft and issue full risk report (including the complete Risk Register), plus extracts as required

Implementation:
- Perform agreed actions and report progress, and identify need for new actions
- Identify secondary risks, issues or problems, as well as new risks
- Modify the project schedule and budget to include new or replanned actions
- Update the Risk Register with the current status of each risk and progress on agreed actions

Review:
- Minor review
  - Hold facilitated risk meeting to review all red and draft risks, plus amber risks if time allows.
  - Identify and assess new risks, appoint risk owners and develop responses
  - Update the Risk Register and project plan to take into account risk actions
  - Revise and define risk actions and appoint risk action owners
  - Draft and issue summary risk report
- Major review
  - Review all current risks and draft risks through facilitated risk workshop
  - Identify and assess new risks, appoint risk owners and develop responses
  - Revise and define risk actions and appoint risk action owners
  - Update the Risk Register and project plan to take into account risk actions
  - Update the quantitative risk analysis model to determine predicted project outcomes, both pre- and post-response
  - Update risk metrics to allow trend analysis
  - Draft and issue full risk report
  - Review risk process efficiency and effectiveness

Post-Project Review:
- Prepare risk data for the meeting
- Consider risks during risk lessons learned meeting
- Capture conclusions in risk lessons report as input to the main post-project review

FIGURE 14-13: ATOM Activities for a Large Project

CHAPTER 15

....

Simulating Possible Futures (Quantitative Analysis)

One benefit of risk management in general is that it allows consideration of possible futures without the need for a time machine. The ATOM process, as typically applied for medium or small projects, does this in a purely qualitative manner, without using statistical analysis. This approach is perfectly adequate for such projects, but there are circumstances where this is not enough. Some bigger projects—such as those that are inherently risky because they are of high cost or long duration, or are innovative or strategically important—pose a higher level of risk challenge. These projects demand a deeper understanding of risk and therefore more rigorous analysis.

By using well-established statistical analysis techniques and computer software, models can be built that predict future project outcomes that reflect the overall risk of the project. Risk information from the Identification and Assessment steps can be combined with the project's schedule or budget and analyzed with statistical techniques to predict possible futures for the project. This approach to modeling overall project risk is called quantitative risk analysis.

A number of proven quantitative techniques can be used to model possible futures, such as Monte Carlo analysis, decision trees, and influence diagrams. Each of these techniques is appropriate in different circumstances, but in project risk management the most commonly used technique is Monte Carlo analysis, since it allows detailed analysis of the combined effect of risks on project objectives. Monte Carlo analysis is also the method of choice within the ATOM risk process.

There are two common objections to using quantitative risk analysis, and Monte Carlo in particular:

1. Some think the techniques are too difficult and not worth the time and effort required. While this might have been true in the past, the availability of easy-to-use software tools removes much of this objection. The principles of quantitative risk analysis are also not difficult to understand or apply (see below), and potential users should consider whether the return is worth the investment or not.

2. A second objection is that the results of Monte Carlo analysis are always pessimistic. This belief arose largely from the traditional practice of analyzing only the effects of negative risks (threats) on the project, where the only possible variation in outcome is to be late or over budget. When the risk process includes both threats and opportunities, modeling outputs are neither pessimistic nor optimistic, but are more realistic and reflect the true risk exposure of the project.

The benefits of using quantitative risk analysis over and above qualitative assessment can be summarized as follows:

- Considers the combined effect of risks (both threats and opportunities) on project outcomes, recognizing that risks do not exist in isolation and that they will interact in a number of ways

- Predicts future performance against key objectives (usually time and cost), indicating the range of possible outcomes from best case to worst case, and calculating what should be expected if no further action is taken (the statistical mean or expected value)

- Gives a view of the overall project risk exposure arising from the totality of risks that might affect the project

- Provides a consistent baseline for sensitivity or what-if analysis to explore the effectiveness of planned responses

- Uses unambiguous numbers to describe uncertainty, rather than labels such as high, medium, or low, which can be interpreted differently by different people

- Exposes key risk drivers (i.e., risks that have the greatest influence on the overall outcome of the project), allowing management attention to focus on the riskiest parts of the project

- Answers questions when the answer is a number, including probabilities of achieving project targets, amounts of required contingency, likely spend rate, etc.

The ATOM process is scalable to all types of projects, and categorizes projects into three sizes: small, medium, and large. Quantitative risk analysis as part of ATOM is rarely needed for small projects, optional for medium projects, but usually required for large projects. This chapter presents practical guidelines for using Monte Carlo analysis on large projects, focusing on a description of the principles and process that is independent of any particular software tool.

Introducing Monte Carlo Analysis

Monte Carlo analysis is based on the generation of random numbers, allowing the random sampling of a range of possibilities from predefined input data in a risk model. The input data must reflect the degree of uncertainty in the project, based on the risks exposed in the risk process. A single analysis is formed from many iterations, each of which runs through the risk model once to produce one outcome calculated from a randomly chosen sample drawn from the input data. An analysis can calculate thousands of outcomes that reflect the range of what is possible, based on the uncertainties reflected in the input data, and these will include the best and worst possible outcomes and all values in between. The results from a Monte Carlo analysis are typically presented in two forms:

1. A histogram that shows the range of possible outcomes and the number of times a particular outcome was achieved

2. An S-curve, which plots the range of possible outcomes against the cumulative probability of achieving a given value

Figure 15-1 shows a histogram from a quantitative risk analysis, with the number of occurrences for each outturn value plotted against the left-hand y-axis. This is overlaid with the cumulative S-curve from the same data, plotted against the right-hand y-axis.

To apply quantitative risk analysis to a project effectively, a number of key steps must be applied. These are summarized below, and then explained in more detail later in this chapter.

Define the purpose of the analysis. The overall project objectives have already been determined during the Initiation step of the generic ATOM process and documented in the Risk Management Plan. Using this information, the particular emphasis and purpose of the quantitative analysis can be determined. The scope of the analysis might only cover schedule risk or cost risk, or an integrated view may be needed. Quantitative analysis can also be applied to other objectives, such as internal rate of return (IRR) or net present value (NPV).

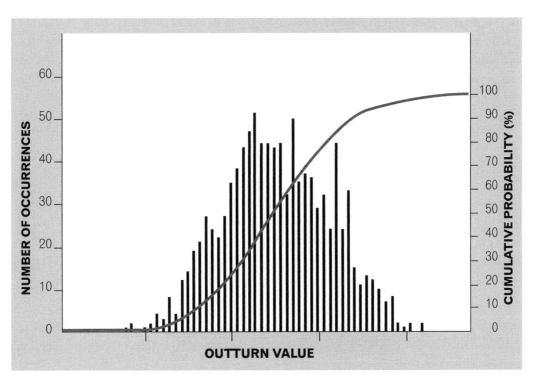

FIGURE 15-1: Example Monte Carlo Histogram and S-Curve

Develop the risk model or models. For a schedule risk analysis, it is usual to base the risk model on the critical path network for the project. A cost risk analysis model is usually based on the cost breakdown structure (CBS), which is often set out in a spreadsheet. A single integrated risk model can be created for analysis of both schedule and cost risk by using the critical path network and ensuring that all project costs are included within the schedule.

Generate input data and build analysis models. Once the initial model has been developed, the data required for the analysis can be derived and input. This must reflect all relevant risks, including threats and opportunities, and can include both variability (presented as ranges of values) and the possibility of alternative options (modeled using stochastic branches—see below).

Initial analysis—run model and validate initial results. The completed model is then analyzed by running a large number of iterations. An initial view of the model's robustness should be taken in order to check that no errors were made in inputting data and that nothing illogical has been included. Any errors should be corrected before proceeding further.

Secondary analysis—run model including risk responses. The risk model is adjusted following further data gathering to include the effect of risk responses and actions. Repeating the analysis assists in understanding the effectiveness of planned responses.

Produce and interpret analytical outputs. The final outputs from the analysis present the range of possible outcomes, allowing assessment of the likelihood of achieving project objectives, and exposing the main risk drivers.

Decide on appropriate course of action and report results. The outputs produced should be carefully considered and the need for any resulting actions decided upon. Actions could include anything from completely restrategizing the project to minor adjustments to the logical sequence of the project's activities. As a final step in the process, a report is produced detailing the analysis, including the results obtained and any resultant decisions or recommended changes.

Quantitative Risk Analysis in the Project Life Cycle

Like project risk management in general, quantitative analysis can be used at any time in the project life cycle. A number of points in the project are particularly appropriate for a quantitative analysis as part of the ATOM process. Quantitative risk analysis within ATOM uses information from the qualitative assessment, and therefore cannot be performed before the Assessment step. The various places in the project life cycle where quantitative risk analysis is undertaken are described in the following paragraphs.

Preproject. In the case of a client organization, a quantitative analysis of the data included in the business case is carried out before the project is approved or sanctioned in order to determine the risk associated with the project. This provides important data to inform key project decisions before the project even starts.

For contractor organizations, a quantitative analysis assists in deciding whether to bid by determining the most likely duration or outturn cost and comparing this with the client's requirements. Based on this result, an informed decision can be made on whether to bid, at what price, and with what contingency.

Project start. As soon as the project is approved, the feasibility of the plan is tested and, as a result, a more a robust plan developed. In doing this, further insight is gained on the main risk areas and how they can be managed.

At regular intervals during the project life cycle. The Risk Management Plan defines the review cycle of the project, and for large projects this includes a series of Major Reviews. Each Major Review should update the analysis using the risk model set up during the first quantitative risk analysis, to reflect the current project strategy and status, as well as current levels of risk exposure.

At a major change. The ATOM process includes a Major Review whenever a major change occurs on a large project; this review should also include a quantitative analysis to determine the change in risk exposure resulting from the project change.

Quantitative Risk Analysis in the ATOM Process
Quantitative risk analysis depends on information generated by the Assessment step. The results of quantitative risk analysis inform Response Planning. However, it is also valuable to use the risk model to predict the effect of planned responses on risk exposure, so the quantitative risk analysis should be repeated after these have been defined. Indeed, the results of the post-response analysis may reveal that additional response planning is required. This means that quantitative risk analysis is intertwined within the various steps of the ATOM process, as shown in Figure 15-2.

Getting Started
A number of inputs are required prior to starting a quantitative risk analysis for a project:

- The project critical path network and/or CBS

- The fully populated project Risk Register—this might not include all planned responses depending on where in the ATOM process quantitative analysis is being undertaken

- Quantitative risk analysis software tool

Conducting quantitative risk analysis is impossible without using a software tool. Some organizations have developed bespoke tools for quantitative risk analysis, but there are many such tools available on the market, and it is usually better to buy one. However, care should be exercised when deciding which tool to use. Factors to consider when selecting a tool include:

- Ensure that the tool can support the generic ATOM process.

- Determine specific functionality, including support for schedule risk analysis, cost risk analysis, or integrated risk analysis.

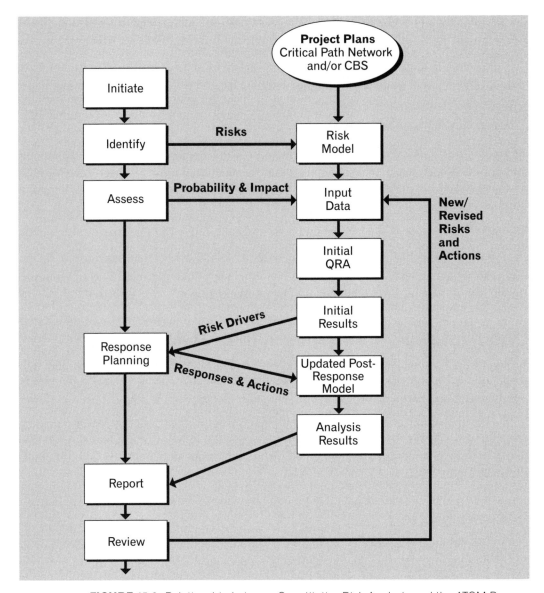

FIGURE 15-2: Relationship between Quantitative Risk Analysis and the ATOM Process

• If quantitative analysis is required, determine additional functionality, including support for different distribution types, stochastic branching, and correlation.

• Consider integration issues to ensure that risk tools can be used seamlessly with other project scheduling and estimating tools.

• Review ability to produce required reports and outputs and how easily these can be customized.

• Identify user base, whether individuals, multiuser, or multisite.

• Consider training needs and how training will be achieved.

• Ensure that appropriate support is available.

- Build in growth potential.

- Choose a tool that does what you do or what you want to do. Do not allow the tool to dictate or change the risk management process that has been adopted.

Who needs to be involved?

A number of key people need to be involved in the quantitative analysis, including the risk champion, project manager, project sponsor, risk owners, and project support staff (such as planning engineers, cost engineers, or estimators). As with other aspects of the ATOM risk process, the risk champion takes the lead in performing quantitative analysis, though some organizations might use a specialist risk analyst skilled in statistical modeling and using quantitative analysis software tools to support the risk champion.

Creating the initial model(s)

The risk champion prepares the initial risk model(s) in liaison with the project support staff and risk analyst (where present), and validates the model with the project manager.

It is theoretically possible to carry out Monte Carlo analysis using a risk model containing many hundreds of items, and quantitative risk analysis tools are able to process these vast amounts of data. However, large numbers of elements in a risk model create two problems: the overhead of generating input data and statistical issues arising from complex models. It is therefore best to keep the number of elements in a risk model to a minimum number that reflects a realistic representation of the project. For most projects, including large ones, this should be less than 100, though up to 200 elements can be required for very complex projects. Where the complexity of a large project cannot be accommodated in a smaller number of risk model elements, it is usually possible to split the model into a number of smaller submodels for analysis, and then combine the results later, thus keeping the overall number of elements to less than 200.

When creating risk models, it is important that they encompass all uncertain areas of the project. For a schedule risk analysis the starting point is the project schedule, and a cost risk analysis starts from the CBS. However, the full detail in the starting schedule or CBS might not be required for a quantitative risk analysis. Detail should be kept in or added to the risky areas of the project as determined from the risk breakdown structure (RBS) and work breakdown structure (WBS) mapping undertaken during the qualitative risk assessment step. Less risky areas of the plan (for example, routine review meetings or regular reporting) can be summarized to reduce the level of detail.

There may be some areas of the project where the precise detail of the work is not yet fully defined, or where different options exist. A risk model can include alternative logic elements to reflect the uncertainty relating to future decisions. This is done using stochastic branches, either probabilistic or conditional, to model optional activities that might be required under certain circumstances. Figures 15-3 and 15-4 give examples of these branches.

Planning permission is required for the project to proceed. However planning permission is only approved without comment on 50% of occasions. 40% of the time planning will be approved subject to amendments. 10% of the time planning will be rejected and plans will need to be revised and resubmitted.

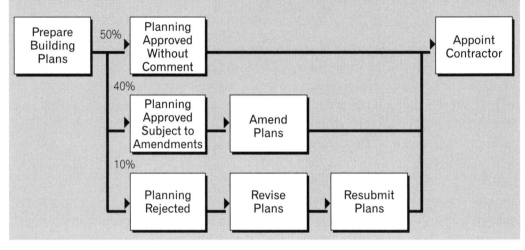

FIGURE 15-3: Probabilistic Branching

The procurement strategy for the project is based on the use of competitive tendering and the use of contractors. However, it is recognized that this approach must not delay the project. Therefore, two alternative strategies have been determined. If the initial design is not approved until after July 1st but before July 31st, a contract will be negotiated with a preferred supplier. If the initial design is not approved until after July 31st, then an in-house design team will be assembled.

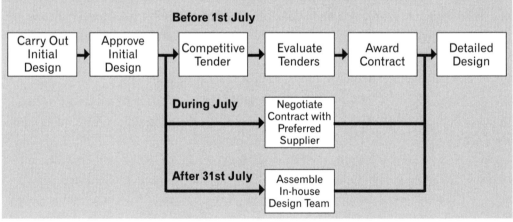

FIGURE 15-4: Conditional Branching

Mapping risks to model

Once the initial risk model has been prepared, the risks contained in the Risk Register are mapped to schedule activities or spreadsheet budget items. Some risks will map on a one-to-one basis, i.e., one risk affects only one activity or budget item, whereas other more generic risks might apply to several activities or budget items.

Some key risks in the Risk Register might not map clearly to existing elements in the risk model, particularly where such risks describe unusual events outside the planned activities. These risks may be included in the risk model using stochastic branches (usually

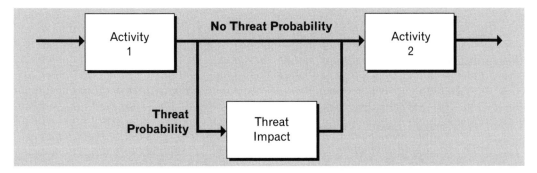

FIGURE 15-5: Modeling Threats with Probabilistic Branching

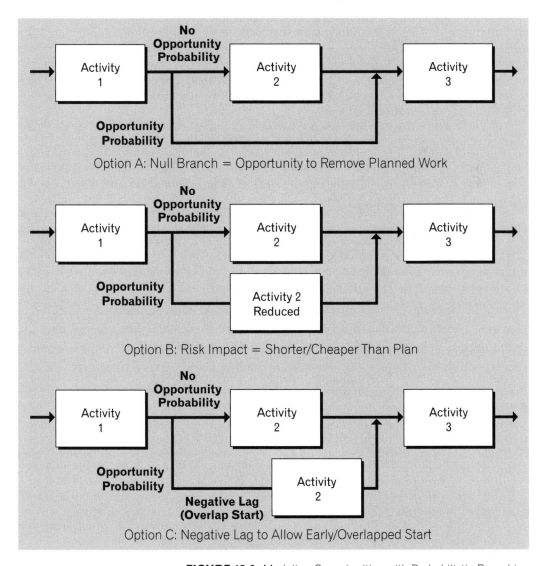

FIGURE 15-6: Modeling Opportunities with Probabilistic Branching

probabilistic). Examples of using branches to model both threats and opportunities in this way are illustrated in Figures 15-5 and 15-6.

Finally, risks will likely be in the Risk Register that are not included in the scope of the quantitative risk analysis, and these exclusions should be recorded. These may include "acts of God," or risks that have an extremely low probability, or risks where the impact is so low that there is little point in modeling them.

The risk champion records the mapping of risks to risk model elements, because this is a key input to the quantitative risk analysis. A suggested form for this is presented in Figure 15-7, where risk mapping is recorded using the left-hand four columns.

ACTIVITY	PLAN VALUE	MAPPED OPPORTUNITIES	MAPPED THREATS	MIN	ML	MAX	Distribution Type	Correlation Group

FIGURE 15-7: Example Risk Mapping Form

Correlation groups

The default condition for a Monte Carlo analysis is to assume total randomness for all uncertain variables throughout the risk model. This does not, however, reflect reality, as there are many internal influences within a risk model. Two activities might be influenced by the same risk, or one element might directly influence others. This needs to be reflected in the risk model using correlation groups.

Failure to include correlation in a risk model allows elements to vary independently, when in reality this would not be the case. For example, if the risk "contractor productivity may be significantly less than planned" was mapped to several activities in the risk model, then we should expect productivity for all activities on which the contractor was working to be similar. Absence of correlation reduces the spread of results calculated during the analysis, with random uncertainty in uncorrelated elements canceling out. In reality, risks are interdependent, and planned activities are also related. These relationships must be included in the risk model, creating correlation groups to link activities and risks that can affect each other. Such links might be driven by the existence of common causes or external dependencies, or where a single risk affects several elements of the model. In these cases the Monte Carlo tool's ability to sample randomly must be constrained.

A correlation group identifies elements in the model where sampled values are related, either positively or negatively, using a correlation coefficient (between −1 and +1, or from −100% to +100%) to model the strength of the relationship. In the absence of better data, it is common to use values of 0.7 or 0.8 (70% or 80%).

The risk champion identifies potential correlation groups, based on the following:

- Elements in the risk model affected by linked risks (using the RBS)

- Tasks performed by a common resource (using the organizational breakdown structure (OBS))

- Similar types of tasks (using the WBS)

- Generic risks affecting multiple risk model elements

- Causal relationships between risk model elements

Allocation of tasks to correlation groups can be recorded in the right-hand column of the risk mapping form (see example in Figure 15-7).

Initial data gathering

Once the initial risk model(s) have been created, the risk champion (and risk analyst) work with nominated risk owners to confirm risk mapping and ensure that the structure of the model is realistic. This can be done either in a workshop or a series of interviews. risk owners also comment on the use of branches and correlation groups in areas of the risk model relating to their areas of responsibility.

The risk champion and risk owners must then prepare distributions for risk model elements, reflecting the risks mapped to each element. The most common distribution type is the three-point estimate, which can be derived using a simple approach based on making adjustments from the current planned value, as illustrated in Figure 15-8. A three-point estimate (credible minimum, most likely, and credible maximum) is usually represented using a modified trian-

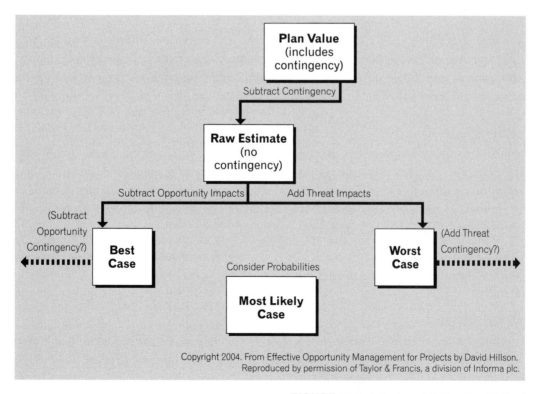

FIGURE 15-8: Adjustment Estimating Method

gular distribution (see below). If the quantitative risk analysis includes the effect of planned responses, the input distributions must reflect this. A three-point estimate derived in this way can be recorded in the right-hand columns of the risk mapping form (Figure 15-7).

In some cases it might not be possible or appropriate to use the three-point estimate, so other distributions may be used. The ones most commonly used are shown in Figure 15-9 and briefly described below. Use of one of these distribution types to model the effect of risks on a task in the risk model can be recorded on the risk mapping form (Figure 15-7).

MODIFIED TRIANGULAR OR TRIGEN

The modified triangular distribution is a continuous distribution representing the three-point estimate. This distribution is most widely used in risk models, since it recognizes estimating uncertainty by requiring minimum and maximum values that are not absolute values. It is common to assume a 5 percent chance that the minimum value will be exceeded and a 5 percent chance of the maximum being exceeded. These percentiles may be changed to represent different levels of uncertainty in the estimate.

UNIFORM DISTRIBUTION

A uniform distribution is a continuous distribution where it is possible only to estimate minimum and maximum values. This is typically used when there is considerable uncertainty over the duration of an activity or the value of a budget item, and therefore a most-likely value cannot be estimated.

CURVES

A variety of curves can represent the distribution of uncertainty around a risk model element. The most commonly used curves are normal, beta, and lognormal (shown in Figure 15-9). Although they are clearly more realistic representations of uncertainty, these curves are hard to define and so they should only be used when there is good information on the variability of a particular risk model element.

DISCRETE OR SPIKE

Sometimes a risk model element can only take particular values, i.e., it is not a continuous distribution. These are known as discrete or spike distributions and should be used when there are only a fixed number of possible values and where other values cannot exist; for example, if an approval committee meets once a week, a decision can only be made after one or two or three weeks, but at no time in between.

Once all consultation has taken place, the risk champion produces the final risk model(s), which is then validated by the project manager.

Analysis

Analysis takes place in two discrete stages. The initial analysis uses the model in its raw state without any consideration for planned responses or actions that might change the project's risk exposure. The second stage repeats the process, usually more than once, taking into account planned responses and actions.

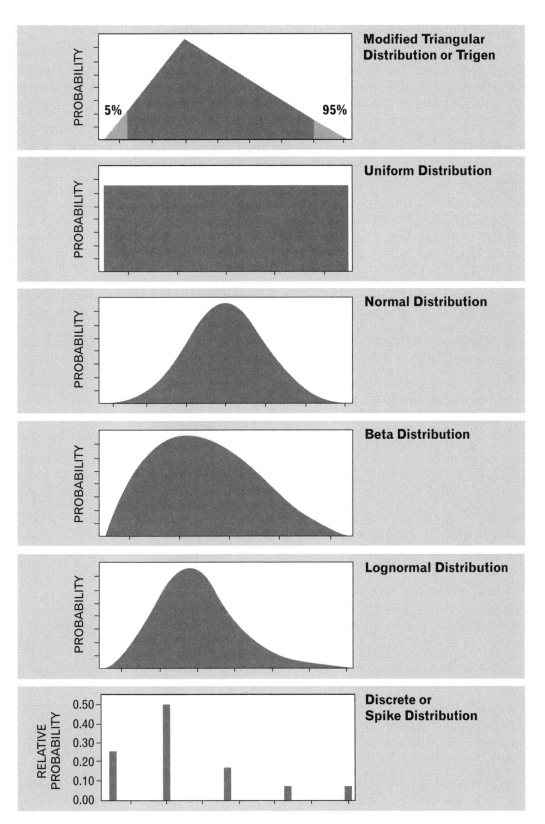

FIGURE 15-9: Typical Distributions Used in Monte Carlo Analysis

Initial analysis

Once the model has been completed it is analyzed or "run" using the Monte Carlo tool to randomly sample from the input data (both distributions and stochastic branches) and calculate the range of possible outcomes. Quantitative risk analysis tools can process large amounts of data very quickly, so the number of iterations necessary to achieve good results is almost irrelevant. Typically 10,000 iterations are used to ensure that all possible outcomes are sampled in a complex risk model, but this can be reduced significantly if the model is relatively simple—perhaps to only 1,000 iterations. Results from the initial analysis are used to check the validity of the model, including any input errors.

Secondary data gathering and secondary analysis

The data in the risk model is adjusted by carrying out data-gathering interviews with risk owners. The focus of these interviews is to determine where values for individual model activities and other parameters such as stochastic branches might have changed as a result of the actions that are to be implemented. Repeating the analysis with this revised data provides a prediction of the expected effectiveness of planned responses in improving the overall risk exposure of the project.

Upon completion of the analysis most computer tools will produce a number of standard outputs or reports.

OUTPUTS: THE S-CURVE

The main output from a Monte Carlo analysis is a cumulative probabilistic distribution function known as the S-curve. This might be supported by a histogram that presents the incidence with which each particular result was obtained. The S-curve allows analysis of the combined effect of both estimating uncertainty and explicit risks on objectives. S-curves can be created that relate, in the case of schedule risk analysis, to the completion of the overall project, interim milestones, subprojects, or major activities; in cost risk analysis they can be produced for the final outturn cost or the cost of major budgetary items or subprojects. Examples of S-curves for time and cost can be seen in Figure 15-10.

OUTPUTS: CRITICALITY ANALYSIS

A number of other outputs can be obtained from the Monte Carlo analysis that give additional information in more detail than the S-curve. The first relates only to quantitative analysis of schedule risk, and is known as criticality analysis. A schedule has at least one critical path, which is the longest route from beginning to end and determines the overall project duration. During a schedule risk analysis, however, the Monte Carlo simulator makes multiple runs through the plan, randomly varying activity durations according to the input data that reflects the uncertainty and mapped risks. Some activities will take longer than the original planned duration while others will be shorter. As a result, the critical path will almost certainly vary during the analysis because previously critical activities might be completed in a shorter time while noncritical activities are extended. In fact, during the many iterations of a risk model a number of alternative critical paths might be followed.

For each activity in the risk model, it is possible to calculate a criticality index, defined as the

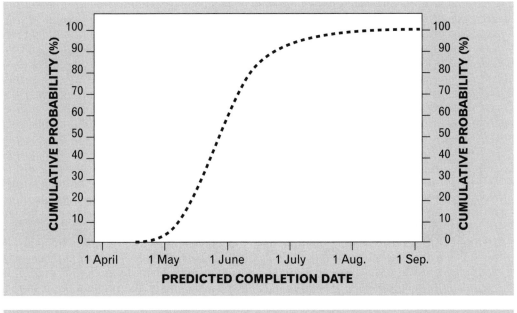

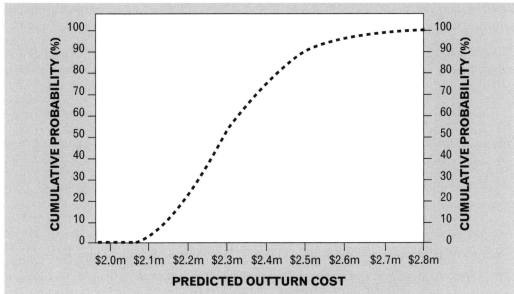

FIGURE 15-10: Example S-Curves for Time and Cost

number of times that an activity appears on the critical path, and usually expressed as a percentage of the total number of iterations. Therefore, an activity that is always critical has a criticality index of 100 percent, while one that can never be on the critical path has zero criticality. The activities of interest are those with criticality between 1 and 99 percent, as they might become critical under certain circumstances. Ranking activities by criticality index highlights those activities most likely to drive the overall duration and completion date, and therefore require focused risk management attention. By concentrating on the threats and opportunities mapped against high-criticality activities, the degree of schedule risk can be reduced effectively. A sample criticality analysis diagram is shown in Figure 15-11.

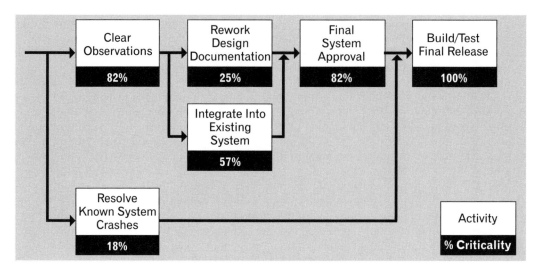

FIGURE 15-11: Example Criticality Analysis Diagram

OUTPUTS: CRUCIALITY ANALYSIS

Another useful analysis of detailed risk drivers relates the degree of variability in a particular element of the risk model with the variation in the overall project outcome. Termed *cruciality*, it can be applied to both schedule and cost risk analysis, expressed as a correlation coefficient (between −1 and +1) indicating the relationship between each activity or risk and the total outcome.

Elements with high cruciality (sometimes referred to as sensitivity) are key drivers of risk, because a large change in the element produces a correspondingly large change in the overall outcome. This is equally true of both threats and opportunities, since highly crucial threats have a large adverse effect on the overall project, while highly crucial opportunities have the biggest overall upside impact.

As in the case of criticality analysis, elements in the risk model can be ranked by cruciality to indicate which are the most significant causes of risk to the overall result. This information is often presented graphically as a tornado chart to highlight the major risk drivers. Schedule activities, cost items, or risks with high cruciality should be treated with priority when determining areas for further risk management attention and action. An example tornado chart can be seen in Figure 15-12.

OUTPUTS: EYEBALL PLOT

If an integrated schedule-cost risk analysis has been undertaken then one further output is normally available, known as an eyeball plot. The eyeball on the plot encloses all possible outcomes of the project by plotting the project's predicted completion date against its predicted cost. The minimum duration and cost, maximum duration and cost, and the most likely duration and cost are plotted. The eyeball represents all the possible outcomes. The larger the eyeball the greater the uncertainty in the project; see Figure 15-13.

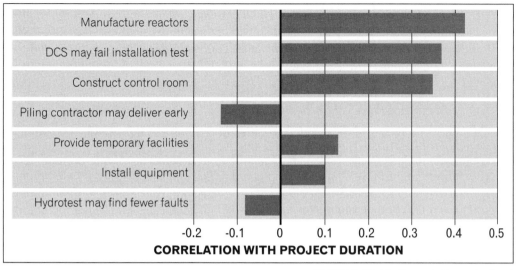

FIGURE 15-12: Example Tornado Chart

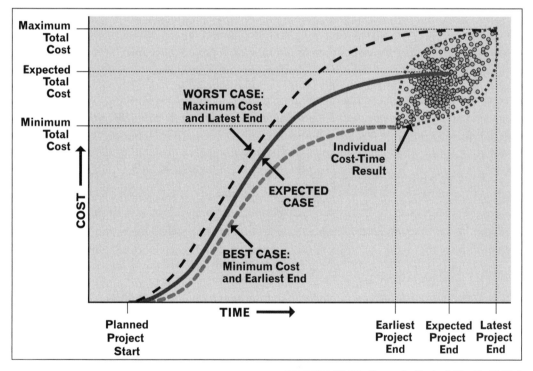

FIGURE 15-13: Example Eyeball (Football) Plot

Interpreting Outputs

The basic or standard S-curves can be used to understand the range of possible outcomes for any objective: The greater the range the more uncertain the outcome. Values can also be read from the S-curve corresponding to a particular percentage likelihood that these will be achieved. Commonly-used values include the 10th, 50th and 90th percentiles (P10, P50, P90). These can also be described as confidence levels, because they represent the chance of meeting a specific value. In particular, the degree of confidence that objectives might be achieved can be expressed as a percentage. The mean value represents the expected outcome given the input data with the level of risk included in the model. Proper interpretation of S-curves can assist in the determination of appropriate contingency levels for both time and cost. Finally, the overall project risk can be assessed using an S-curve because it reflects the extent of uncertainty in the project (from the range of possible results between best case and worst case), and indicates the degree of confidence associated with achieving project targets.

Overlapping S-curves can be prepared that represent the risk model without risk responses included, and including all responses or individual responses on a progressive basis. A series of such S-curves can be overlaid to show the effect of addressing specific risks one at a time as well as the effect of responding to all risks. These are often referred to as "onion ring diagrams" (as described in Chapter 14 and shown in Figure 14-10).

Criticality indices can be used to determine which activities might become critical if risk is unmanaged. The project manager should concentrate on activities with highest criticality, exploring the underlying reasons for this, determining the main risk drivers, and developing actions to address the subcritical paths.

Tornado diagrams based on cruciality can be used to target the individual risk model elements (activities or risks) that have the most effect on overall project outcomes. Reducing the variability in these has a direct effect on the uncertainty of the project.

An eyeball plot gives a view of the overall project risk. The larger the eyeball, the greater the overall uncertainty in project outcome. Depending on the scales used, the angle of the eyeball indicates whether the project is more susceptible to time risk or cost risk. Assuming that the horizontal (x) axis represents time and the vertical (y) axis represents cost, then the closer the eyeball is oriented towards the horizontal the more time risk is prevalent, and the closer it is oriented towards the vertical the greater the cost risk. It is possible to overlay eyeball plots from different risk analyses to demonstrate changes in risk exposure as the project proceeds. An example is shown in Figure 15-14, which indicates how the chance of achieving project targets improves with time.

Using Results

The results from quantitative risk analysis can inform key decisions throughout the project life cycle. The results can provide vital information when deciding whether the project should be undertaken at all or whether a bid should be submitted. Results can also play a significant part in selecting or modifying the project's implementation strategy.

If the results of the analysis suggest that there is very little chance of achieving a key project objective, such as the project's estimated completion date or outturn cost, this does not necessarily mean that all is lost. The project manager, in conjunction with the project team, should consider how to increase the chance, perhaps by changing the project's strategy, reducing its scope, or modifying performance requirements.

The results of the analysis can also focus on the key risks (i.e., the worst threats and best opportunities) where management action will be of the greatest benefit. In addition, the main risk drivers can be identified, namely those with the highest criticality and/or cruciality, allow-

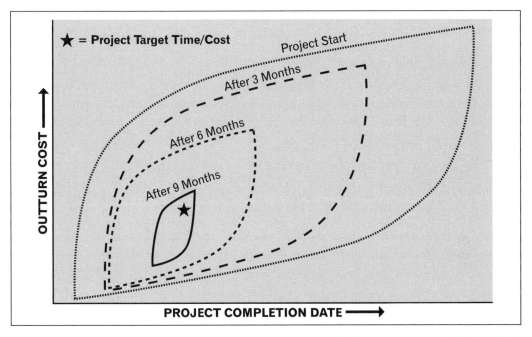

FIGURE 15-14: Overlaid Eyeball Plots

ing development of responses to tackle these as a matter of priority.

Using analysis results also helps in determining the effectiveness of planned responses by comparing analysis results pre- and post-response, perhaps with an onion ring diagram. This again helps to focus attention and may lead to a change in response strategy if the predicted effect of planned responses is not sufficiently significant.

One of the many distinct benefits of risk management is the setting of realistic and achievable targets. The results of quantitative analysis can be used to set overall and interim targets/milestones and appropriate levels of contingency. This is especially useful when using quantitative risk analysis pre-project. Different targets can be set, including stretch targets with a lower (but not impossible) chance of achievement to motivate and challenge the project team to higher levels of performance.

Finally, analyzing changes in risk exposure associated with proposed major changes aids in deciding whether the change should be accepted or not; if the change cannot be rejected then the effect it will have on project objectives with and without further responses will be understood.

Reporting

The final outputs from a quantitative analysis are generally presented either in a standalone risk analysis report, or included as a subsection of the full risk report that follows either the First Risk Assessment or a Major Review. In either case, the following contents should be addressed:

- **Executive summary.** This summarizes the key findings, main conclusions, and recommendations from the main body of the report in at most a single page, omitting all unnecessary detail.

- **Purpose, scope, and objectives of this quantitative risk analysis.** The main purpose of the analysis is described, highlighting its place in the risk process.

- **Project status summary.** (If this is a subsection, it will already have been included in the main body of the report.) This section briefly summarizes the current status of the project, including progress against the project schedule and budget, delivery of products, major issues that have arisen, etc. This summary sets the context within which the risk analysis was undertaken.

- **Key findings.** The chance of meeting targets (e.g., schedule and cost objectives) along with the main risk drivers. In addition, anything particularly unusual in the results is discussed and the underlying reasons are described.

- **Detailed results.** S-curves are presented first since these are the main analytical output. Interpretation of the S-curves includes the range of possible outcomes, the expected values for completion date and outturn cost, and the likelihood of achieving project targets. Onion ring overlays of S-curves determine main risk drivers, as do tornado charts, criticality diagrams, cruciality diagrams, and eyeball plots. Pre-response and post-response analyses are presented and discussed to indicate the effectiveness of planned responses, with recommendations on whether additional response planning is required. Each type of output is presented in this section with its own analysis and commentary, highlighting any notable features of the results or anything requiring particular management attention.

- **Conclusions and recommendations.** Summary of what was found and what should be done. Based on the interpretation of outputs, the recommended responses and actions required to maximize the chances of project success are listed and discussed.

- **Appendices.** These present supporting information and other detail not included in the main body of the report, and may include:

  - **Mapping information and model data.** Details of how risks were mapped into the project plan or cost estimate, and the resulting input data generated for use in the risk model.

  - **Detailed outputs.** The body of the report includes the main analytical outputs, but more detailed supporting outputs, such as statistical tables, might be included in an appendix.

  - **Background information.** Any assumptions or exclusions made during the quantitative risk analysis are listed, together with any special conditions or characteristics of the project that influenced the risk analysis.

  - **Risk Register.** For a standalone risk analysis report, it may be useful to include the Risk Register in an appendix for reference purposes.

Conclusion

The steps required to perform quantitative risk analysis within the ATOM process are summarized in Figure 15-15. Quantitative risk analysis (QRA) plays a key part in the overall risk management process for a large project. Some view it as optional icing on the cake, while to others it is the essential be all and end all of risk management. In ATOM, quantitative risk analysis has a more pragmatic place: it is not needed on all projects, rarely used on small projects, optional for medium-size projects, but usually required for large projects, where the stakes are inevitably higher.

There are undoubtedly benefits available from using quantitative risk analysis, though these come at a cost, which is usually only justifiable for large projects. This is why ATOM requires these techniques only for projects where the investment in quantitative risk analysis is likely to provide a valuable return.

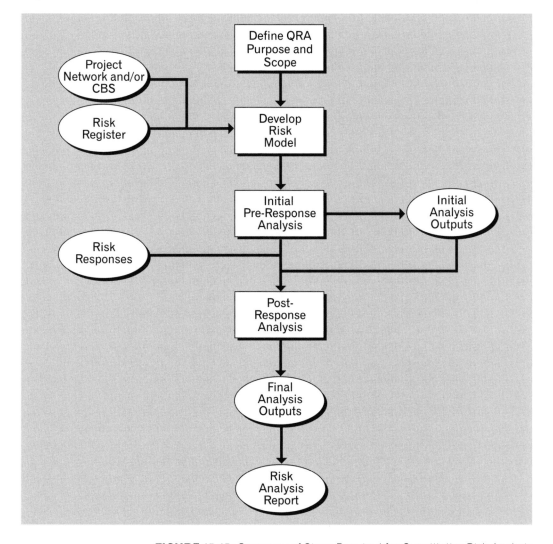

FIGURE 15-15: Summary of Steps Required for Quantitative Risk Analysis

Next Steps

The ATOM process presents a pragmatic perspective on project risk management that was produced by practitioners for practitioners. The emphasis is on what works, with a simple framework and practical guidelines on how to use proven tools and techniques.

This final chapter covers how to take the basic ATOM process out of the book and into practical application in the workplace. It answers the question, "Okay, so I've read the book—now what shall I do?" A number of steps are recommended, as summarized in Figure E-1. As with everything else about ATOM, these steps are simple and pragmatic, and based on the wide experience of multiple practitioners over many years.

Step 1: Appoint an Organizational Risk Sponsor

One of the key Critical Success Factors (CSFs) discussed in Chapter 2 is a supportive organization. One expression of this is the appointment of an organizational risk sponsor to lead the introduction of risk management into the business. Ideally this is a senior manager with broad experience across the organization and who is widely respected at all levels. He or she also needs to have a reasonable working knowledge of the risk process and a clear vision of the place of risk management in the organization. This key individual must have the time and energy to commit to making risk management effective across the business, working with others in the organization as required. The organizational risk sponsor manages the introduction of risk management, and requires the authority to define and implement the necessary changes, and the ability to engage staff at all levels to cooperate with the initiative.

This person's appointment should be announced widely throughout the organization so people know what is expected of both the organizational risk sponsor and themselves.

Step 2: Tailor the ATOM Process

A main attraction of ATOM is that it is applicable to any project of any size in any industry or business sector, meeting the requirement of the CSF for a scalable process (see Chapter 2). The ATOM process can be tailored based on project size, and is presented here in three versions:

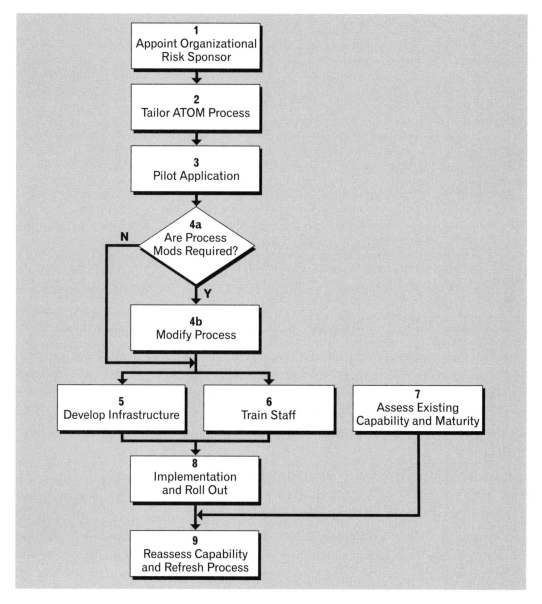

FIGURE E-1: Recommended Next Steps

1. A reduced ATOM process suitable for small projects, integrating risk activities into the routine management of the project with minimal additional overhead

2. The standard ATOM process for medium projects, adding specific risk activities to the normal project process

3. An extended ATOM process for large projects, using quantitative risk analysis and a more rigorous review cycle to address the increased risk challenge

However, projects come in all shapes and sizes, and expecting them all to fit neatly into three categories is somewhat simplistic. As a result, most organizations will find it necessary to customize ATOM to meet their particular needs, though some will be able to apply the small, medium, or large versions directly.

Tailoring the ATOM process requires a review of the types of projects typically undertaken by the organization. A standard project sizing tool should be developed (as described in Chapter 3), and used to assess a wide range of previous projects. This gives an indication of the distribution of projects between the ATOM categories of small, medium, and large. The version of the ATOM process corresponding to the largest concentration of projects should be used as a starting point for a tailored risk process. For example, if 70 percent of the organization's projects are in the small category, that should form the basis for the tailored process.

Starting from one of the three ATOM variants, the process is reviewed by a representative group of project stakeholders, led by the organizational risk sponsor, and process modifications are made as required. These might include changing some of the techniques recommended in the standard ATOM variant, or modifying the reporting requirement, or making specific role allocations for the risk process. This should result in production of an organization-specific risk management process based on one of the three versions of ATOM, but reflecting the needs of most of the projects most of the time. This tailored process can be used as the baseline for managing risk on the majority of projects, though the organization should aim to have all three variants available to deal with their small, medium, and large projects.

Having customized the ATOM process in this way, a set of process documentation is produced following the organization's documentation standards.

Step 3: Pilot Application

The tailored version of the ATOM risk process should be piloted on a typical project to validate its appropriateness, demonstrate its applicability to the specific business of the organization, and deliver the benefits to the pilot project. The process can then be refined in the light of the pilot experience. The pilot project should be carefully chosen to be representative of the majority of projects undertaken by the organization. It is important to ensure the full commitment of all project stakeholders in using their project as a pilot for the risk process, because lack of buy-in can jeopardize a successful implementation. A short briefing for project stakeholders from the organizational risk sponsor is useful for introducing the process, clarifying the tools and techniques to be used, and emphasizing the importance of the pilot.

Facilitating the risk process on the pilot project might require external support, perhaps from other parts of the organization skilled in risk management, or from outside consultants.

The pilot project should implement the tailored risk process in full, following the process documentation closely. All project stakeholders are encouraged to take a full and active role in the process, and to note any areas of difficulty that might require modification after the pilot stage is complete.

Step 4: Modify Process (if required)

At the end of the pilot project (or at a suitable interim milestone), the organizational risk sponsor conducts a review meeting, which is attended by key project stakeholders. This meeting reviews the tailored ATOM risk process as actually implemented on the pilot project, and considers all comments from those involved. If possible, decisions are made in the meeting regarding required changes to the risk process. Following the review meeting the organizational risk sponsor settles any outstanding issues, and then ensures that agreed changes are incorporated into the process documentation.

Step 5: Develop Infrastructure

Once the tailored ATOM risk process has been piloted and reviewed, and any agreed changes have been fully documented, the organization must ensure that the infrastructure necessary to support the risk process is provided. Chapter 2 indicates that appropriate methods, tools, and techniques are another CSF for effective risk management, and these must be present if implementation of the risk process is to work.

A key area of infrastructure is the provision of software tools to support the various steps of the risk process. As discussed in Chapter 2, a prerequisite for this is determining the level of implementation required by the organization, which is decided via the pilot project step. For a simple implementation, the organization might decide to support the risk process using basic spreadsheets and risk databases. More complex implementations might justify purchase of a dedicated risk software package, though this should be done with care, considering selection criteria in advance (including those outlined in Chapter 15 for quantitative risk analysis tools) and scoring each candidate package against the requirement. The organizational risk sponsor decides which tools are appropriate, and arranges for their provision.

Another important aspect of infrastructure is developing suitable templates for the risk process. ATOM provides a range of generic templates in Appendices A and B that can either be used directly or modified to meet the specific requirements of the organization's tailored risk process. The organization should produce a range of templates, including the following:

- Risk Management Plan
- Risk Register
- Risk checklist
- Risk breakdown structure (or prompt list)
- Risk reports

These templates should be made widely available for use by all projects across the organization, perhaps via an intranet or shared knowledge database.

Having decided on tools and templates, attention must be given to how these will integrate into other systems and processes, particularly those used for routine project management. It is important for risk management to be a fully integrated part of how projects are managed. The interfaces between the risk infrastructure and the rest of the project support system largely determine how successfully this is achieved.

Step 6: Train Staff

The final CSF detailed in Chapter 2 is the need for competent people to perform the risk process, operate the tools and techniques, and make appropriate risk-based decisions. As a result, staff training is an important element of implementing a tailored ATOM process. This training should be developed specifically around the organization's customized ATOM process.

A variety of stakeholders participate in the risk process, and each requires a different type of training. A multilayered training program should be developed, with targeted messages to each stakeholder group at a range of levels depending on their responsibilities within the risk process. This might include different types of training for senior managers (benefits awareness), project/program managers (risk process management), project team members (risk process implementation), and risk specialists such as risk champions and risk analysts (risk skills training). Ongoing mentoring and coaching may also be necessary to resolve issues as they arise and to provide implementation assistance.

If the organization has in-house training capability, it should be engaged to provide the required training; otherwise, suitable external support should be sought.

Step 7: Assess Existing Risk Management Capability

Prior to full implementation and rollout of ATOM, the organization assesses its existing level of risk management capability and maturity. This assessment provides a baseline against which improvement in the organization's ability to manage risk will be measured.

Several tools are available to assess general project management capability, and some of these include project risk management. It is better to use a specific risk management assessment framework, such as the Risk Maturity Model (RMM). This model assesses the project risk management capability of an organization against four attributes (culture, process, experience, application), and places the organization on a spectrum with four levels of maturity (naïve, novice, normalized, natural). A similar assessment can be conducted for subsets of the organization, such as a department or project team.

This assessment of organizational risk management capability and maturity is used to define the starting point for introducing ATOM into the organization, and the assessment is repeated afterwards to demonstrate the results of the implementation.

Step 8: Implementation and Rollout

The agreed customized ATOM risk process as documented within the organization's quality system is then implemented on all projects and across the business, led and supported by the organizational risk sponsor, who notes early experiences in order to capture lessons to be learned and enable ongoing development of the process.

A structured communication campaign is recommended, led by the organizational risk sponsor, taking the message of project risk management throughout the organization, and encouraging everyone to play their part. The specific details of this campaign depend on the nature of the organization, but it should focus on sharing the principles, processes, and benefits of the adopted approach to managing risk on projects. It might include some or all of the following components:

- Senior management awareness briefings

- Road show presentations

- Articles in company publications and newsletters

- Items on the organization's external web site and intranet

- Workplace posters and leaflets

- Special promotions

During the rollout it should be emphasized that the organization wishes to continue to learn as progressively more experience is gained with implementing risk management on various projects. A feedback mechanism is put in place to receive constructive criticism and positive suggestions for improvement from staff who are starting to use risk management on their projects. The organizational risk sponsor ensures that all feedback is considered and acted on appropriately, and that originators of suggestions are kept informed of the progress of their comments.

Step 9: Reassess Capability and Refresh Process

After a period of implementation (perhaps 6 to 12 months), the level of risk management capability and maturity is reassessed, using the same framework described in Step 7, in order to demonstrate improvements and indicate areas requiring continued attention. Immediate adjustments are made as required to ensure maximal risk management effectiveness, with consequential changes to risk procedures, tools, templates, and training.

In addition, it is recommended that every organization refresh its approach to risk management after approximately two to three years, to ensure that staff remain motivated and committed to proactive management of the risks facing their projects. The organizational risk sponsor leads a structured review, addressing all aspects of risk management on projects (and possibly more widely), and identifying areas requiring adjustment or improvement. For example, new risk techniques or refresher risk training for key staff might be considered.

Conclusion

While a simple scalable process such as Active Threat and Opportunity Management (ATOM) offers a robust framework for management of risks on projects, any organization serious about risk management needs to do more than just blindly follow a process. The steps outlined in this epilogue assist in applying the generic ATOM approach to the specific risk challenge faced by a particular organization.

Risk management is not difficult, because it is simply structured common sense. By taking the steps described here and implementing ATOM across the full range of projects conducted by the organization, the undoubted benefits of effective risk management can be reaped, leading to increased predictability of project outcomes, more successful projects, enhanced customer satisfaction, improved team motivation, reduced waste, increased profit, and clear competitive advantage. ATOM offers the means to manage project risk and meet the challenge of uncertainty; using it guarantees improved success.

Templates and Examples

<TEMPLATE> RISK MANAGEMENT PLAN FOR THE <PROJECT-NAME> PROJECT

Prepared by: <Project Manager>

Approved by: <Project Sponsor>

Reference: <>   Version: <>   Date: <>

INTRODUCTION

This document is the Risk Management Plan for the <project-name> project, defining the risk management process to be employed throughout the life of this project. The project manager is responsible for reviewing and maintaining this Risk Management Plan throughout the project to ensure that the risk process remains appropriate to deal with the level of risk faced by the project.

PROJECT DESCRIPTION AND OBJECTIVES

<Brief description of the project, including its background and purpose>

The scope and objectives for the <project-name> Project are summarized as follows:

- <list all objectives, including time, cost, scope, quality, performance, functionality, reputation, business benefits, safety, etc.>

<Comment on relative prioritization of project objectives>

AIMS, SCOPE, AND OBJECTIVES OF RISK PROCESS

The <project-name> project risk management process aims to manage all foreseeable risks (both opportunities and threats) in a manner that is proactive, effective, and appropriate, in order to maximize the likelihood of the project achieving its objectives, while maintaining risk exposure at an acceptable level.

"Acceptable risk" is defined for the <project-name> project as <clear definition of how much risk is acceptable to key stakeholders such as the project sponsor, perhaps in terms of how many "high" threats can be present in the project, or maximum acceptable Threat P-I Score and minimum acceptable Opportunity P-I Score, or extent of allowable delay or additional cost>.

The risk process will aim to engage all project stakeholders appropriately, creating ownership and buy-in to the project itself and also to risk management actions.

Risk-based information will be communicated to project stakeholders in a timely manner at an appropriate level of detail, to enable project strategy to be modified in the light of current risk exposure.

The risk management process will enable project stakeholders to focus attention on those areas of the project most at risk, by identifying the major risks (both opportunities and threats) potentially able to exert the greatest positive or negative influence on achievement of project objectives.

The risk management process covers all activities undertaken during the lifetime of the project.

<Clarify whether the risk process is intended to cover internal project risks only, or whether it

FIGURE A-1: Risk Management Plan Template

extends to supplier risks, corporate risks, program risks, business risks, etc. Also clarify what types of risk are included; for example, technical risks, commercial risks, management risks, external risks, etc. Consider using a risk breakdown structure (RBS) for this (see Appendix B). Where some sources or types of risk are excluded, state how these will be dealt with if they are identified.>

APPLICATION OF THE ATOM PROCESS

<Either refer to the standard ATOM process document, or summarize briefly the approach to be used, perhaps using text as below. Comment on whether or not the risk process is expected to include quantitative modeling. Detail the frequency with which the risk process will be updated.>

This project is considered to be <small, medium, or large> in accordance with the agreed project sizing tool. For this project a <reduced, standard, enhanced> ATOM process will be applied.

The following ATOM process will be used for the <project-name> project:

- Initiation: clarifying and recording objectives for the project being assessed, and defining the details of the risk process to be implemented, documenting the results in a Risk Management Plan

- Identification: exposing and documenting risks that might affect project objectives either positively or negatively

- Assessment: either qualitatively describing risks individually so they can be understood and prioritized, and/or quantitatively modeling the effect of risks on project outcome, to determine which areas of the project are most at risk

- Response Planning: determining appropriate strategies and actions to deal with identified risks, with a nominated owner to address each risk

- Reporting: communicating the dynamic status of risk on the project to all stakeholders

- Implementation: implementing agreed response strategies and actions and checking their effectiveness

- Review: updating the risk assessment at regular intervals through a series of major and minor reviews

- Post-Project Review: where lessons are learned for both the improvement of risk management and project management in general

The Initiation phase will be completed before the project commences, then the remaining steps in the risk process will be cyclic, repeated regularly throughout the life of the project. The First Risk Assessment will be completed within <> of project start, and reviews will be performed <weekly/monthly/trimonthly/etc.> thereafter. <Describe use and planned periodicity of major and minor reviews should be included here>.

RISK TOOLS AND TECHNIQUES

<List the tools and techniques to be used for the risk process, perhaps using the words below.>

The following tools and techniques will be used to support the risk management process on the <project-name> project:

- Initiation

  - Risk management plan (this document), issued at project start and reviewed regularly by the project manager during the project.

- Identification

FIGURE A-1: Risk Management Plan Template *(continued)*

- Risks (both threats and opportunities) will be identified using the following techniques:

  - Brainstorming with all members of the project team plus representatives of key suppliers

  - Analysis of all project assumptions and constraints, both implicit and explicit

  - Review of a standard risk checklist

  - Ad hoc identification of risks by project team members at any time during the project

  - Initial Risk Register to record identified risks for further assessment, following the standard format

- Assessment

  - Probability and impact assessment for each identified risk, using the project-specific scales defined in Appendix A

  - Double P-I matrix to prioritize risks for action, using the standard risk scoring calculations based on probability (P) and impact (I)

  - Top risk list for priority management attention

  - Risk categorization using the standard risk breakdown structure (see Appendix B) to identify patterns of exposure

  - Risk register update to include assessment data

- Response Planning

  - Response strategy selection as appropriate for each identified risk, including owner allocation

  - Identification of specific actions and action owners

  - Risk register update to include response data

- Reporting

  - Risk report to project sponsor and steering group/project board

  - Provision of ad-hoc reports to stakeholders and project team as required

- Implementation

  - Implementation of response strategies via their agreed actions

  - Monitoring of the effectiveness of agreed actions and updating of project plans

- Review (see section below on risk reporting)

  - Risk workshops as part of a major review to identify new risks, review progress on existing risks and agreed responses, and assess process effectiveness

  - Risk review meeting as part of minor review to identify new risks, review progress on existing risks and agreed responses

- Post-Project Review

  - A lessons-learned meeting to capture all lessons learned relating to risk management on the project

FIGURE A-1: Risk Management Plan Template *(continued)*

ORGANIZATION, ROLES, AND RESPONSIBILITIES FOR RISK MANAGEMENT

<Define the roles and responsibilities for various staff in relation to the risk process, perhaps using the words below.>

The responsibilities of key project stakeholders for risk management on the <project-name> project are defined in individual terms of reference for each job role, and summarized as follows:

Project sponsor

- Actively support and encourage the implementation of a formal risk management process on the project

- Set and monitor risk thresholds and ensure these are translated into acceptable levels of risk for the project

- Attend risk workshops, identify risks and ownership of risks

- Review risk outputs from the project with the project manager to ensure process consistency and effectiveness

- Review risks escalated by the project manager that are outside the scope or control of the project or require input or action from outside the project

- Make decisions about project strategy in light of current risk status to maintain acceptable risk exposure

- Ensure that adequate resources are available to the project to respond appropriately to identified risks

- Release "management reserve" funds to the project where justified to deal with exceptional risks

- Report risk status regularly to senior management

Project manager

- Manage the overall risk management process; ensure that foreseeable risks (both threats and opportunities) are identified and managed effectively and proactively to maintain an acceptable level of risk exposure for the project

- Determine the acceptable levels of risk for the project by consultation with the project sponsor

- Approve the Risk Management Plan prepared by the risk champion

- Promote the risk management process for the project

- Participate in risk workshops and review meetings, and identify and own risks

- Approve risk response plans and their associated risk actions prior to implementation

- Apply project contingency funds to deal with identified risks that occur during the project

- Oversee risk management by subcontractors and suppliers

- Report risk status regularly to the project sponsor and project board/steering committee, with recommendations for appropriate strategic decisions and actions to maintain acceptable risk exposure

- Highlight to senior management any identified risks that are outside the scope or control of the project, or that require input or action from outside the project, or where release of

FIGURE A-1: Risk Management Plan Template *(continued)*

"management reserve" funds might be appropriate

- Monitor the efficiency and effectiveness of the process in conjunction with the risk champion

Risk champion (this might be a full-time or a part-time role)

- Responsible for overseeing and managing the overall risk management process on a day-to-day basis
- Prepare the Risk Management Plan
- Facilitate risk workshops and risk reviews, at which risks are identified and assessed
- Create and maintain Risk Register
- Interview risk owners to determine risk responses
- Responsible for ensuring the quality of all risk data
- Analyze data and produce risk reports
- Review progress with risk owners of risk responses and their associated actions
- Advise the project manager on all matters relating to risk management
- Coach and mentor team members and other stakeholders on aspects of risk management

Risk owner

- Develop responses to risks in the form of risk actions, which are assigned to action owners
- Monitor the progress on their risk responses
- Report progress on responses to the risk champion via the Risk Register

Action owner

- Implement agreed actions to support response strategies
- Report progress on actions to the risk owner and recommending any other actions needed to manage the risk

Project team member

- Participate actively in the risk process, proactively identify and manage risks in his/her area of responsibility
- Provide inputs to the project manager for risk reports

RISK REVIEWS AND REPORTING

Risk exposure on the <project-name> project will be reviewed <state frequency of Major and Minor Reviews> during the life of the project. At these reviews new risks will be identified and assessed, existing risks will be reviewed, progress on agreed actions will be assessed, and new actions and/or owners will be allocated where required.

The effectiveness of the risk process will be reviewed as part of a Major Review to determine whether changes to the approach, tools, or techniques are required. Where process changes are agreed by the project manager and risk champion, this Risk Management Plan will be updated and reissued to document the revised process.

<Detail the frequency and content of risk reports, perhaps using words similar to those below.>

FIGURE A-1: Risk Management Plan Template *(continued)*

A risk report will be issued <state frequency> by the project manager to the project sponsor after each Major or Minor Review. See Appendix C for the contents of a full risk report following a Major Review, and Appendix D for the contents of a summary risk report following a Minor Review.

Project team members and other stakeholders will be provided with an extract from the current Risk Register after each review, listing those risks and actions for which the individual is responsible.

On completion of the project, a risk section will be provided for the <project-name> project lessons learned report, detailing generic risks (both opportunities and threats) that might affect other similar projects, together with responses that have been found effective in this project. Input will also be provided for the project knowledge database, to capture risk-related lessons learned from this project.

APPENDIX A: Definitions of Probability and Impacts
<Define scales for probability and impact to be used for this project, in a similar format to those below. The probability scale below may be used unchanged, but the impact scales must be replaced with values specific to the particular project and that reflect agreed risk thresholds for this project.>

SCALE	PROBABILITY	+/– IMPACT ON PROJECT OBJECTIVES		
		TIME	COST	QUALITY
VHI	>90%	>20 days	>$200K	Very significant impact on overall functionality
HI	71–90%	11–20 days	$101K–$200K	Significant impact on overall functionality
MED	51–70%	4–10 days	$51K–$100K	Some impact in key functional areas
LO	31–50%	1–3 days	$10K–$50K	Minor impact on overall functionality
VLO	11–30%	<1 day	<$10K	Minor impact on secondary functions
NIL	<10%	No change	No change	No change in functionality

(Note: When using these impact scales to assess opportunities, they are to be treated as representing a positive savings in time or cost, or increased functionality. For threats, each impact scale is interpreted negatively; i.e., time delays, increased cost, or reduced functionality.)

FIGURE A-1: Risk Management Plan Template *(continued)*

APPENDIX B: Standard Risk Breakdown Structure (RBS)
<Define hierarchical structure of sources of risk that might affect this project. The example Risk Breakdown Structure (RBS) below might be used as a starting point.>

RBS LEVEL 0	RBS LEVEL 1	RBS LEVEL 2
0. PROJECT RISK	1. TECHNICAL RISK	1.1 Scope definition 1.2 Requirements definition 1.3 Estimates, assumptions, & constraints 1.4 Technical processes 1.5 Technology 1.6 Technical interfaces 1.7 Design 1.8 Performance 1.9 Reliability & maintainability 1.10 Safety 1.11 Security 1.12 Test and acceptance
	2. MANAGEMENT RISK	2.1 Project management 2.2 Program/portfolio management 2.3 Operations management 2.4 Organization 2.5 Resourcing 2.6 Communication 2.7 Information 2.8 HS&E 2.9 Quality 2.10 Reputation
	3. COMMERCIAL RISK	3.1 Contractual terms & conditions 3.2 Internal procurement 3.3 Suplers and vendors 3.4 Subcontracts 3.5 Client/customer stability 3.6 Partnerships and joint ventures
	4. EXTERNAL RISK	4.1 Legislation 4.2 Exchange rates 4.3 Site/facilities 4.4 Environmental/weather 4.5 Competition 4.6 Regulatory 4.7 Political 4.8 Country 4.9 Social/demographic 4.10 Pressure groups 4.11 Force majeure

FIGURE A-1: Risk Management Plan Template *(continued)*

APPENDIX C: Sample contents list for a full risk report

EXECUTIVE SUMMARY

SCOPE AND OBJECTIVES OF REPORT

PROJECT STATUS SUMMARY

OVERALL RISK STATUS

TOP RISKS, ACTIONS AND OWNERS

DETAILED RISK ASSESSMENT
    High/Medium/Low Risks
    Causal Analysis (Mapped To RBS)
    Effects Analysis (Mapped To WBS)

CONCLUSIONS AND RECOMMENDATIONS

APPENDICES
    COMPLETE RISK REGISTER
    PRIORITIZED RISK LIST
    (OTHER RESULTS AS REQUIRED)

APPENDIX D: Sample contents list for a summary risk report

EXECUTIVE SUMMARY

SCOPE AND OBJECTIVES OF REPORT

OVERALL RISK STATUS

TOP RISKS, ACTIONS AND OWNERS

CHANGES SINCE LAST REVIEW

CONCLUSIONS AND RECOMMENDATIONS

APPENDIX
    COMPLETE RISK REGISTER IN PRIORITY ORDER

FIGURE A-1: Risk Management Plan Template *(continued)*

RBS LEVEL 0	RBS LEVEL 1	RBS LEVEL 2	EXAMPLE RISKS	Could this risk affect our project? Yes No Don't know Not applicable
0. PROJECT RISK	1. TECHNICAL RISK	1.1 Scope definition	Scope changes may arise during project. Redundant scope may be discovered.	
		1.2 Requirements definition	Client may introduce significant change during project (positive or negative). Internal inconsistencies may exist within requirements. Key requirements may be missing from formal requirement specification.	
		1.3 Estimates, assumptions, and constraints	Basis of estimating may be wrong. Planning assumptions may be invalidated during project. Imposed constraints may be relieved or removed.	
		1.4 Technical processes	Standard processes may not meet requirements of specific solution. New processes may be required. Processes may be improved and made more effective.	
		1.5 Technology	New technology may be developed during project lifetime. Technology changes may invalidate design.	
		1.6 Technical interfaces	Unexpected interactions may occur at key interfaces. Data inconsistencies across interfaces may require rework. Key interfaces may be reduced.	

FIGURE A-2: Example Risk Checklist (Based on a Risk Breakdown Structure)

RBS LEVEL 0	RBS LEVEL 1	RBS LEVEL 2	EXAMPLE RISKS	Could this risk affect our project? Yes No Don't know Not applicable
0. PROJECT RISK	1. TECHNICAL RISK	1.7 Design	It may prove impossible to meet some requirements within design limitations. Reuse of existing design elements may be possible.	
		1.8 Performance	Final solution may not meet performance requirements. Some performance requirements may be mutually exclusive.	
		1.9 Reliability and maintainability	Target reliability criteria may be unattainable with chosen solution. The use of innovative technology may improve reliability. Maintainability requirements may impose unacceptable design constraints.	
		1.10 Safety	ALARP solution may impose additional cost. Changes in safety regulations may require significant redesign.	
		1.11 Security	Security implications may be overlooked during design. Government regulations may change during project.	
		1.12 Test and acceptance	Test protocols may reveal significant design error requiring rework. Client may withhold final acceptance for reasons outside contract.	

FIGURE A-2: Example Risk Checklist (Based on a Risk Breakdown Structure) *(continued)*

RBS LEVEL 0	RBS LEVEL 1	RBS LEVEL 2	EXAMPLE RISKS	Could this risk affect our project? Yes No Don't know Not applicable
0. PROJECT RISK	2. MANAGE- MENT RISK	2.1 Project management	Project management systems may not be adequate to support project requirements. Poor decision-making may result in inappropriate task allocation. Adoption of best-practice risk process may improve project performance.	
		2.2 Program/ portfolio management	Project may be given inappropriate priority within the program. Other projects may divert key resources. Other projects may be canceled and release resources.	
		2.3 Operations management	Design may expose weaknesses in existing products or processes. Business-as-usual demands may reduce project funding or contingency.	
		2.4 Organization	Reorganization may impact project organization (negatively or positively). Changes in corporate structure may affect project (negatively or positively).	
		2.5 Resourcing	Key resources may be unavailable when required. Specific skills may not be available when required. It may be possible to recruit existing subcontract staff permanently.	
		2.6 Communication	The client's requirement may be misunderstood. Project reporting needs may change during project. Key stakeholder interests may change (positively or negatively).	

FIGURE A-2: Example Risk Checklist (Based on a Risk Breakdown Structure) *(continued)*

RBS LEVEL 0	RBS LEVEL 1	RBS LEVEL 2	EXAMPLE RISKS	Could this risk affect our project? Yes No Don't know Not applicable
0. PROJECT RISK	2. MANAGE-MENT RISK	2.7 Information	Client may fail to provide required information on time. Client-supplied information may be inadequate to support project.	
		2.8 HS&E	Health and safety legislation may change during the project. An accident or incident may occur, delaying the project.	
		2.9 Quality	The number of defects found during integration may not match expectations (higher or lower). Quality circles may result in significant effort reduction. Effective quality management may reduce rework.	
		2.10 Reputation	Corporate reputation incident may damage support for the project. Senior management may lose confidence in project team. Improved reputation may increase availability of funds and resources.	
	3. COMMER-CIAL RISK	3.1 Contractual terms and conditions	Client standard terms may prove unacceptably onerous. Contractual terms may contain internal inconsistencies. Harmonized client/subcontractor terms may reduce risk exposure.	
		3.2 Internal procurement	Other departments may not deliver as expected. Required skills may not be available from other departments. Internal support may increase as the project progresses.	
		3.3 Suppliers and vendors	A key supplier may go out of business. Mergers between suppliers may erode competitiveness. Vendors may be able to deliver ahead of schedule.	

FIGURE A-2: Example Risk Checklist (Based on a Risk Breakdown Structure) *(continued)*

RBS LEVEL 0	RBS LEVEL 1	RBS LEVEL 2	EXAMPLE RISKS	Could this risk affect our project? Yes No Don't know Not applicable
0. PROJECT RISK	3. COMMER- CIAL RISK	3.4 Subcontracts	Key subcontractors may refuse to work together. Subcontract staff may take industrial action (strike). Partnering with selected subcontractors may improve working relationships.	
		3.5 Client/customer stability	Client may change business focus and withdraw support for project. Changes in client personnel may require additional project management effort. Client may be bought out or merge with a more supportive company.	
		3.6 Partnerships and joint ventures	Our partner may have competing commercial interests. The joint venture may break up.	
	4. EXTERNAL RISK	4.1 Legislation	Changes in legislation may impose changes in the solution (positive or negative). Legal requirements may add unforeseen design requirements.	
		4.2 Exchange rates	Exchange rates may change during the project (favorably or unfavorably). Key suppliers may invoice in foreign currency.	
		4.3 Site/facilities	Site access may prove more difficult than expected. Required facilities may not be available on site. New transport arrangements may ease project logistics.	
		4.4 Environmental/ weather	Weather may be unseasonable (better or worse than expected). Unexpected environmental conditions may affect progress (positively or negatively).	

FIGURE A-2: Example Risk Checklist (Based on a Risk Breakdown Structure) *(continued)*

RBS LEVEL 0	RBS LEVEL 1	RBS LEVEL 2	EXAMPLE RISKS	Could this risk affect our project? Yes No Don't know Not applicable
0. PROJECT RISK	4. EXTERNAL RISK	4.5 Competition	A key competitor may launch a competing product and invalidate the project. Key staff may be poached by competitors. Key competitor may withdraw from the market.	
		4.6 Regulatory	Regulatory requirements may impose unexpected design constraints. Significant changes in regulation may occur during the project (positive or negative).	
		4.7 Political	Political factors may influence senior management support for the project. A change in government may result in changed priorities or legislation (positively or negatively).	
		4.8 Country	Local resources may lack the required skills. Currency instability may undermine the business case for the project. Local government interest in the project may change (positively or negatively).	
		4.9 Social/ demographic	Changing social imperatives may impose additional requirements. Public perception of the project may change (positively or negatively).	
		4.10 Pressure groups	Extremists may disrupt project progress. Lobby groups may promote the cause of the project.	
		4.11 Force majeure	Force majeure event may occur, disrupting the project. Occurrence of force majeure may create an opportunity to address underlying issues.	

FIGURE A-2: Example Risk Checklist (Based on a Risk Breakdown Structure) *(continued)*

APPENDIX B

....

Further Templates and Examples

ATOM presents a practical "how to" method that is applicable to any project of any size. To aid practitioners in putting ATOM into practice, this appendix provides a range of templates and examples to support each step of the ATOM risk process. Some of these templates and examples can be used without modification, while others require tailoring to the specific requirements of the project and organization. Further details on how to use each template and example are given in the relevant chapter.

The templates and examples in this appendix are listed below.

B-1: Example project sizing tool

B-2: Stakeholder analysis template

B-3: Typical agenda for an Initiation meeting

B-4: RACI chart template

B-5: Sample Project-Specific Probability-Impact Scales

B-6: Sample double Probability-Impact Matrix

B-7: Sample Risk Breakdown Structure

B-8: Sample agenda for a First Risk Assessment/two-day risk workshop

B-9: Assumptions and constraints analysis template

B-10: Sample Risk Register format

B-11: Sample contents list for a full risk report

B-12: Sample agenda for a Major Review workshop

B-13: Sample agenda for a half-day risk review meeting

B-14: Sample contents list for a summary risk report

B-15: Typical agenda for a Post-Project Review meeting

B-16: Example risk mapping form

This project sizing tool divides projects into three categories (small, medium, and large), to indicate the appropriate level of risk management process. Two shortcuts are used: Projects with value less than $50K are automatically defined as small, and projects valued at more than $5M are defined as large. Projects valued between $50K and $5M are assessed against the ten criteria below. For each criterion the closest description is selected, and the corresponding criterion score is recorded at the right of the row (one of 2, 4, 8, or 16). Criterion scores are totaled to give an overall project score, indicating project size as follows:

≥75	*Large project*	An extended ATOM risk management process is required.
35–74	*Medium project*	A standard ATOM risk management process is required.
<35	*Small project*	A reduced ATOM risk management process is required.

CRITERION	CRITERION VALUE= 2	CRITERION VALUE= 4	CRITERION VALUE= 8	CRITERION VALUE= 16	CRITERION SCORE
Strategic importance	Minor contribution to business objectives	Significant contribution to business objectives	Major contribution to business objectives	Critical to business success	
Commercial/ contractual complexity	No unusual commercial arrangements or conditions	Minor deviation from existing commercial practices	Novel commercial practices, new to at least one party	Groundbreaking commercial practices	
External constraints and dependencies	None	Some external influence on elements of the project	Key project objectives depend on external factors	Overall project success depends on external factors	
Requirement stability	Clear, fully defined, agreed objectives	Some requirement uncertainty, minor changes during project	Key project objectives depend on external factors	Requirements not finalized and subject to negotiation	
Technical complexity	Routine repeat business, no new technology	Enhancement of existing product/ service	Novel product/ project with some innovation	Groundbreaking project with high innovation	
Market sector regulatory characteristics	No regulatory requirements	Standard regulatory framework	Challenging regulatory requirements	Highly regulated or novel sector	
Project value	Small project value (<$250K)	Significant project value ($250K–$1M)	Major project value ($1M–$3M)	Large project value (>$3M)	
Project duration	Duration <3 months	Duration 3–12 months	Duration 1–3 years	Duration >3 years	
Project resources	Small in-house project team	Medium in-house project team	Large project team including external contractors	International project team or joint venture	
Post-project liabilities	None	Acceptable exposure	Significant exposure	Punitive exposure	
				OVERALL PROJECT SCORE	

FIGURE B-1: Example Project Sizing Tool

STAKEHOLDER	AREA OF INTEREST	Attitude (+/−)	Power (+/−)	Interest (+/−)	Stakeholder Type

Instructions:

In the first two columns, list all key stakeholders and their interest (or stake) in the project.

For each stakeholder, identify whether their attitude toward the project is supportive or resistant (+ or −), whether their power to influence the project is high or low (+ or −), and whether their level of interest in the project is high or low (+ or −).

Based on these three parameters, categorize each stakeholder into one of eight types, as follows:

ATTITUDE	POWER	INTEREST	TYPE
+	+	+	Savior
+	−	+	Friend
+	+	−	Sleeping Giant
+	−	−	Acquaintance
−	+	+	Saboteur
−	−	+	Irritant
−	+	−	Time Bomb
−	−	−	Tripwire

FIGURE B-2: Stakeholder Analysis Template

TIME ALLOWANCE (hours)	CONTENT
½	1. Introductions
¼	2. Background to the project
½–1	3. Clarification of project objectives: scope, time, cost, quality, other objectives
¼	4. Scope and objectives of the risk management process
¼	5. Application of the ATOM risk management process
¼	6. Tools and techniques to be used
½	7. Roles and responsibilities for risk management
¼	8. Reporting and review requirements
¼	9. Definitions of scales for probability and impacts (P-I scales)
¼	10. Risk thresholds
¼	11. Potential sources of risk to this project
¼	12. Next steps

FIGURE B-3: Typical Agenda for an Initiation Meeting

	Stakeholder 1	Stakeholder 2	Stakeholder 3	Stakeholder 4	Stakeholder 5	Stakeholder 6
Risk task 1						
Risk task 2						
Risk task 3						
Risk task 4						
Risk task 5						
Risk task 6						
Risk task 7						
Risk task 8						
Risk task 9						

Key:

R = Responsible   **A** = Accountable/Approve   **C** = Consult/Communicate   **I** = Inform

Instructions:

Identify key stakeholders and record in column headings.

List key risk process tasks in the first column.

For each task, identify which key stakeholder is responsible for its completion (mark as R), and to whom they are accountable for task completion and/or from whom the task requires approval (mark as A). Any stakeholders to be consulted during the task are marked C, and those to be informed of its results or outcome are marked I.

FIGURE B-4: RACI Chart Template

SCALE	PROBABILITY	+/– IMPACT ON PROJECT OBJECTIVES		
		TIME	COST	QUALITY
VHI	71–99%	Greater than <d>	Greater than <s>	Very significant impact on overall functionality
HI	51–70%	<c> to <d>	<r> to <s>	Significant impact on overall functionality
MED	31–50%	<b> to <c>	<q> to <r>	Some impact in key functional areas
LO	11–30%	<a> to <b>	<p> to <q>	Minor impact on overall functionality
VLO	1–10%	Less than <a>	Less than <p>	Minor impact on secondary functions
NIL	<1%	No change	No change	No change in functionality

FIGURE B-5: Sample Project-Specific Probability-Impact Scales

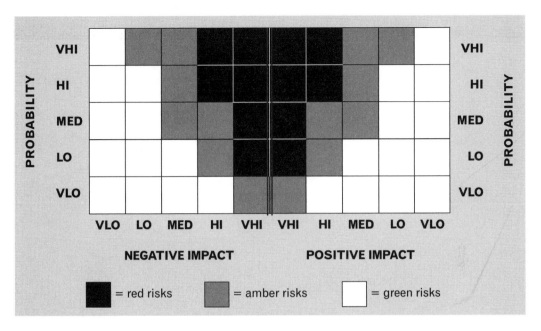

FIGURE B-6: Sample Double Probability-Impact Matrix

RBS LEVEL 0	RBS LEVEL 1	RBS LEVEL 2
0. PROJECT RISK	**1. TECHNICAL RISK**	1.1 Scope definition 1.2 Requirements definition 1.3 Estimates, assumptions, & constraints 1.4 Technical processes 1.5 Technology 1.6 Technical interfaces 1.7 Design 1.8 Performance 1.9 Reliability & maintainability 1.10 Safety 1.11 Security 1.12 Test and acceptance
	2. MANAGEMENT RISK	2.1 Project management 2.2 Program/portfolio management 2.3 Operations management 2.4 Organization 2.5 Resourcing 2.6 Communication 2.7 Information 2.8 HS&E 2.9 Quality 2.10 Reputation
	3. COMMERCIAL RISK	3.1 Contractual terms & conditions 3.2 Internal procurement 3.3 Supplers and vendors 3.4 Subcontracts 3.5 Client/customer stability 3.6 Partnerships and joint ventures
	4. EXTERNAL RISK	4.1 Legislation 4.2 Exchange rates 4.3 Site/facilities 4.4 Environmental/weather 4.5 Competition 4.6 Regulatory 4.7 Political 4.8 Country 4.9 Social/demographic 4.10 Pressure groups 4.11 Force majeure

FIGURE B-7: Sample Risk Breakdown Structure

DAY 1

Morning

1. Introductions
2. Confirm project objectives
3. Confirm scope of risk process for this workshop
4. Workshop ground rules
5. Risk management briefing (if required)
6. Expectations and Results
7. Identify risks
   Brainstorm risks using the risk breakdown structure

Afternoon

   Analyze assumptions and constraints to generate further risks
   Standard risk checklist to identify any further/final risks
8. Rationalize risks
9. Describe risks using risk metalanguage
10. Record identified risks (during workshop or after meeting)

DAY 2

Morning

11. Explanation of assessment scheme (recap)
12. Assessment of probability and impacts
13. Risk categorization

Afternoon

14. Nomination of risk owners
15. *If time, develop initial responses to priority risks*
16. Close the workshop

FIGURE B-8: Sample Agenda for a First Risk Assessment/Two-Day Risk Workshop
(Including Identification and Assessment Steps)

Assumption or Constraint	Could this assumption/constraint prove false? (Y/N)	If false would it affect project? (Y/N)	Convert to a risk?

Instructions:

List all project assumptions and constraints in the first column.

Identify whether each might prove false (Y/N), and whether a false assumption/constraint might affect the project (Y/N).

Where both answers are yes, mark the assumption/constraint as a risk.

FIGURE B-9: Assumptions and Constraints Analysis Template

Project Number:			Client:
Project Title:			Project Manager:
Risk Ref.	RBS Ref.	WBS Ref.	Risk Owner:
Risk Type: (T/O)	Risk Status: (Draft/Active/Closed/Deleted/Expired/Occurred)		
Risk Title:			
Risk Description:			

Cause of Risk	Effect on Objectives		
	Objective	Impact Rating Nil/VLO/LO/MED/HI/VHI	Impact Description
	Time		
	Cost		
	Quality		
Probability Rating Nil/VLO/LO/MED/ HI/VHI	Other		
Date Risk Raised:	Date Risk Closed/Deleted/Expired/Occurred:		

Risk Response—Preferred Strategy:			
Action(s) to Implement Strategy	Action Owner	Action by Date	Status

Comment/Status:

FIGURE B-10: Sample Risk Register Format

EXECUTIVE SUMMARY

SCOPE AND OBJECTIVES OF REPORT

PROJECT STATUS SUMMARY

OVERALL RISK STATUS

TOP RISKS, ACTIONS AND OWNERS

DETAILED RISK ASSESSMENT
    High/medium/low risks
    Causal analysis (mapped to RBS)
    Effects analysis (mapped to WBS)

CONCLUSIONS AND RECOMMENDATIONS

APPENDICES
    COMPLETE RISK REGISTER
    PRIORITIZED RISK LIST
    (OTHER RESULTS AS REQUIRED)

FIGURE B-11: Sample Contents List for a Full Risk Report

TIME ALLOWANCE (hours)	CONTENT
½	1. Introductions
3	2. Review current risks
1	3. Review draft risks
1	4. Consider new risks
–	5. Update Risk Register (done during steps 1–4)
½	6. Review risk process effectiveness
¼	7. Close workshop

FIGURE B-12: Sample Agenda for a Major Review Workshop

TIME ALLOWANCE (hours)	CONTENT
¼	1. Introductions
2	2. Review red risks
½	3. Review draft risks
½	4. Consider new risks
	5. *Review amber risks if time permits*
–	6. Update Risk Register (done during earlier steps)
¼	7. Close meeting

FIGURE B-13: Sample Agenda for a Half-Day Risk Review Meeting

EXECUTIVE SUMMARY

SCOPE AND OBJECTIVES OF REPORT

OVERALL RISK STATUS

TOP RISKS, ACTIONS AND OWNERS

CHANGES SINCE LAST REVIEW

CONCLUSIONS AND RECOMMENDATIONS

APPENDIX
    COMPLETE RISK REGISTER IN PRIORITY ORDER

FIGURE B-14: Sample Contents List for a Summary Risk Report

TIME ALLOWANCE (hours)	CONTENT
¼	1. Introductions
½	2. Review final Risk Register
2	3. Identify risk-related "lessons to be learned"
½	4. Summarize "lessons to be learned"
¼	5. Close the meeting

FIGURE B-15: Typical Agenda for a Post-Project Review Meeting

ACTIVITY	PLAN VALUE	MAPPED OPPORTUNITIES	MAPPED THREATS	MIN	ML	MAX	Distribution type	Correlation group

FIGURE B-16: Example Risk Mapping Form

Glossary of Terms and Abbreviations

accept: A *risk response* strategy that is not proactive toward a *risk,* but prepares for and deals with the *impact* of a risk should it occur. This may involve use of a *contingency plan.* An acceptance strategy can be selected for either *threats* or *opportunities.*

action owner: The person responsible for implementing an agreed *risk action* and reporting progress to the *risk owner.*

APM: Association for Project Management.

Assessment: Part of the risk management process where the *probability* and *impact* of identified risks are assessed in order to prioritize risks based on their position on a *Probability-Impact Matrix,* and where risks are categorized using the *risk breakdown structure* and other frameworks.

assumption: A future uncertainty that is treated as a fact for the purposes of planning or decision making.

assumptions and constraints analysis: A technique for *risk identification* based on identifying and testing *assumptions* and *constraints* to determine their stability and sensitivity.

ATOM: Active Threat and Opportunity Management. A generic project risk management process that is scalable and applicable to any type of project.

avoid: *A risk response strategy* directed toward a *threat,* which aims to eliminate the uncertainty, usually by implementing *risk actions* to remove its potential cause.

cause: An existing certain event or set of circumstances that may give rise to one or more *risks.* A cause is the first element of a *risk description* using *risk metalanguage.*

CBS: Cost breakdown structure.

checklist: A structured list of *risks* that have been identified during previous projects and that can be used as an input to *risk identification.*

consequence: See *effect.*

constraint: A condition of the project, usually imposed externally, that restricts the options open to the project.

contingency: Amount of time or money set aside against *accepted* risks, or to make allowance for unforeseen risks, to be used to compensate for the negative consequences of *threats* that occur, or to be used to take advantage of the positive consequences of *opportunities* that occur. (See also *management reserve.*)

contingency plan: Appropriate *responses* defined in advance but implemented only if/when a risk actually occurs or when planned responses fail to have the intended effect. Contingency plans can be developed for either *threats* or *opportunities*.

correlation: A mechanism for relating groups of tasks and/or risks within a *risk model* to reduce the allowable degree of variation during a *Monte Carlo analysis*. Related tasks and/or risks are called a correlation group. The statistical sampling within a correlation group is driven by a predefined correlation coefficient. Also called *dependency*.

Critical Success Factor (CSF): A condition that is required to ensure success, and whose absence leads to failure.

criticality: A measure of how often an element in a *Monte Carlo* quantitative schedule *risk model* appears on the critical path, expressed as a percentage of the overall number of iterations during the simulation. A criticality index between 0% and 100% for each task in the *risk model* is calculated automatically during the analysis.

cruciality: A measure of the relationship between variation of each task or risk in a *risk model* and variation of the overall project outcome, usually expressed as a correlation coefficient (from -1 to +1). The results of a cruciality analysis are often presented in a *tornado chart*. Also known as *sensitivity*.

CSF: See *Critical Success Factor*.

decision tree analysis: The *quantitative risk analysis* technique for assessing the value of alternative actions, taking into account the costs of taking the action, the likelihood of future uncertain events that may occur if the action is taken, and estimates of resulting rewards or costs. The decision made is usually the one that yields the greatest *expected value* (or the least expected cost). A decision tree may be evaluated using *Monte Carlo analysis*.

Delphi technique: An anonymous facilitated technique used for *risk identification* based on the consensus opinions of experts.

dependency: See *correlation*.

double Probability-Impact Matrix (double P-I Matrix): Two *probability-impact matrices* presented alongside each other, with one showing *threats* and the other showing *opportunities*. The typical double P-I Matrix shows threats on the left matrix and opportunities on the right, with the opportunity matrix flipped horizontally to bring both red zones together in the center of the double P-I Matrix. See also *Probability-Impact Matrix*.

effect: The possible outcome of a risk if it occurs. Effects are negative for threats and positive for *opportunities*. Effects form the third element of a *risk description* using *risk metalanguage*. (Also called *consequence* or *impact*.)

EMV: See *Expected Monetary Value*.

enhance: A *risk response strategy* directed toward an *opportunity*, which aims to increase *likelihood* or *consequence*, or both, above the *risk acceptance threshold*.

enterprise risk management (ERM): Integrated application of risk management across the entire business, addressing all levels of risk, including strategic, business, corporate, reputation, portfolio, program, project, technical, safety, etc.

ERM: See *enterprise risk management.*

EV: Expected value; used to evaluate a *decision tree.*

expected monetary value (EMV): See *expected value (EV).*

expected value (EV): (1) The statistical average or weighted mean of a distribution, approximating to the 50th percentile calculated during *quantitative risk analysis* using *Monte Carlo analysis,* which represents the outcome that would occur on average given the input data. (2) A measure of *risk exposure* calculated as the product of *probability* and *impact.* Since probability is dimensionless, the units and sign of expected value are the same as the units and sign of the impact. Sometimes also called *expected monetary value (EMV).*

exploit: A *risk response strategy* directed toward an *opportunity,* which aims to eliminate the uncertainty by implementing *risk actions* to ensure that the opportunity occurs.

eyeball plot: An output from an integrated time-cost *quantitative risk analysis* using *Monte Carlo simulation,* which presents all possible time-cost pairs (usually for project duration and total project cost) calculated from the analysis, together with a best-fit ellipse (the "eyeball"). Sometimes also called a *football plot* (especially in the U.S.).

First Risk Assessment: The initial performance of *risk identification, assessment,* and *response planning* during the ATOM risk management process.

football plot: See *eyeball plot.*

frequency of occurrence: A measure of *likelihood* for a specific *risk* that could occur repeatedly over a given period of time or in a given number of trials. Frequency of occurrence is usually expressed as number of occurrences per unit of time or per total number of trials.

heuristic: A frame of reference used as a shortcut when making decisions. In the risk process, heuristics usually operate subconsciously, and include availability, stereotyping, anchoring and adjustment.

impact: The resulting change to one or more objectives that will happen if a risk occurs. See also *effect.*

Implementation: The step in the risk process where agreed *risk actions* are performed by *action owners,* the *Risk Register* is updated, and *risk reports* are prepared.

influence diagram: A structured approach to *quantitative risk analysis,* which presents the topic of the analysis using entities, outcomes, and influences, and which represents the relationships and effects between them. An influence diagram may be evaluated using *Monte Carlo analysis.*

inherent risk: The *risk* as originally identified before *risk actions* have been implemented. (See also *residual risk.*)

Initiation: The initial phase of the risk management process in which the scope and parameters of the particular risk analysis are determined. Decisions made during risk process initiation are recorded in a *Risk Management Plan.*

IRR: Internal rate of return.

issue: An event (usually negative) that has occurred, is affecting achievement of an objective, and usually cannot be addressed directly by the project manager. Sometimes also used for an ill-defined matter of concern that might give rise to *risks.*

likelihood: The chance that a particular *risk* will occur. This can be expressed as either a *probability* for a single event or condition, or as a *frequency of occurrence* for repeatable events.

Major Review: A comprehensive process of updating the assessment of risk exposure.

management reserve: Amount of money or time intended to compensate for the consequences of unforeseen risks, usually held outside the project budget. (See also *contingency.*)

Minor Review: A process of updating the assessment of *risk exposure* with minimal effort.

mitigate: See *reduce.*

Monte Carlo analysis: A technique for *quantitative risk analysis* in which the range of possible outcomes is determined by selecting random values from defined distributions within a *risk model.* The process is done on an iterative basis to determine statistical probabilities of particular outcomes.

M_o_R™: *Management of Risk,* published by the U.K. Office of Government Commerce (OGC)

OBS: Organizational breakdown structure.

OGC: U.K. Office of Government Commerce.

onion ring diagram: A series of overlapping *S-curves,* often used to show the cumulative effect of *risk actions* on the result of a *quantitative risk analysis.*

opportunity: Any uncertainty that, if it occurs, would have a beneficial effect on achievement of one or more objectives, such as improved safety and saved time or cost. A positive or upside *risk.*

overall project risk: The exposure of project stakeholders to the consequences of variation in project outcomes. Overall project risk is more than the sum of individual *risk events,* and includes the effects of other sources of uncertainty such as ambiguity and variability. It is best estimated through use of *quantitative risk analysis* techniques.

P-I: Probability-Impact.

PMBOK® Guide: *A Guide to the Project Management Body of Knowledge,* published by the Project Management Institute (PMI®). Chapter 11 presents generic processes for project risk management.

PMI®: Project Management Institute.

PRAM Guide: *Project Risk Analysis & Management Guide,* published by the Association for Project Management (APM), which presents a generic approach to project risk management.

probability: A measure of *likelihood* for a specific *risk.* Probability may be expressed in qualitative terms (e.g., high, medium, or low) or in quantitative terms (as a percentage or a number in the range 0–1).

Probability-Impact Matrix (P-I Matrix): A two-dimensional plot with *probability* as one axis and *impact* as the other. Identified *risks* can be plotted on the matrix to prioritize them into one of a number of zones within the matrix (usually three: red, amber, green). The matrix can be of different sizes, but is usually symmetrical (e.g., 3x3, 4x4, 5x5). The Probability-Impact Matrix can be used to prioritize both *threats* and *opportunities,* usually using a "mirror" double matrix format (see *double Probability-Impact Matrix*).

probability-impact scoring (P-I scoring): A method of scoring individual *risk events* by allocating numerical values corresponding to *probability* and *impact,* and multiplying these to give a *risk score,* which can be used to prioritize risks, calculate metrics, and perform trend analysis.

prompt list: A list of generic headings or categories of types of risk that can be used to structure *risk identification.* It may be presented as a simple linear set of headings, or as a hierarchy like the *risk breakdown structure.*

quantitative risk analysis: A numerical analysis of *risk exposure* based on the *probability* and *impact* of identified risks, which predicts possible outcomes and allows an estimate of *overall project risk.* Quantitative risk analysis techniques include *Monte Carlo analysis, decision trees,* and *influence diagrams.* These techniques often use sensitivity analysis to explore the effects of key risk drivers.

RACI chart: A version of the Responsibility Assignment Matrix that allocates tasks to individuals or groups under four headings: responsible, accountable (and/or approves), consulted (and/or contributes), informed.

RAG: red/amber/green scoring system for risk assessment.

RAM: See *responsibility assignment matrix.*

RBS: See *risk breakdown structure.*

reduce: A *risk response strategy* directed toward a *threat,* which aims to reduce *likelihood* or *consequence,* or both, below the *risk acceptance threshold.* Also known as *mitigate.* (In some processes the term *mitigation* is used for all types of *risk response strategy.*)

residual risk: The *risk* remaining after agreed *risk actions* have been implemented. (See also *inherent risk.*)

Response Planning: Part of the risk management process where appropriate *risk response strategies* are developed, *risk actions* are generated, and *risk owners* and *action owners* are nominated.

responsibility assignment matrix (RAM): A chart showing allocation of particular tasks to individuals or groups, usually formed by relating the work breakdown structure (WBS) to the organizational breakdown structure (OBS). (See also *RACI chart.*)

risk: Any uncertainty that, if it occurs, would have a positive or negative effect on achievement of one or more objectives. Risks include both *threats* and *opportunities.* Risk in projects includes both individual *risk events* and *overall project risk.*

risk acceptance threshold: A measure of the level of *risk exposure* above which action must be taken to address *threats* and *opportunities* proactively, and below which risks may be *accepted.*

risk action: This is an activity implemented by an *action owner* at the request of a *risk owner* in order to implement an agreed *risk response strategy.* The risk action and its associated cost are independent of the actual occurrence of the risk.

risk aggregation: A part of *risk identification* in which risks that are similar, interdependent, or temporally coincident are grouped together for further attention.

risk analyst: A specialist in risk management processes, tools, and techniques (particularly in the use of *quantitative risk analysis*) who may provide expert support to a project.

risk assessment: The process of estimating the *probability* and *impact* of identified risks, and comparing it against a defined *risk acceptance threshold.* (Also known as *risk evaluation.*)

risk attitude: A chosen mental disposition toward uncertainty, influenced by perception. Risk attitudes are adopted by individuals and groups. Risk attitudes exist on a continuous spectrum, but common risk attitudes include risk-averse, risk-tolerant, risk-neutral, and risk-seeking.

risk breakdown structure (RBS): A hierarchical framework presenting possible sources of risk, used to structure *risk identification* and *qualitative assessment.* A generic RBS may be developed covering all types of project, or a specific RBS may be used for a particular application.

risk champion: The person responsible for facilitating the risk management process on a particular project.

risk description: A structured statement of *risk,* usually containing three elements: *cause, risk,* and *effect,* often combined using *risk metalanguage.*

risk driver: An uncertain factor that exerts a significant influence over the overall outcome of the project.

risk evaluation: See *risk assessment.*

risk event: An uncertain discrete occurrence that, if it occurs, would have a positive or negative effect on achievement of one or more objectives.

risk exposure: A measure of the overall effect of identified risks on objectives, to describe *overall project risk.* Risk exposure may be expressed quantitatively (for example, in time or cost terms), or qualitatively (for example, high risk, or low risk).

risk identification: A structured process of exposing knowable *risks,* including both *threats* and *opportunities,* and describing and recording them for further analysis.

risk management: The structured process of taking appropriate decisions and implementing appropriate actions in response to known *risk events* and *overall project risk.* (Also used as a generic term for the whole process of initiation, risk identification, assessment, response development, and implementation.)

Risk Management Plan (RMP): A planning document produced during the *Initiation* step that records the parameters of the risk process for a particular project, including: the scope and context of the risk assessment; objectives to be considered; methodology, tools, and techniques to be used; roles and responsibilities; risk acceptance threshold; reporting and update cycle. (Also sometimes known as a risk strategy statement or risk policy.)

risk metalanguage: A structured description of a *risk* that separates *cause, risk,* and *effect.* A typical risk description using risk metalanguage might be in this form: "Because of <cause>, <risk> might occur, which would lead to <effect>."

risk model: A mathematical representation of a project that can be used as the basis for *quantitative risk analysis.*

risk owner: The person responsible for ensuring that an appropriate *risk response strategy* is selected and implemented. This person is also responsible for determining suitable *risk actions* to implement the chosen strategy, with each risk action assigned to a single *action owner.*

risk policy: See *Risk Management Plan.*

Risk Register: A record of all identified risks from the risk management process for a particular project, presented in a standard format, including assessments, agreed responses and actions, and current status. The Risk Register may be an output from a proprietary risk software package, or may be maintained as a standalone document, spreadsheet, or database.

Risk Report: An output from the risk process that records the findings and presents conclusions and recommendations. Different types of report are possible, such as a Full Risk Report including detailed analysis, or a Summary Risk Report presenting less detail, or a risk analysis report presenting the results of a *quantitative risk analysis.*

risk response strategy: A strategy for determining what, if anything, should be done with a *risk.* It leads to specific *risk actions* to deal with individual risk events or sets of related risks. Proactive risk response strategies for *threats* include *avoid, transfer,* and *reduce.* Proactive risk response strategies for opportunities include *exploit, share,* and *enhance.* If a proactive risk response strategy is not possible or cost-effective, it may be decided to *accept* a risk (either threat or opportunity).

risk review: A structured update of the assessment of current risk exposure, which may be undertaken using a dedicated risk review meeting or as part of the routine project review process. Risk reviews can be conducted at various levels of detail (see *Minor Review* and *Major Review*).

risk score: A nondimensional number calculated from the Probability-Impact scoring system, which can be used to prioritize risks, calculate metrics, and perform trend analysis.

risk strategy statement: see *Risk Management Plan.*

RMP: See *Risk Management Plan.*

ROI: Return On Investment.

scenario analysis: A *quantitative risk analysis* technique used either within other techniques to expose key *risk drivers,* or as a standalone technique to explore outcomes associated with defined sets of possible future situations.

S-curve: A cumulative probability distribution curve produced from a *quantitative risk analysis* using *Monte Carlo simulation,* which presents all possible values calculated from the analysis together with their probability of being achieved. S-curves can be produced for time (e.g., project duration, end-date, or milestone dates), cost (e.g., total project spend), or other variables.

secondary risk: A *risk* that arises as a direct result of implementing a *risk response strategy* or *risk action* for an existing risk. Secondary risks can be either *threats* or *opportunities.*

sensitivity: See *cruciality.*

sensitivity analysis: A *quantitative risk analysis* technique used within other techniques to expose key *risk drivers,* by varying one or more parameters within a *risk model* and determining the extent of the effect on the overall outcome. Sensitivity analysis can be performed on deterministic or probabilistic risk models. Results are usually presented using a *tornado chart.*

share: A *risk response strategy* directed toward an *opportunity* that aims to involve a third party who is better able to manage the specific risk.

stakeholder: Any person or party with an interest in the outcome of the project and/or an ability to exert influence.

stakeholder analysis: The process of determining the degree of interest, influence, and attitude of *stakeholders* toward a particular project.

stochastic branches: Constructs used within a *risk model* defining alternative logic paths that might be followed during a *Monte Carlo analysis.* Two types of stochastic branches are common: the probabilistic branch, where the frequency of sampling for each alternative path is driven by a predefined probability, and the conditional branch, where existence of a path is determined by the status of a predefined condition. Stochastic branches can also be used to model *risks* explicitly.

Strengths, weaknesses, opportunities, and threats (SWOT) analysis: A *risk identification* technique used to structure a risk workshop.

SWOT: strengths, weaknesses, opportunities, threats—the elements of a *SWOT analysis.*

threat: Any uncertainty that, if it occurs, would have an adverse effect on achievement of one or more objectives, such as injury, damage to environment, delay, or economic loss. A negative or downside *risk.*

tornado chart: An output from a *quantitative risk analysis* using *Monte Carlo analysis* that shows the main *risk drivers* in descending order of importance, plotting their *cruciality*.

transfer: A *risk response strategy* directed toward a *threat*, which aims to involve a third party who is better able to manage the specific risk.

WBS: Work breakdown structure.

References and Further Reading

Association for Project Management, *APM Body Of Knowledge,* 5th ed. High Wycombe, Bucks, U.K.: Association for Project Management, 2006; ISBN 1-903494-13-3.

Association for Project Management, *Project Risk Analysis & Management (PRAM) Guide,* 2nd ed. High Wycombe, Bucks, U.K.: APM Publishing, 2004; ISBN 1-903494-12-5.

Australian/New Zealand Standard AS/NZS 4360:2004 *Risk Management.* Published jointly by Standards Australia, Homebush NSW 2140, Australia, and Standards New Zealand, Wellington 6001, New Zealand; ISBN 0-7337-5904-1.

Bernstein, P.L. *Against the Gods—The Remarkable Story of Risk.* New York: Wiley, 1996; ISBN 0-471-12104-5.

British Standard BS6079-3:2000 *Project Management—Part 3: Guide to the Management of Business-Related Project Risk.* London, U.K.: British Standards Institute; ISBN 0-580-33122-9.

BS IEC 62198:2001 *Project Risk Management—Application Guidelines.* London, U.K.: British Standards Institute; ISBN 0-580-390195.

BSI PD ISO/IEC Guide 73:2002 *Risk Management—Vocabulary—Guidelines for use in standards.* London, U.K.: British Standards Institute; ISBN 0-580-401782.

Chapman, C.B. & S.C. Ward. *Project Risk Management: Processes, Techniques, and Insights,* 2nd ed. Chichester, U.K.: Wiley, 2003; ISBN 0-470-85355-7.

Cooke-Davies, T. "Can We Afford to Skimp on Risk Management?" *Project Manager Today* 10, no. 9 (Sept. 1998): 12–15.

Cooper, D.F., S. Grey, G. Raymond & P. Walker. *Project Risk Management Guidelines: Managing Risk in Large Projects and Complex Procurements.* Chichester, U.K.: Wiley, 2004; ISBN 0-470-02281-7.

Dinsmore, P.C. & T.J. Cooke-Davies. *The Right Projects Done Right: From Business Strategy to Successful Project Implementation.* New York: Wiley, 2005; ISBN 0787971138.

Grey, S. *Practical Risk Assessment for Project Management.* Chichester, U.K.: Wiley, 1995; ISBN 0471-93978-X.

Hillson D.A. 1997. "Towards a Risk Maturity Model," *International Journal of Project & Business Risk Management* 1 (no. 1): 35–45.

Hillson, D.A. 2000. "Project Risks—Identifying Causes, Risks and Effects," *PM Network* 14 (no. 9): 48–51.

Hillson, D.A. 2003. "Using a Risk Breakdown Structure in Project Management," *Journal of Facilities Managment* 2 (no. 1): 85–97.

Hillson, D.A. *Effective Opportunity Management for Projects: Exploiting Positive Risk.* New York: Marcel Dekker, 2004; ISBN 0-8247-4808-5.

Hillson, D.A. (ed.). *The Risk Management Universe: A Guided Tour.* London, U.K.: British Standards Institution, 2006; ISBN 0-580-43777-9.

Hillson, D.A. & R. Murray-Webster. *Understanding and Managing Risk Attitude,* 2nd ed. Aldershot, U.K.: Gower, 2007; ISBN 978-0-566-08798-1.

Hulett, D.T., D.A. Hillson & R. Kohl. 2002. "Defining Risk: A Debate." *Cutter IT Journal* 15 (no. 2): 4–10.

Institute of Risk Management (IRM), National Forum for Risk Management in the Public Sector (ALARM) & Association of Insurance and Risk Managers (AIRMIC). 2002. "A risk management standard." Published jointly by IRM/ALARM/AIRMIC, London, U.K.

Institution of Civil Engineers, Faculty of Actuaries & Institute of Actuaries. *Risk Analysis & Management for Projects (RAMP),* 2nd ed. London, U.K.; Thomas Telford, 2005; ISBN 0-7277-3390-7.

Johnson, G., K. Scholes & R. Whittington. *Exploring Corporate Strategy.* London, U.K.: FT Prentice Hall, 2006; ISBN 1405846003.

Murray-Webster, R. & P.W. Simon. 2006. "Risk Management in Action?" Proceedings of first ICCE & IPMA Global Congress on Project Management, Ljubljana, Slovenia.

Murray-Webster, R. & P.W. Simon. *What is the Current State of Project Management?* Hook, U.K.: Project Manager Today Publications, 2006; ISBN 1900391155.

Project Management Institute. *A Guide to the Project Management Body of Knowledge (PMBoK®),* 3rd ed. Philadelphia: Project Management Institute, 2004.

Raz, T. & D.A. Hillson. 2005. "A Comparative Review of Risk Management Standards," *Risk Management: An International Journal* 7 (no. 4): 53–66.

Schuyler, J. *Risk and Decision Analysis in Projects,* 2nd ed. Philadelphia: Project Management Institute, 2001; ISBN 1-880410-28-1.

Simon, P.W. 2003. "The Effective Use of Probability and Impact Grids." Proceedings of *From Diagnosis to Delivery: 6th Risk Conference,* London, U.K.

Simon, P.W. & R. Murray-Webster. 2006. "Driven to Precision." Proceedings of first ICCE & IPMA Global Congress on Project Management, Ljubljana, Slovenia.

U.K. Office of Government Commerce (OGC). *Management of Risk—Guidance for Practitioners.* London, U.K.: The Stationery Office, 2007; ISBN 978-0-11-331038-8.

Vose, D. *Risk Analysis—A Quantitative Guide,* 2nd ed. Chichester U.K.: Wiley, 2000; ISBN 0471-99765-X.

Williams, T.M. 1994. "Using the Risk Register to Integrate Risk Management in Project Definition." *International Journal of Project Managment* 12:17–22.

Williams, T.M. 1996. "The Two-Dimensionality of Project Risk." *International Journal of Project Managment* 14:185–186.

Williams T. M. *Modelling Complex Projects.* Chichester, U.K.: Wiley, 2002; ISBN 0-471-89945-3.

Index

A

accept (risk response strategy), 84, 86, 142, **223***

action owner, 45, 46, 82, 97, 98, 99, 100, 109, 142, 143, **223**

    role of, 47

action windows. *See* impact and action windows

active (risk status), 101, 102, 109, 111, 118, 119, 121, 125, 127, 144, 160

adjustment estimating, 179

agenda

    first risk assessment/two-day risk workshop, 56, 59, 151, 217

    initiation meeting, 43, 213

    major review, 109, 110, 220

    post-project review meeting, 127, 221

    risk lessons learned meeting, 166

    risk review meeting (half-day), 118, 220

APM. *See* Association for Project Management

Assessment (ATOM process step)

    activities, 70–78

    flowchart, 69

    inputs 69, 70

    large projects, 156–160

    outputs, 78–80

    overview, 67–69

    small projects, 140, 141

assessment of probability and impacts, 71–74

Association for Project Management, 32, **223**

assumptions, 61, 62, 139, **223**

assumptions analysis. *See* assumptions and constraints analysis

assumptions and constraints analysis, 61, 62, 139, 218

avoid (risk response strategy), 84, 86, 142, **223**

B

benefits (of risk management), 7, 8, 10, 11, 16

brainstorming, 56, 61

business case, 23, 38, 39, 43, 58, 123

C

capability. *See* risk management capability

cause (of risk), 6, 63, 64, **223**

CBS. *See* cost breakdown structure

change log, 124–128

checklist, 57, **223**

closed (risk status) 101, 102, 112, 113, 121, 125, 127, 144, 160

conditional branching, 176

constraints 61, 62, 139, **223**

constraints analysis. *See* assumptions and constraints analysis

contingency, 44, 170, 173, 179, 186, **223**

contingency plan, 86, 158, **224**

correlation, 174, 178, 179, 184, **224**

cost breakdown structure, 172, **223**

critical success factor, 9, 16–20, **224**

criticality, 182–184, 186, **224**

cruciality, 184–186, **224**

CSF. *See* critical success factor

customizing ATOM, 191–196

D

decision tree, 169

decision tree analysis, **224**

deleted (risk status), 101, 102, 112, 113, 121, 125, 127, 144, 160

Delphi technique, **224**

dependency, **224**. *See* also correlation

distribution types, 174, 179, 180

draft (risk status), 28, 101, 102 102, 111, 119, 135, 144, 145, 150

E

effect, of risk, 6, **224**

* Items in **bold** are glossary entries.